AFFIRMING THE BIRTH MOTHER'S JOURNEY

A Peer Counselor's Guide to Adoption Counseling

wendy lowe and jutta wittmeier
with carmen wittmeier

CALGARY
Pregnancy Care CENTRE
helping women in crisis

Note for Librarians: A cataloguing record for this book is available from Library and Archives
Canada at www.collectionscanada.ca/amicus/index-e.html
ISBN 1-4120-6788-x

*Printed in Victoria, BC, Canada. Printed on paper with minimum 30% recycled fibre. Trafford's print shop
runs on "green energy" from solar, wind and other environmentally-friendly power sources.*

TRAFFORD
PUBLISHING™

Offices in Canada, USA, Ireland and UK

This book was published *on-demand* in cooperation with Trafford Publishing. On-demand
publishing is a unique process and service of making a book available for retail sale to the
public taking advantage of on-demand manufacturing and Internet marketing. On-demand
publishing includes promotions, retail sales, manufacturing, order fulfilment, accounting and
collecting royalties on behalf of the author.

Book sales for North America and international:
Trafford Publishing, 6E–2333 Government St.,
Victoria, BC v8t 4p4 CANADA
phone 250 383 6864 (toll-free 1 888 232 4444)
fax 250 383 6804; email to orders@trafford.com
Book sales in Europe:
Trafford Publishing (uk) Limited, 9 Park End Street, 2nd Floor
Oxford, UK ox1 1hh UNITED KINGDOM
phone 44 (0)1865 722 113 (local rate 0845 230 9601)
facsimile 44 (0)1865 722 868; info.uk@trafford.com
Order online at:
trafford.com/05-1699

10 9 8 7 6 5 4 3

Dedication

This book is dedicated to our two adopted children, and to their birthmothers, whose intense pain and sorrow made possible our dream of family. We wish we had known then what we know now about what these women experienced. Our prayer is that this book will enable Pregnancy Care Center volunteers to support birthmothers through every stage of the adoption and grief process. We have always longed to thank the two amazing women who have changed our lives. May Centers bless birth mothers in the same way that our children's birth mothers have blessed us.

-Adoptive parents and anonymous donors
(who made this book possible)

Contents

CHAPTER ONE

Rationale

*"Open adoption is something really beautiful. Being able to see my
daughter grow up and to see her happy was all I needed to make it okay."*

—Chantal, birth mother, age 30

Tanya[1] came into the Calgary Pregnancy Care Centre with a wide-eyed, wild-haired three-year-old clinging to her leg. The moment the reluctant toddler let go to explore a room filled with toys, her mother began sobbing. Watching the little girl through the window that separated the playroom from the counseling room, the nineteen-year-old told her peer counselor that she had always known that rearing a child by herself would be difficult. She had survived the first two years after Madison's birth, relying on her family's support to complete high school and to find a job that would cover her expenses. Though caring for a baby had pushed her to her limits, Tanya loved her daughter.

Turning away from the glass window, Tanya then described how her mother's relapse into depression had changed everything. Madison, once an outgoing baby, had grown increasingly quiet and withdrawn under her grandmother's care, while Tanya's mother appeared exhausted by the long hours she spent baby-sitting. Sensing the growing tension in the household, Tanya had realized that the time had come to move out and parent on her own.

No one, she explained tearfully, had told her how difficult parenting a toddler would be. In order to afford daycare, she was forced to work additional hours and to drop the two college courses she had started. While caring for an infant had been challenging, the 'terrible twos' proved to be overwhelming. When Tanya arrived home from work, exhausted, she had little energy left to deal with her daughter's clingy behavior, temper tantrums, and seemingly endless thirst for attention. She was a terrible mother, Tanya lamented, unable to provide nutritious food and adequate clothing for her child, and too burned out to really care.

What Tanya said next shocked her counselor. "I want to place Madison for adoption," she stated flatly. "I'm not ready to be a mother."

Keesha arrived at the Centre with an even more disconcerting story. She had given birth at the age of twenty-six and soon discovered that the baby she had believed would give her purpose

---

[1] Throughout the book, names and identifying details have been changed to protect the anonymity of clients.

only further complicated her life. Restless and depressed, Keesha began reverting to old habits, abusing drugs and alcohol and becoming romantically involved with men who shared these interests. Only four months old, Keesha's baby, Annika, was apprehended by Social Services after a concerned neighbor called the police.

Keesha spent the next four years trying to piece her life back together. During this time, Annika was removed from the home on four separate occasions, including the morning Keesha's new boyfriend sexually assaulted the toddler on the bathroom floor. Despondent, Keesha told her peer counselor that the four-year-old was now in her sixth foster home and suffered from recurring nightmares and chronic bedwetting.

During their pregnancies, their counselors learned, neither Tanya nor Keesha had been informed about the adoption option. For Tanya, the choice was between abortion and parenting; the possibility of placing had not even occurred to her before the reality of single-handedly rearing a toddler had set in. Keesha had dismissed the idea immediately. A child should be with its mother, she had reasoned at the time; to 'give it away' would be an act of cruelty that would do irreparable damage to the child.

Ironically, even if Tanya and Keesha had visited a Pregnancy Center during the decision-making stage of their crisis pregnancies, their situations may have changed little. Adoption, one of the choices that should be most frequently promoted, is often avoided by peer counselors. In fact, according to research conducted by the Family Research Council, a nonprofit research and educational organization based in Washington, D.C., one of the most serious problems facing Pregnancy Centers is the overwhelming failure to present the adoption option to clients. In the report, entitled *The Missing Piece: Adoption Counseling in Pregnancy Resource Centers*, author Curtis J. Young states that counselors are generally uninformed about adoption and the choices available today, or are hindered by fears and negative preconceptions.

The result, Young observes, is an extremely low adoption rate in the majority of Centers. There is, in fact, virtually no difference between women who are counseled at a Center and the general population: adoption rates in the United States, in both cases, are estimated at below one percent. Ironically, the women surveyed in the study expressed a greater receptivity to adoption than abortion, though abortion was by far the most widely practiced of the two options.

The failure to present the adoption option can prove costly. In Tanya's case, her initial ignorance surrounding her options would result in a placement several years after her daughter's birth—a placement that would prove traumatic to both mother and child. For Keesha, whose identity was wrapped up in her child, adoption appeared an impossible option, even though she was at risk of permanently losing custody of her daughter. And for many other uninformed women, abortion may appear to be the only feasible alternative to parenting.

WHY CHOOSE ADOPTION?

According to *The Missing Piece*, women often associate adoption with child abandonment, the breaking of trust (the essence of the mother-child relationship), and the exposure of the child to emotional damage. Some women, however, recognize adoption as a way in which to love their children selflessly. Although placing a child is not the right choice for everyone, women who do so may avoid some of the challenges faced by women who choose to parent alone and prematurely.

Research has shown that unmarried mothers are more likely to suffer from depression than other women.[2] A high percentage of these women are poorly educated and at risk of poverty. Thirty-seven percent of unmarried American mothers, one study has shown, do not have a high school degree, while only a mere thirty-one have at least some college experience.[3] In large U.S. cities, forty-one percent of unmarried mothers are poor, and another twenty-eight percent are considered 'near poor.'[4] In the year before their babies were born, the same study shows, thirty-nine percent of unmarried American mothers received welfare or food stamps, twenty-three percent received a housing subsidy, and eight percent received other government transfers, such as unemployment insurance.

The children of single mothers tend to have more difficulties than those raised in intact, two-parent families, and are at higher risk of attachment and learning disorders. There is also a greater risk of sexual abuse: typically, more partners will enter a single mother's home than a woman who has already secured a marriage partner. Furthermore, children who are parented in an unstable home, only to be apprehended or placed after the age of two, often suffer substantial damage.

In contrast, studies show that children raised in adoptive homes typically thrive. According to research conducted by the Search Institute, adoptive adolescents have a self-esteem as high or higher than their peers, are as attached to their parents as siblings who were not adopted, are less likely to have parents who are separated or divorced, and are, in the majority of cases, psychologically healthy.[5]

Birth mothers have also been found, as a whole, to experience more favorable outcomes than those who choose to parent. Columbia University researchers found that unmarried teenagers who place are more likely to complete high school, attend college, secure employment, and find a marital partner than teens who parent. The women studied were less likely to have a subsequent pregnancy out of wedlock, to cohabit, or to require government support. The teenagers who placed also expressed a greater overall satisfaction with life, were less prone to depression, and looked to the future with greater optimism.[6]

OUR EXPERIENCE

Upon reading *The Missing Piece*, we recognized that the experience of most Centers has not been the experience of the Calgary Pregnancy Care Centre, with its significant adoption focus. The Centre, based in one of the two largest cities in the province of Alberta, has made adoption an integral part of its volunteer training, comprising one-eighth of the material covered.

---

[2] The nationwide study, published in the *Child Development* journal in 2002, looked at approximately 1,000 women across the United States between 1979 and 1992.

[3] McLanahan, Sara, et al. "The Fragile Families and Child Wellbeing Study Baseline Report," August 2001.

[4] Ibid.

[5] Peter L. Benson and Anu R. Sharma, et al. "Growing Up Adopted: A Portrait of Adolescents and Their Families," Search Institute, June 1994.

[6] Pearila Brickner Namerow, Debra Kalmuss and Linda F. Cushman, "The Consequences of Placing versus Parenting Among Unmarried Women," *Marriage and Family Review 25*, 1997

Volunteers' fears about adoption are openly addressed, and counselors are equipped to present the option in a positive, non-threatening manner. Clients, in turn, receive ongoing support; the Centre is one of the few to run a successful birth mothers' support group. As a result, the Calgary Pregnancy Care Centre has seen years in which up to ten percent of clients carrying to term have placed their babies for adoption.

The province of Alberta is also an anomaly. Whereas the adoption rate in the United States is approximately one percent and the Canadian rate is two percent, Alberta boasts a rate of four percent. In our view, the combination of effective adoption legislation and the Centre's active involvement has contributed to the unusually high adoption rate.

In the mid-1980s, Alberta developed a privatized open adoption system. Prompted by women's reluctance to release their children to Social Services (which had previously overseen virtually every adoption), the government chose to regulate the trend towards independent adoption by licensing private agencies. The Calgary Pregnancy Care Centre, which began operating in 1985—two years before significant changes were made to the Child Welfare Act—was actively involved in the process.[7] The Centre lobbied as legislation was written around adoption; participated in focus groups and government panels, exploring the ramifications of the proposed legislation; and helped evaluate several aspects of the new legislation as it was put into practice.

Today the Centre continues to be informed and politically active for the sake of its clients. The task of acquiring a wide knowledge base, we believe, is not the sole responsibility of adoption agencies. Because Centre workers are on the front-line, the consequences of failing to provide women with adoption information can be serious: clients may never go to an agency, considering what may have otherwise been a positive option. Even if women choose another option, one that best fits their circumstances, they have the right to know about adoption—and about open adoption, in particular.

Open adoption—a form of adoption in which some degree of contact between the child and its birth mother is maintained—is, of course, a new concept, one that carries an element of suspicion or controversy in many conservative circles. In our view, the imagined horrors of open adoption are not a reality. Although we recognize that open adoption is not an appropriate option for every client, the fact that placing can involve some degree of choice or ongoing contact will make it more palatable to women facing unplanned pregnancies.

We have seen clients who were adamantly opposed to the idea of closed adoption place in a more open scenario. We have received positive feedback to our presentation of adoption information during counseling sessions, even among clients who choose another option. We have worked with birth mothers over the long term, maintaining contact with women whose children are coming into late adolescence and early adulthood. We have seen significant changes in those who avail themselves of our services, successfully undergoing extensive grief counseling, and, in some cases, finding faith or returning to the agency as volunteers.

To fail to educate counselors about positive new trends in adoption, or to neglect to teach clients about the adoption option, is to rob women of what may be a life-affirming, life-changing choice.

---

[7] The CPCC was known, at that time, as the Calgary Crisis Pregnancy Centre (CCPC).

THE MISSING PIECE

According to the Family Research Council, perceptions about adoption are frequently mis-construed. Almost everyone, pregnancy counselors and clients included, is influenced to some degree by the prevalent view in society that placing is a shameful act, one that causes irreparable damage to the child.

For women facing crisis pregnancies, many of these perceptions can be traced back to child-hood. According to research conducted in 1999, the earliest impressions of adoption were, for many of the women interviewed, primarily negative: adoption was typically associated with de-ception and abandonment. Respondents' impressions of adoption did not change over time: the women frequently recounted sensational and extremely negative stories that were propagated by the media.

These earlier associations influenced women when they themselves were faced with un-planned pregnancies. The study pinpoints three emotional equations that show how the major-ity of women perceive adoption:

Adoption = Abandonment
Adoption = The Big Lie
Adoption = An Unbearable Sacrifice

Adoption, in other words, is most powerfully associated with child abandonment, an act of betrayal. Secondly, it is connected with deceit and secrecy—a connection often made through observations made while observing or dealing with adopted friends or relatives. Finally, adop-tion is viewed as an unbearable breaking of the maternal bond, the denial of the powerful incli-nation to nurture, and the loss of dignity and self-worth associated with motherhood.

During the decision-making process, the study reveals, most women will defer back to their earlier associations with adoption, impressions that are firmly rooted. In order to overcome these impressions, Young observes, "communication designed to change how women think and feel about adoption must be able to chip away at those associations and establish new ones" (4).

Surprisingly, research conducted by The Family Research Council also shows that women are more receptive to the idea of adoption than they are to abortion. A representative sample of American women was asked, in a preliminary study in 1997, to consider how likely they would be to counsel a single, pregnant woman to choose abortion, marriage, adoption, or single par-enthood. When asked to rate their preference for each of the four options on a ten-point scale, women were most likely to recommend single parenthood, giving it a 6.1 rating (with one being the least recommended, and ten being the most). Abortion was the least recommended option, being rated a mere 2.3 on the scale.[8]

The researchers were not only struck by the "base-level resistance to abortion" (1), but by the fact that adoption was given a much higher rating of 5.1. For although women were more likely to counsel adoption, actual abortion rates were much higher. This discrepancy led researchers to recognize "an untapped potential for success in motivating women to consider adoption" (1).

---

[7] The marriage option came in third, being rated at 4.4.

Pregnancy Counselors

Part of the missing piece—the inability of Centers to reach the untapped potential—is, according to the 1999 study, related to pregnancy counselors. Although counselors are remarkably committed and empathetic individuals, interviews revealed that they are as prone to the same negative perceptions as the clients they serve. Like other women, in other words, early negative experiences involving closed and secretive adoptions are often transferred to the present.

Even if counselors' earlier impressions are primarily positive, pregnancy workers are typically reluctant to impose the adoption option on women. By discussing adoption, counselors fear that they will lead a client to believe that her ability to parent is being undermined, or that the counselor has a hidden agenda—a financial motive for encouraging her to place. Counselors, being naturally empathetic, are also reluctant to watch clients face the pain of adoption, to share in their distress, or to feel responsible should a client regret her decision to place.

For many counselors, one of the greatest fears is that in presenting the adoption option, they might actually incite a client to abort. These counselors, Young argues, "do not want to risk incurring the potential guilt when it is safer to stay with the near-certainty of clients carrying to term and parenting their babies" (21). Wanting to take the path of least resistance and potential harm, and to maintain trust and rapport with the client, counselors will accept a woman's claim that adoption is out of the question, and view her decision to parent as "a final emotional victory" (22).

In addition to being hindered by fears, the study revealed that counselors lack the expertise and confidence needed to approach the subject of adoption. Few were able to respond to clients' objections or to even open the door to discussion. Once a client had declared her intentions, few believed that her decision could be altered.

Restoring the Missing Piece

When a single woman first discovers that she is pregnant, Young observes, she will typically perceive only two options: abortion and rearing the child alone. Because she is in a state of crisis, a woman who is inclined to abort will have made the choice as a "reflexive response to a threat" (5), with no consideration for the unborn child. At this stage, the decision to abort or to carry is made at a purely emotional level. A client who enters a Pregnancy Center will have made an initial decision and is now seeking reinforcement. However, her uncertainty will provide counselors with a window of opportunity, time in which to encourage her to carefully examine her initial decision.

For a woman who decides to carry, the second stage of decision-making involves the choice between parenthood and adoption. This stage is grueling: she will have months in which to contemplate her decision and to grapple with the advantages and disadvantages of each option. A woman considering adoption must be able, on an emotional level, to give up a piece of her own being: the baby who has become "fused with her self" (10). She must overcome common fears and prejudices about adoption. She must find a source of reliable information and effective assistance.

Women, *The Missing Piece* emphasizes, can overcome the emotional barriers and choose adoption. They can regain "a sense of equilibrium" (12), and "fulfill their need to nurture their children in a very selfless way" (13). Choosing adoption, Young argues, can enable women to "regain their identities as responsible, caring adults" (13), and to place "the welfare of the child above [their] own needs" (14).

Pregnancy Centers, Young concludes, must help restore the missing piece by embracing adoption. If adoption is to become a core value, volunteers and staff must be recruited accordingly. Training must enable counselors to examine and alter their own preconceptions about adoption, and to overcome barriers that prevent them from introducing the option to clients. The Center must not instill in clients the idea that parenting is the only responsible choice, but must openly display information about adoption. Finally, Young argues, the adoption process itself must be formalized to provide women with a sense of closure.

THE ROLE OF CENTERS

Often Pregnancy Centers, fearing that they will be perceived as adoption agencies, will not only fail to present the adoption option, but will do virtually no ongoing adoption counseling with clients. Ironically, while the thought of abandoning a woman who has chosen abortion is considered reprehensible, many Centers will leave another client floundering in her grief—simply because she has chosen the adoption option. Although she will face equally significant and complex grief issues, the client who places is seldom given the support shown to a post-abortive woman. Sadly, both may experience similar repercussions if they fail to grieve, including a tendency to make poor decisions around relationships, to have a replacement pregnancy, or to be unable to move forward.

While a Center's role is not to facilitate adoption, it can play a crucial and unique role as the birth mother's advocate, embracing her even when all other means of support fail. A positive experience for a birth mother will not only result in good choices for her child, but will enable her to become emotionally healthy over the long term. Women who work through their grief become stronger, emotionally and spiritually, acquiring many of the skills needed to make positive life choices. Some clients, in our experience, have even looked back and celebrated the unplanned pregnancy, recognizing that they have grown in ways that they never would have otherwise.

The intent of this book is to help those who seek to better understand birth mothers, the challenges they face, and the unique joy that is theirs. We believe that Pregnancy Centers can successfully present the adoption option to clients and provide a powerful ministry to birth mothers as they work through their grief. The suggestions in the following pages have been tried, tested, and evaluated over the long term. The clients who have participated in the programs offered by the Centre have learned to embrace their role as birth mothers, and have gone on to lead successful lives.

In order to ensure that the voices of birth mothers are heard, we have included firsthand accounts from a variety of women, from a high school student who placed in an open adoption at sixteen, to a forty-five-year-old woman who has never met the daughter she placed in a closed adoption more than two decades ago. These women, speaking from different stages in the adoption process, describe, in their own words, what it means to place a child. Although names and recognizable details have been changed to protect their identities, the stories are their own.[9]

The book includes, too, the views and recollections of other members of the adoption constellation: birth fathers, adoptive couples, and adoptees. The entire adoptive process is examined, from the decision to place and the selection of parents, to the birth and entrustment, to the grief in the days, months, and years to follow and the development of an adoptive relationship over the long term. Other pertinent issues are also addressed, including the spiritual issues that arise from a placement, the complications birth fathers might bring to an adoption, and the additional considerations women must make when they choose to place while parenting other children.

Although written primarily for peer counselors volunteering in Pregnancy Centers, we hope that this book will prove useful to a wider audience. Many lives are, indeed, affected when a woman makes the decision to place. Our hope is that counselors will be better prepared to confidently explore the adoption option with clients, knowing that the choice might be in the best interests of a woman and her child. We hope that adoptive parents will better understand the perspective of a birth mother and what she longs for in an adoptive relationship. We desire to open eyes and minds to the possibility of open adoption. Finally, and perhaps most importantly, we hope that our efforts will enable birth mothers to recognize the significance of their loving sacrifice and to move forward with their heads held high.

---

[9] Unless otherwise noted, interviewees' ages reflect the time the adoption occurred, not when the interview took place.

IN THEIR OWN WORDS

Chantal's Story

"I was twenty-nine when I found out I was pregnant. For the first eight hours, I kept thinking, 'I could just stop this thing. Nobody would know.' Then I came to my senses and knew that I could not go through with an abortion.

"The first person I told was one of my nearest and dearest friends. She phoned out of the blue—she has a history of doing that when I'm in turmoil—and asked how I was doing. When I told her what had happened, she was behind me one hundred percent. She told me to get on a bus, and I spent the weekend at her place.

"I knew that I had to continue with the pregnancy, but I was worried about how I was going to keep this baby. My friend said, 'Often when there're two choices and neither of them looks good, there's a third option.' That's when she mentioned adoption to me.

"I thought, 'No! No! I can't do that!' But then we started talking about it and I decided to go see a counselor at Catholic Social Services.

"I told the birth father about the pregnancy right away because we had been friends for about ten years. His first reaction was that he didn't want to be a part-time dad. We were really straight with each other. The baby was created out of a lovely friendship, but we didn't want to spend the rest of our lives together.

"I spent about a month and a half sitting on the fence, trying to decide whether I was going to keep or place. I had a number of friends saying this, and a number of friends saying that, and I expressed to them that it was very important that they let me sit on the fence and weigh the pros and cons.

"Throughout the whole thing I had been praying lots. God basically said to me, 'When you need to know, you'll know.'

"I found my answer on an evening where my friends and I had gone to the dance bar that my boyfriend and I had frequented. I ran into him and we started talking. He said, 'We're going to have to get some stuff figured out, like money, and where you're going to live, and how you're going to live.'

"As he was talking, my decision was made. A voice in my head said, 'Nope, we don't need to do this, because I'm placing.'

"I went through eight portfolios when I was trying to choose a family. I chose my top three and then thought, 'Oh Lord! How am I going to choose? How do I do this?'

"So the birth father and I went to a meeting with my social worker. She said, 'If I said you had to choose a family within the next five minutes here, would you be able to?' I automatically said yes—and it was the same family that the birth father had at the top of his list!

"I had so many confirmations about my decision and the parents I chose. I knew from the moment I was pregnant that I was having a girl. Growing up, I had always wanted a big brother. When I came across the family's portfolio, it was done from their son's perspective, saying how much he wanted a little sibling. I thought, 'Kaitlyn's going to have the big brother I always wanted!'

"Another confirmation came when I met the adoptive couple and we talked about naming the baby. I said, 'I'd like to have either the first or the middle name, and I'd like it to be Kaitlyn.' They looked at each other and they said, 'That's the very name we were talking about on the way here!'

"Knowing that the decision was made was very helpful. I had some struggles with friends who thought I was just sloughing my responsibility. I actually told one of them, 'If you're making me choose between this decision and the friendship, I'll choose the decision.' That's how right I knew my choice was.

"I spent two whole days with Kaitlyn when she was born. I soaked in every moment; it was incredible. I think she spent only thirty minutes in her bassinet! She even slept with me in the bed. That was something that I had to do. There's no way I could have done it closed and just given her away.

"The placement ceremony was intense. I didn't want to just put Kaitlyn in the car and go my own way. I held her until I actually placed her over. My parents were there, which was very significant. My dad lost it. When that happened, I leaned over to Kaitlyn and I whispered, 'Look what you've done! Thank you!'

"I certainly experienced many emotions after that. I wondered why it had to happen. I was angry that I couldn't get around it and keep her. I was really angry that the birth father didn't make another choice, because had he said, 'Let's get married,' I would've said, 'Yup!' The fact that we loved each other as friends would have allowed us to have a good marriage. And I was sad that Kaitlyn was gone! 'My goodness,' I thought, 'I'm not going to have a relationship with this little one like her mom or dad will!'

"I had an incredible social worker that walked me through step by step, telling me what to expect and preparing me for what was coming. I was able to anticipate the little unexpected things that would have thrown me if I hadn't known.

"The only thing that she was wrong about is that it gets easier. It doesn't. You're able to deal with it better, but it doesn't get any easier. Seeing Kaitlyn grow up is almost harder because I'm not part of it, and I realize that her parents know her better than I ever will. That was a hard lesson to learn.

"But you plug through it. And every time I see Kaitlyn, it's a confirmation. She's so happy and she wouldn't have half of what she has right now if she had been with me on my own. Two people can suffer long term or one person can suffer short term. I chose the one person suffering short-term. And even when I have bad days, it's not because I had to place Kaitlyn. It's because I don't have what I thought I was going to have at this time in my life.

"Kaitlyn has changed my life. I couldn't imagine it without her. I have purpose: she was my purpose for that time. I have a new relationship with God because of her, and a new respect for my life, too. I could have contracted three million different types of STDs. I could be dying of AIDS right now. But I got pregnant. God turned something that I shouldn't have done—or something that could have been really ugly—into the extreme opposite. I can't imagine anything more beautiful than this adoption situation.

"My best friend told me, 'Don't let anyone tell you that placing a baby is any easier than parenting, or vice versa.' I know that it takes a different kind of strength to be a single mom than it does to place a baby. I've explained that to a girlfriend of mine who had a baby when she was sixteen. She said there's no way she could have placed her baby for adoption. I said, 'There's no way I could be a single mom.' We have totally different strengths.

"I find the ignorance around adoption really frustrating. People just think adoption is giving away a baby. It's changed so much! The true nature of the word 'ignorance' is not mean or rude: it means 'not knowing.' Not knowing that you can watch this little baby grow up. Not knowing that you can bring life into the world and not make it a struggle for both of you 24/7 for the rest of your lives.

"There are a lot of babies out there that are aborted because women have this negative conception of adoption. And there are a lot of incredible couples just waiting . . ."

CHAPTER TWO

Options in Adoption

"I would not have been able to get over a closed adoption.
Not knowing where my child is? Forget it!"

—Jacqueline, birth mother, age 23

Decades ago, adoption was shrouded in secrecy. Options were extremely limited; birth mothers remained on the sidelines as decisions were made for them. Adoptions were typically closed. In the hands of private charities, physicians, or government agencies, birth mothers rarely knew the fate of their infants. Their children (with the exception of those placed through interfamily adoptions) seldom found out that they were adopted until adulthood or the death of an adoptive parent.

In the 1980s and '90s, a dramatic, visible shift from closed adoption to open adoption took place. Initiated largely by adult adoptees demanding a right to their records, the movement was embraced by birth mothers who recognized that a degree of openness was, in fact, possible, and that even more openness would be beneficial. Cultural forces sealed the fate of closed adoption as it was once known. With the onset of the information age, evident in private investigators and various Internet sites which reunited adoptees with their birth mothers, secrecy became nearly impossible.

Today, a truly closed adoption is no longer possible: the likelihood of a birth mother being identified and connected with her child is too great. Nevertheless, birth mothers who desire relative anonymity can still choose to avoid meeting adoptive couples or refuse to have contact with their children during the formative years and adolescence.

Should a woman choose open adoption, she may not only meet the adoptive family, but will often maintain some contact with her child. Within the open adoption spectrum, multiple degrees of openness exist. Some women have minimal contact, receiving letters and photographs from the adoptive families; others visit their children on a monthly basis; still others are integrated into the adoptive family, assuming the role of a surrogate aunt or sister figure.

What constitutes 'openness' will vary depending upon the state or province in which the placement occurs. In Quebec, for instance, adoptions are still relatively closed due to the Canadian province's unique Social Services network. If a woman's state or provincial laws do not meet her individual needs, however, she can often place elsewhere. Under the auspices of her local Pregnancy Center, the client can connect with another Center outside of her state or province, obtaining information about residency requirements and other relevant laws. Unless given the option of placing in a very open adoption, some women will not place.

THE NEED FOR CHOICE

The freedom for a woman to make a detailed adoption plan can mean the difference between placing and parenting. Although some women want to ensure that their children have two parents regardless of whether the adoption is open or closed, many believe that placing without obtaining first-hand knowledge of the adoptive family is too risky. Counselors must therefore inform every client about what adoption can look like. Even if a birth mother chooses a comparatively closed adoption, the fact that she made a deliberate and informed choice will enable her to live with that option.

For some clients, especially women with mental health issues or those involved in the sex or drug trade, the probability of having a successful open adoption is remote. If a counselor observes that a woman lacks the stability or maturity needed to maintain an open relationship, she should not foster the expectation that a wide open adoption is within reach. The adoption may quickly close, leaving the embittered client blaming the Center for her misfortune. Still, a well-managed open adoption with very clear boundaries may be possible in some cases.

If a particularly difficult client perceives that she has some choice, she will be less apt to become angry or confrontational. One counselor found that offering women choices 'A,' 'B,' and 'C' often sparked some rational discussion and decision-making in seemingly hopeless situations. During a session, she would first help the woman identify option 'A,' her ideal scenario, which usually involved parenting without intervention from Child Welfare or a government agency. Option 'B' constituted a less palatable but conceivable option—placing in an open adoption and having some contact with the child. Option 'C' represented the worst case scenario, the apprehension of the child and the loss of choice altogether. The counselor would then explain that if the client did not make a plan 'B'—a compromise between 'A' and 'C'—she would risk being left with the most undesirable option.

To a client at risk of having her baby apprehended, option 'B' may prove empowering. When a woman's ability to parent is being questioned, she may still be able to initiate a private adoption if her state or provincial legislation will permit. A woman who places under these circumstances will gain the sense that she has done something for her child, rather than feeling completely powerless. The child, in turn, will be spared the potential trauma of being put through the foster system.

For one twenty-seven-year-old client, the ability to make a choice enabled her to gain some degree of closure. The mother of four children who had been apprehended, she reluctantly admitted that Social Services might intervene upon the birth of her fifth child. Her anger at the governmental agency was obvious. When her counselor raised the topic of open adoption, the woman's interest was piqued. Instead of being forced to relinquish her new son, she decided to give him willingly through adoption.

Although the woman's dreams to parent remained unfulfilled, she was able to select the adoptive parents, plan an entrustment ceremony, and enjoy some limited but ongoing contact with her son. Above all, the client could proudly declare that she had chosen adoption, rather than dealing with the stigma attached to an apprehension by Social Services.

Unfortunately, counselors must be aware that some clients lack the emotional maturity needed to grasp the concept of forming a plan 'B.' Such clients may not even have the basic life skills or functional cognitive processes required to live a productive single life. Although parenting would be out of the question, some women still cannot see past their own wishes.

One distraught client who was six months pregnant came into the Center with her in-home worker. When the client left the room for a cigarette, her worker disclosed that even a dog would be at risk living in the home of the twenty-year-old. The peer counselor saw the client several times and encouraged her to consider making an adoption plan for her unborn child. The woman selected a home. However, since her hopes were set on the remote chance that she would be allowed to parent, the client did not make a firm adoption plan. When the judge ruled against her, her child was apprehended immediately after delivery. What had started out as an open adoption with some choice quickly became closed.

Had the client been able to recognize that no court would allow her to parent, she could have gone through with 'Plan B' and maintained some ongoing contact with her child. Instead, she felt victimized by the system. She called four months after the ruling, pregnant with her second child and residing in a tent in the bush for fear that Social Services would track her down. She refused to see her Pregnancy Center counselor, believing that she would be turned in to the authorities.

It is important for counselors to recognize that in some circumstances, the only thing they can do is stand by a woman's side through an ongoing crisis, remaining a constant support no matter how hopeless the situation. One Pregnancy Center worker describes, firsthand, an experience that forever changed her view of the role of a counselor:

> When Jade first came into the Centre, I knew we were in for a challenge. I can still picture the first time I saw her: she was physically imposing, her anger blatant. She didn't appear to spend much time on her appearance or respect other people's personal space, leaning in too close and speaking too loud. And she quickly enhanced my education as far as street vocabulary and life were concerned.
>
> As her story began to unravel, I realized that this young teen had experienced much pain, and I could understand why she considered herself a world weary adult. She had many emotional issues brought about by the neglect and abuse she had received both in her home and during her years in the foster care system.
>
> Although she knew that the pregnancy wasn't ideal, Jade was looking forward to the birth of her child—someone who would love her and be family to her.
>
> We had a lot to do with Jade during her pregnancy, and everyone involved with her at the Centre agreed that she was in no position to parent this baby. Her family sup-

ports were destructive. The father of the baby was a frightening individual whom she refused to name (for good reason). We did talk to her about the positive potential of adoption for herself and her child; however, it was clear that she had already experienced too many losses and could not even consider it.

We continued to support Jade in whatever way we could and celebrated with her when she gave birth to a healthy baby girl. Like many of our clients, she drifted away from the supports and classes we had to offer but would return when life took a turn for the worse—which was a regular occurrence.

When her daughter was apprehended by Social Services, Jade became a regular visitor to my office. She had little trust for anyone and declared to me that she would continue to see me because she trusted me and felt I'd been good to her. While this may have been a compliment, I wasn't exactly pleased. Jade was not the most pleasant individual to work with. Even worse, I felt that her situation was hopeless: projecting into the future, I was sure that she wouldn't be able to do the things needed to regain custody of her child. I was also concerned about her emotional and mental health, and the fact that she refused to access other resources. Rage and violence were ongoing issues with her. She would get jobs, only to lose them because of her violent temper and her tendency to burn bridges with colleagues who tried to reach out to her.

Over the next few years, Jade regained and then lost custody of her child several times. She often came to my office in a panic, fearing the permanent loss of her child. She also came when she was doing better. Those were the times when I could celebrate with her and affirm her as a worthy human being. She would even listen to some positive input, taking home self-help books or books on parenting.

Jade often came looking for food or bus tickets as well. Although the Centre offers neither, I broke all my normal boundaries and gave her some certificates that could be redeemed at the nearest food store. Even though I realized that she'd probably use them to buy cigarettes, I felt so truly helpless and just wanted to give her something. One day, in the middle of winter, Jade came to the office, coughing and sneezing. She was wearing a light summer jacket that she couldn't even button up. I broke another rule and gave her a coat from our maternity closet, even though she wasn't pregnant. The coat was no fashion statement, but at least it was warm.

Then Jade reached a crisis point. Even though she felt she had been compliant, doing everything she could to become a better parent, she was informed that a court date was being set. Her efforts, although commendable, were not adequate for the well-being of her child, so Social Services was applying for a permanent guardianship order with the intent of finding a permanent foster placement or, ideally, an adoptive family for her daughter.

Her worst fears being realized, Jade panicked, acting out in ways that worked against her. I offered to come with her to court, an offer she accepted with relief. To be honest,

I truly did not want to go. I was sure of the outcome and I was afraid of what might happen since Jade saw parenting her daughter as the only thing that made her life worth living. She felt that all her efforts had been worthless, and saw all government agencies and workers as powerful enemies that were trying to rip her life apart and, in her mind, intent on making her child's life as hopeless as hers felt.

The trial date was set and I kept hoping and praying that by some miracle I would not have to attend, and that Jade would admit she could not win and, in an effort to maintain some dignity, sign the papers and allow her child to find permanence. That was not to be. She expressed to me that she had to fight to the end to try to save her child. For Jade, having her daughter in the care of Social Services brought back all of the painful emotions of her own childhood. She could only imagine the worst happening to her child.

Jade came to my office before the trial, and we took the bus together. She was a nervous wreck and clearly on the verge of a panic attack. I kept encouraging her and trying to make little jokes that might calm her down, since I feared how she might react if she felt cornered. Obviously, the Social Service workers had the same fear as there was a police presence in the courtroom.

I was incredibly proud of Jade that day. From her body language, it was obvious that there were many times that she was coming close to losing control, but instead she would turn around and look at me as I would gesture or mouth, "Stay calm. Breathe. It's okay." She would nod each time and manage to regain her composure. When we left the courtroom, Jade said that she needed to use the restroom. As I was waiting outside, I could hear the slamming of doors and the use of some interesting language. Again, I was proud of Jade because she was venting in a reasonably benign way.

Unfortunately, I dreaded the next day's court session. I knew it would be far worse since the 'experts' would be testifying against Jade. Neither of us slept well that night.

We arrived back in the courtroom early on the second day, and sat alone in the courtroom. Jade took her place in front, and I sat on the first bench directly behind her. That day, I had a series of what I would call 'aha! moments,' revelations that I really didn't want to have but that were absolutely essential.

Even though the proceedings were conducted with dignity and decorum, with everyone behaving professionally, something felt amiss. Yes, the social workers, lawyers, and judge were being much gentler with Jade than I had anticipated. Yes, they obviously felt badly about what had to be done. Yes, they cared about both Jade and her child.

What troubled me was something entirely different. I noticed the court clerk chatting and laughing with one of the lawyers before the trial began. She was young and beautiful, her nails professionally done, her shiny blonde hair styled, every part of her perfectly groomed and made up. She was obviously ready to do this job, which was a new one for her.

I wondered what Jade thought as she sat there, poorly groomed, already crying, wearing what was obviously her best—a torn crocheted top I remember finding with her a long time ago at the Walk-In Closet in preparation for doing a job search. Her shoes, which we had selected at the same place, were torn at the sole and her feet were coming out of them. She was also wearing the coat we had scrounged from the Centre. Her hair was dull, she wore no makeup, and her fingernails were chewed to the point that her fingers appeared raw and painful. Her shoulders were hunched and her body language was oddly both defeated and defiant.

As the trial began and witnesses were called forward, the proceedings became even more painful to observe. First came the social worker, testifying to Jade's failures and her lack of emotional competence and the skills needed to provide even the basic necessities for her child. Next on the stand came the foster mother, a lovely, competent woman who spoke glowingly of how much the child had improved under her care. Then the final blow: the psychologist came to the stand. This obviously well-educated professional spoke of everything Jade lacked—the missing essentials that would make it impossible for her to parent successfully. Then he spoke of the irreversible damage that had already been done in the little girl's life.

I felt removed from the scene, in a sense. I saw for a time what Jade must be seeing, and perceiving, and I felt ashamed. I felt ashamed that I had all the advantages: an education, a job, healthy relationships, and finances that enabled me to live well and to take care of my mental and physical health. I felt ashamed that I would walk out of the courtroom that day back into my comfortable life.

I felt ashamed that I was part of a society and culture that would tolerate the kind of abuse that this young woman had experienced as a child in the system and in her own home. I felt ashamed that this young woman would be given just over four hundred dollars a month to survive on and then be expected to achieve tasks that were virtually insurmountable to someone lacking the basic training and skills that my own children received as a normal part of family and community life.

Jade recently called me. Over the phone, she sobbed as she described how afraid she was to be alone and how fearful she was for her child. She never got to say goodbye. She was also losing her housing and her funding. I felt helpless once again. All I could do was tell her that I was sorry, and that I wished I could make the pain go away.

In the case of this counselor, learning to see the world through the eyes of her client enabled her to maintain a connection even as the birth mother's world fell to pieces. Despite the immense odds faced by her client, the Pregnancy Care Centre worker remains determined to provide Jade—and future clients like her—with whatever ongoing emotional support she needs.

DETERMINING DEGREES OF OPENNESS

When a client is considering adoption, she will need to determine what degree of openness would best suit her. The following questions can help a counselor lead a woman through the preparations needed to make a specific adoption plan:

Would the client prefer to examine the couple's profile or to actually meet them?

Does she want to know the couple's name and address?
Would she prefer to meet in a public place, or would she rather see the home in which her child would be raised?
How much contact would she desire before making a final decision?

What level of commitment is expected?

A letter or a picture once a year for the first two years of her child's life?
Letters and pictures throughout the child's life?
Frequent letters and pictures, and the occasional phone call?
Phone calls on a regular basis in addition to a yearly visit?
Visits on significant dates throughout the year?
Monthly visits? Weekly visits?

What would visitation look like?

A two-hour visit with the couple and child in a public place?
A home visit with the family spanning an entire afternoon?
An allotted time alone baby-sitting the child?
A birth mother/child weekend?

The birth mother must be repeatedly warned, of course, that her expectations may not be met even if the couple she selects agrees to her terms. She cannot interfere with the couple's style of parenting, nor can she demand visitation once the couple obtains legal guardianship. In other words, the adoptive parents have the power to close the adoption, breaking their original promises.

Occasionally, a prospective couple will promise the moon in an attempt to secure a child, and then prove to be disingenuous, closing the adoption entirely. More typically, an adoption will be closed out of geographical necessity: if the adoptive couple moves to another state or province, visits may become irregular, and if the couple moves out of the country, regular visitation will become virtually impossible.

Other couples will close an adoption to strengthen the family's cohesion after a subsequent child is born or adopted. Parents may feel that the open adoption is creating sibling rivalry or accentuating the differences between the adopted and natural children. Problems may also arise when an adoptive couple is dealing with more than one birth mother. In one case, a birth mother watched helplessly as her adoption became increasingly closed. The other birth mother involved had become confrontational and aggressive, causing the adoptive couple to shy away from both women.

Peer counselors cannot offer any guarantees. Adoptive couples are not immune to illness or divorce, or to other circumstances that may alter the family dynamic. Even an excellent match may not work well over the long term. However, the more time a client spends examining the situation and choosing a compatible couple, the better her chances will be of establishing a successful relationship with the adoptive family.

The peer counselor can help to increase a client's odds of success by encouraging the adoptive parents to seek counseling. How receptive adoptive parents will be to open adoption is largely determined by how educated they are around the adoption process. Couples who have had no education regarding open adoption may fail to follow through with their word when conflicts arise.

ADOPTION ALTERNATIVES

Before clients are counseled, it is essential that a Pregnancy Center's executive director obtain information on the adoption laws of that jurisdiction. Family law specialists can be consulted for clarification. [For a list of relevant questions, please consult the appendix.]

There are several avenues of adoption typically available to women seeking to place:

PUBLIC ADOPTION

Government Adoption

This form of adoption is conducted through the auspices of a state or provincial government. Adoptions are arranged by a government department such as Child Welfare, or by agencies, societies, or other organizations funded by the government. Due to its bureaucratic nature, government is often slow to respond to the needs of birth mothers and adoptive couples in the new adoption paradigm. Many of the children surrendered have special needs, having entered the system due to abuse or neglect.

PRIVATE ADOPTION

Private Agency

In a private agency adoption, professionals facilitate the adoption. The adoption agency, which may be non-profit or for profit, connects the birth mother with the adoptive couple for a fee that is usually paid by the couple. Both parties are able to make the critical decisions concerning the match, including how open the adoption will be.

In becoming acquainted with these agencies, Pregnancy Center workers should obtain the following information:

---

[10] If the state or province has a process in place for licensing agencies, Pregnancy Centers should carefully research the implications of referring to a non-licensed agency.

What requirements or credentials must agency workers have?
Is the adoptive couple required to pay a fee?
What costs, if any, must a birth mother cover?
What services can birth mothers expect?
Is the Agency licensed?[10]

Private Direct

In this type of adoption, birth mothers have a direct connection to a couple and the adoption is facilitated through the services of a lawyer. The adoptive couple will generally pay the legal fees.

Third Party or Private Independent Adoption

A third party private adoption is one is which an independent party, whether a doctor, lawyer, or pastor, acts as an intermediary between the birth mother and the adoptive couple. In some jurisdictions, third party adoptions are illegal, as they are considered the brokering of babies. Financial compensation for the birth mother may or may not be permitted as well, although in some cases, a woman who is not allowed to receive compensation can be provided with funds to cover her living expenses.

Third party adoptions can pose some serious problems. Some jurisdictions allow a birth mother to place with a family before a home study has been completed, therefore putting a child's safety at risk. Furthermore, the bonding between parent and child can be disrupted if a home is deemed unfit and the child removed.

Even more common is the risk of interfamily or community conflict. Many unwed women are urged to place by relatives, friends, or adoptive couples within their social circles or communities. Unduly pressured, these birth mothers can make decisions hinged on the advice of others, placing with couples they would have otherwise ruled out. In interfamily situations in particular, the birth mother's anxiety can create conflict, pitting one family member against another, or isolating the woman from those who insist her 'decision' was for the best.

In one incident, a pastor arranged a third party independent adoption. Thinking that he was doing a tremendous deed by bringing an unwed teenager together with a childless couple in the community, and convinced that God orchestrated the union, the pastor was ill prepared when disaster struck. After giving birth, the woman, who had received no grief counseling, opted to keep the child. Caught between an angry birth mother and a devastated adoptive couple, the distraught pastor brought both parties to a local Pregnancy Center in an attempt to repair the damage. His hopes were in vain: the teenager no longer felt accepted by her faith community and in addition to becoming a single mother, decided to abandon one of her major support systems.

Because less mature clients will be more susceptible to pressure, counselors must be prepared to take the necessary steps to protect them. If a woman considering a third party adoption speaks highly of a prospective couple, for example, her counselor should still insist that a home study be done. Clients should also be strongly encouraged to choose the type of adoption most conducive to protecting both their needs and those of their baby.

The client should also be advised that the adoptive parents are required to pay her legal bills in addition to their own. However, the same lawyer should not represent both parties due to a conflict of interest.

OTHER CONSIDERATIONS

When examining her options, a client must be informed about the role the birth father may play in the adoption proceedings. A putative father (the father of a child born to a woman to whom he is not married) may have the legal right to be notified about the adoption. In some cases, his signature may be required before the adoption can proceed.

An estranged wife may discover surprising obstacles when creating an adoption plan. Even if she has been separated from her husband for a decade, the law may consider him to be the baby's father. Similarly, a woman who has been living common-law may, in some jurisdictions, be shocked to discover that her partner has legal rights to her child, even though he is not its biological father.

When sharing information, it is essential that counselors advise clients to seek legal counsel, paid for by the adoptive couple. Although peer counselors can provide general information, they will not have the legal expertise or authority to deal with clients' specific situations.

IN THEIR OWN WORDS

On Open Adoption...

"Open adoption is definitely better than closed. If the adoptive parents have any health concerns about Elizabeth, they call me. She is going to know who I am. She's going to know that I cared for her. She even has a face to hate, if she wants.

"I really didn't want a knock at the door twenty years later, saying, 'Why did you do this to me?'"

—*Jacqueline, birth mother, age 23*

On Closed Adoption...

Michelle's Story

"I was eighteen and had just graduated from High School when I found out I was pregnant. It was November, 1979. I went in to see my family doctor and he said, 'You're Catholic, so you can't have an abortion.' I said, 'Okay.' (I was very compliant in those days.)

"I went to a friend's house that night because I couldn't go home, but trusting her was a poor choice on my part. It was Friday and she wanted to go to the bar. I said, 'Okay.'

I was a zombie that night. I remember people coming up to me asking if I was okay and I said, 'Yeah, I'm fine.'

'I'm fine' quickly became my standard quote.

"I couldn't see myself parenting. I was eighteen, and I know a lot of eighteen-year-olds parent nowadays, but my attitude back then was that I really wanted a mother and a father for my baby. Financially, I couldn't do it, and I honestly didn't think I was mature enough.

"When my family found out, they wanted to know who the birth father was so that my brothers could go and beat him up. We weren't dating anymore and an old girlfriend of his had just come back into town, so I was basically told, 'If she sees us together, you don't know me.' I said, 'Okay.'

I went to the only pregnancy agency I could find. They told me there was no type of housing in town for women in my situation. The only thing I could find was a government-run home for unwed mothers in the city. I had already decided that placing was something I wanted to do. When you're from a small town, you're afraid everyone's going to find out. I had hurt my family enough. I thought leaving town was the best thing to do. I look back and wonder, though, because that's when I needed my family the most.

"I left town when I was almost five months pregnant, when people were already starting to talk. The home I stayed at was run like a big group home—you had your chores and were sent to classes to keep you busy. We were on a first name basis only. I don't think they wanted us to bond with each other. You're basically there for your pregnancy and when you leave, you're gone. I felt totally isolated. My family only came up to visit maybe once or twice a month.

"People often talk about their social workers. I don't have a lot of recollection of mine. I don't even remember her coming to the hospital, though I know she did. I know I met with her once to talk about what kind of parents I was looking for. Today, you have so much choice when looking for a family. Back then, I basically had a choice of religion.

"The best way to describe the social worker was 'cold.' We just met and signed the papers. I was also told not to name my daughter, since the family would probably change her name anyway. She was simply called 'BGG'—'Baby Girl Groeling.' I still think of her as that.

"Before I went to hospital, they said, 'Don't go see your baby. There is a photographer there that will take pictures, but don't do that. It's not a good idea.'

"After labor, they put me in a room that was nowhere near the maternity ward. I went into the maternity ward at one point and asked if I could hold my daughter. I sat in the rocking chair and held her. So many people had told me not to do that, but I couldn't walk away without seeing her.

"I took a cab away from the hospital by myself. I remember looking back at the hospital and thinking, 'I've gone through nine months of hell—the attitudes, the sneers, the glares, the comments, the pain of labor—and I'm walking away with nothing.' I had gone through so much and had nothing to show for it.

"I started college in the fall. All I did was study the first year. By my second year, I was taking drugs, drinking, and sleeping around. I didn't connect any of my destructive behavior to the pregnancy, and things got worse and worse and worse.

"I was really looking for that feeling of being loved. After all I had gone through, I didn't feel loved: I felt pushed down. I liked knowing that people were attracted to me. I didn't use birth control, but amazingly, I didn't get pregnant again.

"For so many years, when it wasn't the alcohol or the drugs, it was the work. I worked so hard, believing I had to be the best. It was almost like making up for what I had done. But at some point I realized that I didn't have to push myself, or prove myself to anyone.

"I came to the Pregnancy Care Centre and went to a birth mother's support group. At the very first one I attended, I shared my story with a group of women. I was fine, I had no problem—until the very end when the leader said, 'Okay, everyone. Bring out your pictures!' I was hanging onto the seat and doing everything I could to fight back tears. That's when I realized that there were a lot of emotions still there.

"After a closed adoption, you carry around the secret and everything that happened to you—how people treated you, the shame, and the guilt. The turning point came when I heard someone say to another birth mom, 'Be proud of who you are. Be proud of your choice.' I actually started crying because I had never heard anyone say that to me. I thought, after so many years, that I could accept my choice—I could be proud of my choice.

"Over the last couple of years I've had to deal with anger and reach acceptance. I can't change the past. I can't change the people. I can't change the way I was treated. I can't blame the whole adoption process back then because they thought they were doing what was best for pregnant women.

"I had always found my own ways—my own rituals—for dealing with my grief. I would always light a candle on my daughter's birthday. Things like that would help me remember. I figured it's not one of those things you're ever going to forget, so you might as well take that time and remember it!

"On my daughter's twenty-first birthday, I decided to do something different. Rather than having a time of grief and sorrow, it would be an opportunity for me to celebrate her birth. Even if I decide to locate her someday and she refuses contact, she cannot take away the fact that I chose life for her.

"I haven't hired anyone to track her down. There's a part of me that really wants to, because I'm curious about what her life has been like and who she is. But I also want to respect where she is at in her life. I don't know when the best time would be to initiate that contact. There might not be a perfect time because there are no guarantees. When I find her, she might reject me, which is something I want to be fully prepared for.

"There was no way to walk through the grief process years ago. I honestly believe there are many women out there who are still suffering. All these secrets. All these years."

Stephen's Story

"I was sixteen when I found out my girlfriend was pregnant. We had been very sexually active from the time we were both fifteen. We had broken up temporarily, and when we got back together, Susan was no longer on the pill. We hadn't even planned the sexual encounter.

"Susan didn't realize that she was pregnant until three months later. She didn't show much at all at any time during the pregnancy, so most people didn't know she was pregnant—not even her parents. She hid it for seven months.

"Back then, abortion wasn't even thought of: it was expensive and the perception was that you had to go down to the States to get it done, and even then it would be done in a back alley. So Susan's family doctor arranged an adoption and assured us that the parents chosen were solid ones. He warned Susan not to hold the baby or be in the same room with it after it was born.

"I was at the hospital during the birth, but I was not allowed in the delivery room. Afterwards, I remember going to the nursery and looking through the window at our baby. It was on the far side of the nursery, so I couldn't see it very well at all. I also remember some sadness around Susan not holding her baby, though I don't remember her ever crying.

"They were careful to ensure that we did not connect with the baby. I can't say that I looked at the baby and had any real thoughts. I had made a decision in my own mind that this really was the best thing for everyone. I wasn't overly upset. I think it would have been much harder if we had had a chance to hold him and connect with him. At the time, I just put that experience away. I told no one. Back then, I honestly didn't have any intricate feelings about anything.

"Susan got pregnant a second time, and we chose to abort. We didn't want to put her parents through the pain of another pregnancy. With all the shame surrounding pregnancy, we took the easy way out. Abortion was possible, by then, and it was much cleaner and simpler than adoption. I was a non-Christian and I didn't consider it a life, so I never had the sense of loss around the abortion that I have had around the adoption.

"It was only ten years ago, when I went to a treatment center for men with addiction problems, that I began to feel. They would ask us on a daily basis, 'How do you feel?' I didn't know. But as I moved through a lot of grief in my recovery process, I began to feel a sense of loss. I went through a year and a half of spontaneous crying and, at times, gut-wrenching crying. There was just a ball of feelings—not any one feeling. But I think that the adoption was a part of it, though how much, I cannot say.

"I have thought at different times about contacting my son and seeing how he turned out. In some of the work I do, I see kids who were adopted out that have serious problems. The tearing away from a mother is very traumatic for a child. I just wondered how my son processed it, and if he has any questions.

"I spoke with Susan once twenty-five or thirty years after we placed. I was thinking of posting our names on the Internet and I asked if she would be interested. She was shocked to hear from me after so long and was uncomfortable with the idea, so I didn't follow up with her. I would still like to post as much information on the Internet as I can gather, because who knows, maybe our son is looking to see who his parents were. He would be in his thirties today and I would love to have a relationship with him.

"In retrospect, I think that my heart was turned towards my girlfriend and my child during the pregnancy. It would have been nice, though, to have had a place where we could have gone as a couple to talk about what was going on. Susan was able to talk to her doctor, but I couldn't talk to anybody! The world basically says to men, 'You don't have a choice. She can do whatever she wants to do, and you can't do anything about it.'

Clare's Story

"Twenty-two years ago, my husband and I agreed that we wanted to adopt. We applied through the government system, knowing that it could take years. We ended up adopting both of our children through private closed adoptions.

"It all began when I met a nurse at a party one night. We got talking about children, and she said, 'If I ever hear of a baby that needs a home, I'll phone you.'

"That was Saturday, and she phoned Tuesday morning! I still think she was an angel, because I couldn't tell you her name if I tried, and she has completely disappeared.

"When we heard about the newborn boy, we sent in a friend of ours who was a lawyer—one that we felt had some compassion. The lawyer basically went in and (this sounds crass) sold us to both the birth mom and her parents.

"I can't imagine what the young mother—she was just seventeen—went through. There was no counseling, no understanding of how to help her through this time of grief and confusion.

"We found out about the baby boy on Tuesday morning, and adopted him Friday night! It was quite wild! The lawyer brought little Paul home at eleven o'clock at night. I didn't have a diaper pin, a bottle—anything! A girlfriend of mine came whipping over with all of the necessities because she didn't want me or my husband out on the road in the middle of winter. She was afraid we'd crash the car because we were so excited.

"I was a little wiser with our second child. When it came time to have a baby, I simply wrote everybody I knew and said, 'Please start praying!' A friend of ours who had just opened an obstetrics office the month before had a lady walk in who was four months pregnant. She asked if he knew anybody who would be interested in parenting her child.

"She was thirty-three and had just separated from her husband. Her husband was not the birth father, and she felt that it was the most prudent thing to release for adoption.

"When our friend told us about this woman, we were thrilled and started a correspondence through the lawyer. At the eleventh hour, after our little girl Ana had been born, her biological grandmother came in to see the baby and tried to convince her daughter to keep the baby (we heard this all through the lawyer). The birth mom said, 'No, I made this decision in a rational moment. My hormones are making me irrational, but I need to carry on with my plan.'

"We sent the birth mom flowers, saying 'thank-you' and 'God bless you.' Apparently that, for her, was the deciding factor. No one in this woman's life had ever sent her flowers.

"In the case of both our son and daughter, the birth parents asked to meet us. We ago-
nized about that. Both times, we came back and said that we didn't feel it was the right
thing at this time. When it came time for our children to know about their past, we explained, we wouldn't hold anything back. If they ever wanted to find their birth moms,
we would encourage them. At the time we were very naïve about what that might look
like, since it wasn't something that was being done at all.

"Our daughter came home with a letter from her birth mom. It basically said that when
the time came, she wanted Ana to know she was placed not because her mother didn't
love her, but because she loved her so much that she wanted her to be raised in a home
with a mother and a father. She thanked us for agreeing to raise her beautiful daughter
and asked God to bless us. That letter was so special to us that we put it in a safety deposit box downtown.

"Of our kids, Ana had the most difficult time. When she hit puberty, she began to struggle with depression. She wasn't sleeping at night, she was irritable and angry, and the
friendships she had were becoming non-existent. One night she had a real meltdown:
she started sobbing and said, 'Why did my birth mother hate me so much?'

"I knew then that the seed of all this angst was her adoption. So I gathered her up in my
lap and said, 'But oh, she loved you so much.' I then told her about the letter.

"We took Ana down to the bank so that she could see the big wrought iron doors and the
two keys it took to open the safety deposit box. This letter was very, very precious, and
she looked at it like it was a gold brick. This was her birth mother's handwriting and her
words! That calmed her down.

"Unfortunately for her, that's all she has—this letter.

"One day Ana came home from school and said, 'Mom, did my birth mom give me a
name? My friend is adopted and her birth mom gave her a name.'

"My heart broke because I had been sent her adoption order and it just said 'Baby Girl' on
it. I had to look Ana in the eye and say, 'She didn't. But I suspect it's because nobody told
her that she could. Nobody gave her permission to give you a name.'

"Ana often had a fantasy family when she was younger. She talked about having four
brothers in Vancouver and would tell people at length about them. I think that this other
family that was thriving elsewhere without her was her birth family in her mind.

"My son was quite a bit older before his search began. When he was little, he loved his
adoption story so much. I told how he came home wrapped in a white blanket and when
I peeled the blanket back, there was this beautiful little pink cherub face. He'd just look
at me and say, 'Oh, tell me again.'

He was confronted at the age of five by a little girl who said, 'You know, you're adopted.'
My heart stopped as I waited for his response.

"He looked at her with a smile on his face and said, 'Yes! And I was just a little baby.'

When Paul got older, he always said that being adopted didn't bother him. It was in the
middle of a very busy afternoon when he was sixteen that he said, 'By the way, I'd like
to find my birth mom.'

"I thought, 'How on earth could he toss that out so flippantly?' Later that night, we
talked and I gave my son the name that had appeared on the adoption order (which had
also been sent to me by mistake years earlier). His mom had given him a name, which I

could tell was a huge, huge gift to him. That was all he needed at that point.

"I told him where to look on the Internet if he wanted to do some research. He hasn't done that yet.

"So far, neither of my children have sought out their birth mothers. The one fear I have is that when they do, Paul and Ana will be met with something less than joy—that their birth mothers won't want to meet them. I've tried to prepare them for that as the years go by.

"At this stage, I would love to meet both the birth moms and sit down with the baby books so they can see the life their children had. I think it would be a huge encouragement for them to see that they did the right thing: their children had a family that loved them, parents that are still together, extended family, and so many opportunities.

"I would also love to see what the birth mothers look like and how they think. I think that will be important for Paul and Ana one day. Right now, they have nobody they're genetically connected to, and I know it's hard on them.

"If I could change anything, I definitely would have met the birth families as requested. I also think that open adoption would have been beneficial in many ways. It's hard knowing that somewhere out there are two women who have no clue about what happened to their kids."

Ana's Story

"I was three days old when I was put up for adoption. I'm almost eighteen now, and I grew up always knowing I was adopted.

"I knew that my birth mother was married, but not to my birth father: she had an affair. She didn't want to have an abortion, so she thought it would be best to put me up for adoption.

"My parents didn't think they could have kids, so they adopted my brother, and then they adopted me.

"I don't remember anything negative whatsoever about being adopted when I was little. It was natural. But when I was older—in junior high—and people started asking questions, I started to question too. People constantly asked questions like, 'Why would your mom give you up for adoption? Did she just not love you?'

"I always wondered that. My mom (the one that adopted me) always told me, 'No, your mom put you up for adoption because she loved you so much that she wanted you to have two parents and a good home.' But I didn't really believe that for a while.

"I felt alone, like nobody really understood what I was going through. My adoptive parents didn't understand because they had never been adopted, and I don't think they really knew what to say or to do.

"I mostly balled my feelings up. I had a lot of built-up emotion in grade six and seven. I went to a Christian school and that really didn't help because everyone came from really good homes. I was the only person who was adopted. And during those two years, being adopted was all I thought about.

"When I imagined my birth family, I always thought that my birth mom would have married my birth father—that she would have left her husband and gotten a divorce. I thought about how cool it would be if they had more kids and I had little brothers and sisters.

"My birth mom wrote a letter and it's in my safety deposit box. It was in her handwriting and it had an impact on me. It reconfirmed the fact that she didn't just give me away—she loved me.

"When I was younger, I gave my adopted dad the hardest time, maybe because he was the one who would punish me when I did something wrong. The worst thing I ever said was, 'You're not my real dad. I hate you! I'm going to find my birth parents.'

"I think my adoptive mom felt sad when I was younger and said, 'I'm definitely going to meet my birth parents!' I had no reason to say that; I just said it. Now that we're able to have an adult talk, though, I honestly think that she's behind me and would support my search.

"I'm almost eighteen and I can decide whether or not to find my birth family. At this point in my life, I know they're not the ones who raised me—they're not my parents. I want to know stupid little things, like how I got my looks, but I don't feel a connection. I feel like my mom's my mom, and my dad's my dad, and my brother's my brother.

"I would like to find out the basics, but I'm not that good with emotional things. I would want to talk to my birth mother about the circumstances, but not about how she felt. That's not my thing!

"I asked my mom the other day if my birth mother would even remember my birthday and she said, 'Of course!' Now that I'm turning eighteen, maybe she's thinking, 'Wow, she's eighteen—an adult.' She'll probably be wondering if I'll look for her.

"I think about my birth dad too. I know some men are a lot less emotional than women, so I've thought of meeting him before I meet my birth mom because it will be a less emotional thing.

"It would be cool to find out if I have siblings, but for me, the hardest thing would be if they didn't know they had a sister, or if they didn't ever want to meet me. I would really like to wait a few years before I do anything.

"I would never adopt—unless, maybe, it was a child from a Third World country or an orphan. Honestly, right now I don't want to have kids, which is part of it. And I don't think I'd be the right person to raise an adopted child because I don't think I'd know what to do with the issues that come up. If something happened to me, I seriously could not handle another kid going through that process.

"I don't know if I would have preferred an open adoption; it's really hard to imagine. If my birth mom had given me more than a letter, I think it would have been harder because I would always be wondering where she is.

"I'm glad there were no secrets though! That would have been terrible growing up thinking that you're part of a family and then finding out that you're not! I would have thought, 'Who are you people?' That's a big secret. If your parents aren't telling you that, then what else aren't they telling you?

"I'm not angry with my birth mother for placing me for adoption. I was angry when I was younger, but that was mostly about not knowing what really went on."

CHAPTER THREE

Pregnancy Centers and Adoption Agencies

"It was lifesaving—meeting my peer counselor. Being open, and informed, and referred to the adoption agency was very important."

—Sandra, birth mother, now age 38

One of the most disheartening things to occur in Pregnancy Centers is the failure to embrace the role that can be played in the adoption process. When a client chooses to place, she is often connected with an agency and then turned over to a professional social worker for counseling. The assumption is made that the client will receive good care.

In reality, the client may receive only minimal care. Should a Pregnancy Center counselor remain involved, however, she can play a unique role that complements the role of the agency worker. While the agency worker serves both the birth mother and the adoptive couple, the Pregnancy Center counselor can act as the birth mother's primary advocate. In referring a client to an adoption agency and believing that the center's mandate has ended, Centers fails to recognize that the birth mother may need an advocate during the process, one who does not need to balance competing agendas.

While most agencies try to accommodate the birth mother's needs, agency workers must serve two parties. Although agencies would have no business without birth mothers, they are financially dependent on adoptive couples, and, in a conflict of interest, the paying customer may hold more sway. And while many adoption agencies would prefer to have long-term relationships with birth mothers, fiscal realities can sometimes preclude this possibility.

In some cases, agencies will also make choices that simplify the process for the adoptive couple or the agency. The resulting guidelines and policies do not always serve the birth mother's best interest. Ignorant of her rights, the woman may feel used and mistreated.

In one case, the birth mother told the adoption agency of her wish to meet the adoptive couple before the baby was born. She did not want ongoing contact, but a single face-to-face meeting. Complications around the pregnancy made her request impossible: she delivered prematurely and agreed to let the adoptive couple take the baby home from the hospital. When the time came for the birth mother to sign the papers, she reminded the agency of her request. She was shocked to find that both the agency and the adoptive couple were resistant. "I let them leave the hospital with my baby," the distraught client told her Pregnancy Center counselor, "and they won't even meet me!"

The peer counselor quickly found that an adoption agency policy dictated that meetings of this nature could only take place prior to delivery. Recognizing that these circumstances were exceptional and that the birth mother could not be faulted for her premature delivery, the Pregnancy Center counselor stepped in as an advocate. The counselor encouraged the woman to discuss the matter with the lawyer overseeing the signing of the papers. He immediately advised her not to sign the papers until her request was honored. When the meeting finally took place, the adoptive couple proved to be everything of which the birth mother had dreamed. She signed the papers and returned home knowing that her baby was in a safe, loving home.

Each client needs a person with whom she can vent, expressing her doubts, anguish, and fears. A birth mother may believe that her agency worker favors the adoptive couple, or does not wish to hear her complaints. Her concerns may be valid: an agency worker will sometimes side with the adoptive couple. After interviewing a wonderful couple that wants a baby more than anything else in the world, the worker may long to work magic for them—a typical human response. In return for making their dreams come true, the worker may assume an almost god-like position in the adoptive couple's eyes. In reasonably closed adoptions especially, the agency worker may be perceived as the one who has made the adoptive couple parents—not the birth mother.

The birth mother, in contrast, can appear far less attractive to the agency worker. In her case, the adoption is a painful process that often overlaps with other unpleasant issues with which she may be dealing, including conflict with her family or the birth father, an incomplete education, and issues involving drug or alcohol use. The birth mother's grief and anger will be evident, and she will not revere the worker. Rather, she may perceive her to be the cause of her intense pain. The worker, in such cases, must make a conscious decision not to take the birth mother's responses personally.

However good the adoption agency, the birth mother will also become aware of a disconcerting loss of control over her situation. At the beginning, when she is still in the decision-making period, both the adoptive couple and the adoption agency will jump through hoops to ensure that the birth mother is comfortable and happy. This 'honeymoon' period will end once the baby is born and the adoption is finalized. The birth mother will lose the power to withhold the child should she become unhappy, and may feel that she has become a secondary citizen. In fact, many birth mothers are afraid to even express their discontent at this stage for fear that the adoption agency will pass this information on to the adoptive couple, who will, in turn, limit contact with her child.

For a birth mother in this situation, having an advocate can be empowering. It is therefore imperative that the Pregnancy Center counselor repeatedly emphasize, from the beginning, that the counselor's single role is to advocate for the client. The Center will continue to care for the woman, regardless of whether she chooses to place, parent, or abort. The Center will not end the counseling relationship if a woman changes her mind. The Pregnancy Center, the client should be assured, is at arm's length from the adoption process.

Similarly, the counselor should emphasize that care will continue after a placement no matter how angry or embittered the birth mother may be. The peer counselor will not be shocked if a client expresses her full anger. However, Pregnancy Center workers must be careful to take any accusations the client makes against the adoption agency in stride. In the process of grieving, a birth mother may unfairly project her anger on to the agency worker, the person who is facilitating the process that is causing her tremendous pain. The worker may be exceptionally talented and still harshly criticized: the issue is often the birth mother's grief, not the worker's conduct.

A peer counselor can often help the client maintain a positive relationship with the adoption agency. In one case, the counselor encouraged an angry client to write a letter to the agency. When the letter was complete, the counselor and client discussed its contents, and the counselor pointed out how much damage an angry letter could cause. The client rewrote the letter, making positive suggestions in a constructive manner. The response was equally positive: the agency made the changes that the client had suggested, and the client was delighted to have made a difference to other birth mothers placing through the agency.

PROFESSIONAL ETHICS

Since a peer counselor serves as the birth mother's primary advocate, extreme care must be taken to avoid situations where a conflict of interest might occur. The following guidelines will help counselors prepare for potentially dangerous scenarios:

Birth mothers

Requests for the peer counselor to adopt

On occasion, a client will ask her peer counselor to adopt her child. When this happens, the Center's executive director must be informed immediately. Only in exceptional circumstances is a request of this nature appropriate. If an attempt is made to arrange an adoption with a volunteer at the Center, the board of directors must be immediately notified.

Centers should also examine their policy around whether women who are actively seeking to adopt can be permitted to counsel.

Adoptive couples

Prior knowledge about the adoptive couple

In small communities in particular, the client may choose an adoptive couple that the peer counselor knows well. When a counselor discovers this coincidence, she must immediately disclose the fact that she knows the couple and offer to find another counselor to work with the client. The counselor must then report this conflict of interest to the executive director immediately.

In some cases, the client will actually be comforted by the fact that her counselor knows the couple, or may view it as a non-issue. A peer counselor who is comfortable with the situation (and does not see the couple on a regular basis) can continue to work with the client, but must not disclose any information to the adoptive couple. Furthermore, she must not look at the couple's file, or give an opinion on whether the birth mother has made an appropriate choice.

If, within the staff or volunteers, one counselor knows the adoptive couple with whom another counselor is dealing, this fact should be disclosed. Neither person should share any further information about the birth mother or the couple. Over the course of debriefing one afternoon, one counselor discovered that she already knew too much about an adoptive couple. "Don't say anything more," she warned the other counselor. "It might very well ruin my dinner with them tonight!"

Meeting the adoptive couple

Some birth mothers will ask their peer counselors to attend the first meeting with a potential adoptive couple. The counselor must remain focused on her mandate: she is there to support the client, not to strike up a friendship with the couple, to decide whether the couple is an appropriate match, or to take over the meeting. A gregarious counselor might believe that her input and leadership is easing the tension between a shy client and an awkward couple. However, her enthusiasm, optimism, and over-involvement can prevent the two parties from bonding properly.

Even worse, the birth mother may place her baby with a couple simply because she knows her counselor approves, leaving the Pregnancy Center worker in a position of responsibility. Even with the best screening, adoptive parents who will fail to honor their initial commitments or who are less than ideal may slip through the process. Ultimately, a birth mother who has been pressured into making a decision may blame her counselor for the negative outcome.

A counselor who cannot restrain herself in a social situation should not attend these meetings.

Further encounters with the adoptive couple

If a counselor has met with an adoptive couple, she should avoid any further contact that may be deemed inappropriate. If the couple phones with questions about the birth mother or the status of the adoption, for example, the counselor should explain that the information can only be disclosed by the adoption agency.

If the birth mother asks her counselor to meet with the adoptive parents to resolve an issue or to explain why the adoption will no longer take place, the counselor should refuse to act as a go-between. The Center should contact a third party, such as the adoption agency worker, for help in handling a situation of this sort.

Counselors must continue to honor the confidentiality of their clients years after an adoption takes place. For example, a counselor is not free to discuss the issue simply because five years have elapsed. In one case, a counselor encountered an adoptive couple at the Pregnancy Care Centre's annual fundraising drive. During the festive event, a woman who was not attending the function approached and asked if she could have her six and eight-year-olds' faces painted. The woman expressed interest in the Centre, and then revealed that both her sons were adopted. When the counselor heard the children's names, she realized that she had counseled their birth mother. Although she longed to identify herself and marvel at the coincidence, the counselor maintained her composure. She even refrained from telling the birth mother that she had stumbled upon her children.

Unsolicited phone calls or messages from prospective adoptive couples

A counselor working with birth mothers will receive mailed profiles and bios, and phone calls from couples seeking to adopt. Under no circumstance should the counselor refer a birth mother to a couple. However, the counselor can refer the couple to an adoption agency and share general information about adoption. The counselor can also reassure callers that unwed mothers are being informed about the adoption option, and advocate for birth mothers by explaining the process from their perspective.

In one unique case, a peer counselor informed a caller about her options and gave her the names of several adoption agencies. Six years later, the counselor discovered that the adoptive mother chosen by a client had striking similarities to the caller from years back. The uncanny resemblance was not coincidental: the adoptive mother had called years ago and received information that would lead to the adoption of her baby girl.

In order to be effective, each Center should have, on hand, the names and numbers of licensed adoption agencies and contact information for international adoption. The names of recent books on adoption can also be shared over the phone or through the mail. A Center can even designate someone to do general educational information sessions on adoption for couples considering this avenue. Some Centers have found that this service turns prospective and adoptive couples into long term supporters of Pregnancy Centers.

Adoption Agency Workers

Client confidentiality

Although Pregnancy Center counselors do not claim to be professionals, they must operate with the highest professional standards. Part of maintaining a high standard involves being hyper vigilant in terms of client confidentiality.

A peer counselor should not have detailed conversations with adoption agency workers unless the client has signed a waiver of confidentiality form. Even after the client's permission has been procured, the counselor should be guarded about what she shares and does not share with an agency worker.

Similarly, if an agency worker phones and discloses information about a client, the peer counselor should stop the conversation immediately. The conversation should not continue until the adoption agency obtains the client's written consent to waive confidentiality.

Advocating for the birth mother

Counselors should always strive to nurture a positive, respectful, collegial relationship with agency workers. However, they should not shy away from advocating for the birth mother, regardless of how much tension is caused. If a birth mother makes a request that is reasonable and within her legal rights, the counselor must advocate on her behalf.

For example, one Center encouraged clients to breastfeed if they so desired, and to consider taking their babies home from hospital for a week before placing. These practices interfered with the adoption agency's policies. Nevertheless, recognizing its responsibility to birth mothers, the Center politely declined the agency's requests to comply with its policies.

A COMPLEMENTARY RELATIONSHIP

The majority of adoption agencies genuinely care for their clients, and will strive to facilitate adoptions that meet the best interests of birth mothers, adoptive couples, and children. Although Pregnancy Centers and adoption agencies play different roles in the adoptive process, their individual services can prove mutually beneficial.

IN THEIR OWN WORDS

"I really got along with the adoption agency, but I realize now that I liked coming to the Centre better. I had major anger towards the agency because they were the people who actually did the adoption. The Centre was a neutral ground; there wasn't anyone who was directly involved."

—*Nicki, birth mother, age 17*

"There were some really good things about the agency. They gave me a large selection of parents to choose from and they didn't hurry me to make a decision. They were good in setting up appointments to meet with the potential couples: it was really based on what worked for me. They always offered me the option to change my mind. They also suggested the Pregnancy Care Centre to me.

"The problem is, adoption agencies are very much there for the adoptive parents: their focus is to place them with the child. Even though it sounds distasteful, the birth parent supplies the child. While I was pregnant, I was very much in the dark about this.

"After I placed, I realized that while the agency had a whole bunch of contact with the adoptive family, they didn't call me or check up on me. If I did talk to them and said I was fine, they would take my word for it and were very happy with that.

"The people at the Pregnancy Care Centre just knew that I wasn't fine. If I said I was, they would grill me more.

"The support group at the adoption agency was a bunch of birth mothers that truly seemed to have not grieved. You could just tell. They were very much, 'Everything's all okay.'

"The birth mothers at the Centre have grieved, and they've grown from the experience."

—*Emily, birth mother, age 25*

"The agencies need to do more to prepare couples that are in the adoptive process. It takes awhile to get your head around the concept of open adoption. It would be so much easier if a mentoring couple was paired with an adoptive prospect, and walked them through the process of thinking it through."

—*John, adoptive father*

CHAPTER FOUR

Opening the Door to Adoption

"I was afraid that if I placed, my son might end up in a bad family and would hate me."

—Aurora, birth mother, age 16

On occasion, a pregnant woman will enter a Pregnancy Center determined to learn how to place her child for adoption. In most cases, however, the mere mention of the word 'adoption' will evoke the following response: "I couldn't possibly carry my baby for nine months, only to give it away." Convinced by the apparent solidity of the woman's conviction, most peer counselors will avoid bringing up the delicate subject again.

The reluctance to provide relevant information or to challenge faulty assumptions about adoption is to commit a grave disservice to clients. Family Research Council research has revealed that while women who seek counseling hope to have their initial choices affirmed, they have yet to reach a final decision. A woman who suspects that she is pregnant will typically experience an immediate predisposition to either carry to term or abort. Grappling with anxiety and uncertainty, she may reassess her alternatives if presented with useful information and support.

In order to help a client make an informed decision, a counselor should not shy away from a discussion about the adoption option. Before exploring this alternative, however, the counselor should first examine her own beliefs and biases about adoption. To be effective, a counselor must be convinced that adoption can be a loving and responsible choice, and will commit—long term—to supporting a client who decides to place. A mature counselor will also show a willingness and motivation to continually learn more about the subject, recognizing the limitations of basic Pregnancy Center training.

Before beginning a session, it is crucial for a counselor to clarify her agenda. The client should be informed that the Pregnancy Center is not an adoption agency, nor does it reap financial benefits if a child is placed. She should be assured that she will be supported regardless of what decision she makes and that only she can decide what is best for her. Impress upon her that the Center is not working on behalf of infertile couples or adoption agencies; its purpose is to support women in crisis pregnancies.

To avoid giving the impression that the adoption option is being foisted upon her, it can be helpful to ask the client for permission to discuss the subject. Explain that a counselor has a responsibility to provide information about all of the alternatives. A woman who has decided to place for adoption will be given information about parenting. Likewise, a woman who has dismissed the possibility of adoption will still be offered information. A good choice is made when each of the alternatives has been thoroughly examined.

COMMON ADOPTION FEARS

When faced with the claim that a client could never carry a baby to term, only to 'give it away,' a counselor should gently challenge the woman's presuppositions. Recognizing that a woman's first exposure to adoption—whether through a childhood friend, a relative, or the media—will color her view, create a dialogue that will bring these early impressions into the open. By asking the right questions, a peer counselor can help a woman identify fears and re-evaluate assumptions in light of current information. A discussion can be prompted by a single question:

What about adoption makes it seem like such a difficult choice for you?

At this point in the conversation, a client will typically respond in one of five ways:

I couldn't stand 'not knowing' about my child.

What if my child was abused or hurt?

What if my child hated me for giving him up?

I couldn't go through that kind of pain.

I don't want to get fat, or have stretch marks—and then have nothing to show for it.

A counselor can then address these common objections to adoption by replacing myth, or outdated information, with fact:

THE FEAR OF 'NOT KNOWING'

As Curtis J. Young observes in The Missing Piece, most of the women interviewed in the study had little knowledge regarding the modern adoption scenario. The majority was unaware of the options available to birth mothers. Few knew how much control birth mothers can now have over the adoption process, or that it is possible for a birth mother to receive periodic information about her child.

When a woman expresses fear about not knowing where her child is and whether it is being well cared for, a counselor should point out the differences between adoption in the past and adoption today. Several decades ago, birth mothers knew virtually nothing about their children's fates and were frequently haunted by their experiences. Women placing for adoption today, in contrast, have an amazing amount of information available and often witness, first-hand, the lives their children lead. The 'unknown' is no longer a reality in most cases.

A counselor can share the stories of former clients who have placed. A variety of adoption scenarios should be presented to give the client an idea of how open an adoption can be, while giving her a realistic view of the restrictions some birth mothers face. The names of former clients, of course, should always be changed to ensure client confidentiality.

THE FEAR OF CHILD ABUSE

A client that expresses concern about her child's safety should be applauded. However, the counselor can point out, once again, the difference between adoption past and present. Whereas social service agencies once relinquished babies to any warm and willing body, consequently placing some children in homes where horrendous abuse occurred, prospective parents are now carefully screened. Adoption agencies take every possible precaution due to issues surrounding legal liability. Furthermore, the current demand for infants ensures that babies go to carefully screened families, unlike past scenarios where infants were dropped into any available home. And, most importantly, birth mothers themselves now play a significant role in the process, and can often choose who will parent their babies.

It may be helpful to remind the client that children who live with their biological parents have not had the benefit of having either parent screened. An adopted child, in contrast, is given an additional safety net when unsuitable candidates are turned away by the adoption agency.

A particularly astute client may question why some statistics show that adopted children have more significant problems or experience less success than those raised in natural homes. A counselor can point out that some statistics do not relate solely to newborns that have been placed, but involve older children. Adoptions through social service agencies, for example, often involve children who had been apprehended from their natural homes because of abuse or neglect. Such children are typically adopted after being shifted through the foster care system and therefore exhibit the effects of multiple traumas. Studies of newborns, in contrast, show no significant differences between natural and adopted infants.

THE FEAR OF REJECTION

A woman may express concern about what her child will think of her as it grows older. She may fear that it will not understand why she chose adoption and may consequently hate her for making the decision. As Young observes in The Missing Piece, many women associate adoption with abandonment and are therefore convinced that an adopted child would feel betrayed, even if it clearly understood that its adoptive parents could provide a superior quality of life.

In the past, an adoptive couple would simply tell a child that its birth mother was too young to be a mother. Nothing more could be said; adoptive parents were given virtually no information about their child's biological parents. Today, however, an adoptive couple will have likely met the birth mother and can pass on detailed information to the child. Even more reassuring to a concerned client is the fact that many birth mothers have the opportunity to explain their decisions to their children, whether in person or in a letter. When given detailed information about the birth mother and her reasons for placing, a child will undoubtedly recognize that the decision was made out of love.

THE FEAR OF UNBEARABLE PAIN

In some women's minds, placing their children would be "just too painful." As The Missing Piece reveals, many women fear that nine months of pregnancy will create an irrevocable mother-child bond, one that cannot—and should not—be severed. On a deeper level, the study states, women feel that they would be unable to endure the embarrassment and judgment of carrying a baby conceived out of wedlock to term, only to 'give it away.'

A client may identify what she perceives as the costs of adoption: returning home from the hospital empty-handed, missing all of the 'firsts' in her child's life, and not being able to see her child grow up. A counselor can point out that many women who come to the Center for post-abortion counseling mourn these very losses. Years after having an abortion, women typically lament, "I wonder what my child would have been like. No one told me how painful this was going to be." Both adoption and abortion, in other words, put a pregnant woman in the position of having to experience significant grief.

The choice to parent also entails a degree of loss of which many clients may be unaware. As with abortion grief, parenting grief may seem abstract. A counselor can point out that a client's social network will likely change when her friends lose interest in the novelty of her baby. A young mother will also lose her carefree status, carrying adult responsibilities at a time when her peers are spontaneous and adventurous. Furthermore, having a child may hinder future romantic relationships; some men may be unwilling to commit because of the complications that arise. Every woman who chooses to parent faces, along with much joy, a degree of loss. A young, single mother has much to lose.

Women who place for adoption for the right reasons and receive proper counseling during the pregnancy and after the placement consistently speak of a positive, albeit painful, growth experience. Although the grieving process is extremely difficult, few of these women, when evaluating their choices later in life, would change their minds.

FEAR OF THE PHYSICAL SIDE EFFECTS OF PREGNANCY

However insignificant this concern may seem when compared to others—such as the fear of the neglect and abuse of an adopted child—some women find the physical consequences of adoption to be particularly unpalatable. Carrying a child to term can result in permanent stretch marks, weight gain, and fluctuating hormones. The prospect of a painful delivery is no more appealing. Finally, the thought of 'giving away' her child after all of the physical side costs can be too much to bear. A woman may believe the adoption process too fraught with loss to be worth the physical marks.

Counselors may find this objection difficult to counter, as pregnancy inarguably exacts a physical cost. However, a counselor can call the client to a sense of maturity, reminding her that although the difficult things in life are costly, they can also be the most rewarding. The counselor can also assuage some of the client's anxiety. She can be reminded, for example, that she is not required to gain copious amounts of body fat, but can limit her weight gain through appropriate exercise and healthy eating habits. Although stretch marks may be inevitable, the client can be encouraged to see them for what they are: badges of honor.

A young woman in particular may have a difficult time associating the changes in her body with the creation of a new human life. She may view her unborn child as an alien, something foreign that is taking over her body. For this reason, a counselor should strive to connect the client's mind with her heart, helping her to recognize that the unpleasant side effects she is experiencing are also the beginning of something miraculous. Extreme caution should be taken when discussing the unborn: a woman who chooses abortion or has had one in the past will be especially sensitive to inflammatory language, language that is never appropriate in a counseling session.

A TIME TO DECIDE

Before the first session ends, impress upon the client the importance of making a decision. Some women postpone the decision-making process and eventually parent out of default. Others follow their gut instinct to place and fail to examine the parenting option, only to discover, months later, that they are not prepared to deal with the grief that accompanies adoption. Encourage the client to carefully examine each of the alternatives, and then come to a point where she can make and celebrate her decision.

A Mother's Greatest Fear

According to the Family Research Council's 1999 study, most women equate adoption with three things: the abandonment of a child, deception, and unbearable sacrifice.* The most powerful association, that of abandonment, compels women to question the integrity and character of other women who have 'given up' their 'unwanted' infants. Also significant is the connection, in women's minds, between adoption and 'the big lie'—a violation of trust in the mother-child relationship. Adoption is, from this perspective, inextricably linked to secrecy and deceit. Similarly distressing is the association made between adoption and an unbearable sacrifice. Placing a child for adoption is, at an emotional level, equivalent to a woman parting with a piece of herself.

Counseling tip: In a good counseling session, each of these fears should be addressed.

Who Chooses Adoption?

The more emotionally mature a woman, the more likely she is to be open to adoption, the Family Research Council study has revealed. In order to view adoption as a potential alternative, a woman must be able to differentiate between herself and her child. In addition to taking responsibility for the pregnancy, she must recognize her duty to ensure that her child's individual needs will be met.

Emotionally immature women, the survey shows, place their needs above the needs of their children. Many women were able to recognize that adoptive parents have the resources to provide for a child and have much to offer emotionally. However, respondents typically contradicted themselves, immediately arguing that adoptive parents might abuse or neglect the child, and could never love a child more than its biological mother.

Counseling tip: In order to help a client differentiate between child and self, first ask her to list the pros and cons of abortion, parenting, and adoption in relation to herself. Then ask her to list how her child would benefit or suffer from each of these decisions. The creation of separate lists can highlight the difference between mother and child

What Clients Look for in a Counselor

Women, according to Family Research Council research, do not want to be pressured into choosing adoption, or to be counseled by someone who might profit from the decision to place. By the same token, they do not want to be undermined should they decide to place, and resent the unspoken assumption that every woman will inevitably wish to parent.

An ideal counselor, explained the women interviewed, is one with whom they can connect on an emotional level. Although a counselor may not have experienced an adoption first-hand, respondents observed, she would be more effective if she had children of her own. Maintaining trust is also essential; a counselor, according to these women, should offer support without judgment and give meaningful advice without pushing an agenda.

Counseling tip: A peer counselor should repeatedly remind the client that the Pregnancy Center does not have an agenda.

IN THEIR OWN WORDS

On fears about adoption...

"I knew nothing about open adoption. I was afraid that if I placed, I would have a knock at the door twenty years later and face a very, very angry child."

—*Jacqueline, birth mother, age 23*

"I was very much in the dark about open adoption. Everybody I knew who was adopted was from a closed adoption. Everything I read was about closed adoption. It's not until I went to an agency that I found out about open adoption."

—*Emily, birth mother, age 25*

On outside pressures...

"My friends thought I was being selfish, mean, and nasty. How could I possibly give away my flesh and blood?"

—*Jacqueline, birth mother, age 23*

"When I first brought up the whole idea of adoption, everyone was like, 'I could never do that. I would never do that!'

"The worst comment came from this one lady who lived two blocks down from me. She said, 'You don't know how this baby's going to turn out when it's born because it was conceived in sin.'"

—*Sandra, birth mother, now age 38*

"Recently someone told me how selfish I was to 'give up' my child because I 'didn't want to take care of him.' I told them, 'That's your opinion, but it's a very stupid opinion, thank-you very much.'

"If I can't take care of my child, why should I keep him, giving him a below-standard life? Why would I choose to live with a child in a one-bedroom hole in downtown Edmonton and be scared to keep my door unlocked?

"People really need to realize that women who give their children for adoption aren't thinking about themselves. They're thinking about their children. They're thinking, 'What can this family give my child that I can't?' It's a huge decision that takes months—even years—to get over. It's not like I just thought, one day, 'I don't want to have a child anymore, so you can take him.'"

—*Aurora, birth mother, age 16*

CHAPTER FIVE

Choosing Adoptive Parents

*"They were healthy mentally, physically, spiritually, and financially. They had a
lot of qualities I wanted, plus. They were a great couple: they deserved a child."*

—Chantal, birth mother, age 30

A birth mother's choice of adoptive parents is one of the most significant decisions she will ever make. Inasmuch as choosing to place reflects a woman's love, the amount of time spent in deciding with whom to place is testimony to the value she has placed on her child.

Counselors will quickly become aware of how much a client's age and stage of life can impact her evaluation of prospective parents. A professional in her mid-twenties will have a different perspective than a client whose main objective is to override the authority figures in her life. Similarly, a client in her thirties will almost inevitably be attracted to a couple far different than the one selected by a woman half her age.

One fourteen-year-old who decided to place, for example, was obsessed with skiing and insisted that the adoptive parents share her passion. When her counselor encouraged her to put more thought into her decision, the client reasoned that the adoptive parents should also be wealthy, so that a want of finances would not hinder their athletic pursuits. Having established these two criteria, the young woman concluded that her baby would have a suitable set of parents. Fortunately for the child, the adoption agency had carefully screened the adoptive couple, who proved to have numerous attributes besides their athletic prowess and wealth.

Although an immature birth mother may lack wisdom and depth in the decision-making process, her counselor should not despair. Leading the client through a series of questions can reveal her values and raise issues that she might otherwise ignore. However superficial her reasoning at fourteen, she will eventually care very much about the quality of the decision she made—and about her counselor's efforts.

One bemused counselor had a client who was delighted to discover that a potential adoptive father did clowning on the side. Attempts to provoke a conversation about values and to encourage the woman to examine other criteria failed miserably: the birth mother repeatedly returned to the merits of the clowning industry. However, the counselor wisely persisted, recognizing that as the client matured, she would regret basing her decision solely on a hobby, however jovial a

44

red-nosed adoptive father might prove to be.

In addition to being influenced by her age and life experience, a client's choice of adoptive parents will almost always be inextricably linked to her own upbringing. A woman who was loved and respected as a child may well choose adoptive parents with a striking resemblance to her own. In contrast, a birth mother that has been reared in a dysfunctional environment will probably select a couple that compensates for her family's deficits. If her parents were alcoholics, she may place considerable emphasis on the adoptive couple's attitudes towards alcohol. Similarly, an outgoing and affectionate couple will have particular appeal to a birth mother whose own parents were cold and unresponsive. In order to help the client recognize the impact her own upbringing will have on her child's future, a counselor can challenge her to examine both the positive and negative aspects of her childhood.

When the client begins searching through the profiles of prospective couples, the counselor should remind her of the serious nature of her decision. If, in the future, her child questions why she chose the couple she did, she will be able to articulate her reasons with confidence.

She should also be repeatedly warned not to place her child with a particular couple out of sympathy or obligation. Her goal is not to make an infertile couple happy, but to find the best possible parents for her baby. The moment a woman considers placing, she may find herself wooed by infertile couples—or those advocating for them. She may face pressure to commit to a specific couple long before she has considered what qualities she is seeking. Since the client will regret a decision made in haste or out of guilt, she should be encouraged to politely inform her suitors that she is not yet meeting with prospects, but can be contacted at a specific time. She can also state that she is making a selection through her agency.

The following is a list of concrete questions that can be used to help the birth mother create a list of criteria. The questions should be covered in one or two sessions before the client begins examining profiles of prospective couples.

Is age a consideration?

Birth mothers often harbor idealistic images of young, attractive married couples in their mid-twenties seeking to adopt. Indeed, teenage clients frequently view people in their mid-thirties as unspeakably old, more fit for the geriatric ward than for pampers and pablum. However, the reality is that many couples marry in their late twenties and do not discover that they are infertile until their mid to late thirties.

A counselor can help a client set a realistic age range, citing the benefits that a more mature couple will offer a child. However, the birth mother should not feel obliged to consider a couple that she feels is too old. An infant placed with parents that are in their mid-forties or even fifties, for example, could face the prospect of losing its parents long before an infant placed with a younger couple.

Are the couple's racial origins important?

In some cases, a birth mother will place great significance on the adoptive couple's ethnic heritage. If a birth mother is carrying a child of a mixed race, for example, she may wish to find parents with a similar background, who will not only understand the unique challenges her child will face, but will share a common appearance. Locating a couple interested in adopting a child of mixed origins is more difficult in the United States than in Canada, where multiracial families are more accepted.

How important is the couple's religious background?

The faith of the adoptive couple is often of utmost importance to a birth mother. If she adheres to a specific faith, she will want her child to follow suit. Mormon clients, for example, seldom consider placing children in homes that do not share the same unique belief system. An atheist, in turn, may not want her child enrolled in Sunday school, and will avoid placing with a family of professing Christians. In contrast, clients with no faith background whatsoever often purposely seek religious couples, believing that additional stability and compassion come with a faith system.

If religion is an issue to a client, a counselor should encourage her to examine the couple's religious background with great care. There may be a vast difference between her definition of a 'Christian' and her social worker's interpretation. One client, for example, went to a Christian adoption agency seeking a Christian adoptive family. Upon meeting a prospective couple, she quickly realized that although they attended church, their faith did not extend beyond the pew. By taking responsibility for carefully screening the couple herself, this birth mother avoided placing her son in a home that was incompatible with her belief system.

When examining the question of religion with a client, the counselor has a responsibility not to impose her own belief system. In some cases, a rebellious birth mother will deliberately make a choice that conflicts with her religious background. One client, reared in a strict Catholic home, insisted that the adoptive couple should have no interest in religion whatsoever, making the absence of faith her most significant criteria. Her Christian counselor wisely honored her choice, recognizing that God's hand was on the child regardless of the birth mother's decision.

If a birth mother has a strong faith, encourage her to spiritually parent her child from afar. Indeed, a woman who prays for her child on a regular basis can experience a strong sense of connection and inner peace.

Into what financial bracket should the couple fit? How important are their vocations?

A birth mother should consider what lifestyle she would like her child to have. Younger clients, who have not yet dealt extensively with finances, can be given information to help differentiate between a professional salary and a blue-collar salary, and to understand, in a concrete way, what it means to live above or below the poverty line. To help an inexperienced client obtain an understanding of how far money will go, a counselor can discuss the costs that parents must consider when feeding and clothing one or more children, paying a mortgage, and planning a family vacation. While $10,000 may sound impressive to a teenager who lives at home and spends her sparse summer earnings on recreation, it will certainly appear less so when placed in a different context.

Clients should be warned, however, that a high income will not guarantee a happy home. Women who come from lower socioeconomic brackets may have less in common with more affluent couples, and these differences may be detrimental in an open adoption. One client who came from a modest background chose adoptive parents strictly on the fact that they were very wealthy. This apparent virtue quickly became a vice in the birth mother's eyes when she realized that she was an embarrassment to her child's parents. As time progressed, she saw adverse qualities in them that she had failed to recognize when she was preoccupied with their financial status. This particular couple, the birth mother observed with regret, placed more emphasis on giving the child material items than in the giving of themselves.

When examining finances, the client should also consider whether she wants one parent to remain at home with the child. Although few families can guarantee that they will be able to consistently depend on a single salary income, their current financial position will indicate whether the decision for one parent to stay at home is feasible.

Is the couple's level of education important?

Ambitious women who have attended university often want their children to be exposed to the arts and culture, and to be stimulated intellectually from the cradle on. These women will place a high priority on both the adoptive couple's education and the expectation that the adopted child will pursue post-secondary studies. Other birth mothers may find other criteria more pressing.

What qualities should the adoptive father have?

Since a birth mother will naturally focus on her 'replacement'—the adoptive mother—advise her to consider the other half of the equation, the adoptive father. A counselor can ask the birth mother what her own father was like, the kind of relationship she shared with him, and what she would change. The more a woman reflects upon her own background, the more real the adoptive parents will become. Younger clients in particular will begin to recognize that the people they interview are human, with individual faults and inadequacies, as well as strengths. If her own father was distant or too rigid, a perceptive birth mother can avoid choosing the same for her child. Many birth mothers became pregnant in their search for male approval and affection; they now have the opportunity to give their children what they themselves craved.

As the client examines the intricacies of her past, the counselor should encourage her to write her thoughts down for future reflection. If she is unable, do so for her, and then relay her thoughts back to her.

Should the child be reared in an urban or rural setting?

Some clients envision having their children raised in a small town or on a farm, away from the crowded, sterile city environment. They also delight in the idea of their children being surrounded by animals, believing that adoptive couples who nurture pets will be more apt to nurture children. A surprising number of birth mothers insist that their children have the opportunity to raise a puppy or kitten, criteria that might appear insignificant to counselors. A woman's wishes should be acknowledged and respected, even if she has idealized notions of life on the farm or in the city.

Should the baby be a first or an only child?

A woman should consider whether she wants her baby to be the eldest (and possibly the only) child of an adoptive couple, or if she would prefer that the infant have a sibling. Many birth mothers delight in giving a couple the excitement of raising their first child, especially since the eldest child will hold the distinction of making the couple parents.

Other women place higher value on ensuring that their children have siblings. Since many infertile couples may only have the opportunity to raise one child due to the shortage of available infants, some birth mothers will often place their children with couples that are already rearing one or more children. A mature birth mother will recognize several benefits in this arrangement: she will have the opportunity to observe how the adoptive couple parents, how open the previous adoptions are, and the couple's respect for the other birth mothers involved.

There are, of course, birth mothers who take a different approach altogether. Upon placing, they go to great lengths to find a sibling for their children. During a counseling session, one birth mother lamented that her infant's adoptive parents were moving too slowly in their search for a second child. She then contemplated strategies that would ensure that the process move swiftly and surely. Another birth mother, upon volunteering at a local high school's program for pregnant girls, inadvertently found a sibling for her son. Her description of the couple she had placed with was so evocative that a pregnant teenager in the audience realized that her search had ended.

What role should the adoptive couple's extended family play in the life of the child?

If a birth mother was an only child, lost her grandparents at an early age, or grew up in a dysfunctional home with limited support from the extended family, she will often carefully examine a prospective adoptive couple's larger family dynamic. The potential for the active involvement of aunts, uncles, grandparents, and cousins in her child's life can be a drawing factor.

Will the adoptive couple be open to raising a child with a disability?

Some clients suffer from a physical or mental disorder with a genetic component. In addition to disclosing their medical histories, these clients must evaluate how receptive the adoptive couple should be to rearing a child with a physical or mental handicap. One lower-functioning client thoughtfully identified the risks associated with the question of disability. "The couple must be okay with a handicapped child," she told her counselor, "because otherwise, if he's not normal at some point in his life, they might reject him."

Another birth mother, a mature seventeen-year-old, had a different perspective. Each couple she interviewed was asked twenty-eight questions, including what they would do if the child was born with an abnormality. One couple she interviewed went against the grain, stating that they would not readily adopt a handicapped child. Although they would accept a child with a minor deformity, they explained, they would have to rethink the decision to adopt if the infant had a profound disability. The birth mother respected the couple's honesty so much that she placed her infant with them.

How open will the adoption be?

The birth mother and the adoptive couple may have very different conceptions of what constitutes an 'open' adoption. The couple may envision meeting the woman every other month in a restaurant, while the birth mother imagines herself assuming the role of a live-in nanny—or practically becoming an adopted child herself. Due to the wide range of expectations, a birth mother should attempt to gauge how receptive a couple is to the prospect of an open adoption, asking them to clearly define their boundaries. If she chooses the couple, ample time should be spent in negotiations.

If a birth mother has only a vague notion of what she wants, or suspects that she will want little involvement in her child's life, she should still be encouraged to request a high degree of openness. Not only will she be able to gauge the couple's level of security surrounding the adoption, but she will provide herself with more options in the future. Remind her that in the adoption scenario, it will be easier to close a door than to open it.

Has the couple dealt with their own infertility issues?

Prospective adoptive parents who have not fully resolved their infertility issues may carry emotional baggage into the adoption. Although a client may feel awkward addressing this highly personal topic, she needs to recognize that her baby should not serve as a replacement for a miscarried child. Her infant is a unique individual and must be valued as such. Furthermore, the birth mother should be warned that couples with unresolved issues are often resistant to open adoption. To a struggling couple, the birth mother's presence can be an unwelcome reminder that the child they hold is not biologically their own.

One seventeen-year-old birth mother interviewed a couple that had had six miscarriages and a stillborn infant in rapid succession. Adoption was clearly an option the couple was seeking only out of desperation. They claimed that they were receptive to an open adoption, but gave obvious indications to suggest otherwise. Young and inexperienced, the birth mother did not understand the complexities of the issues that had surfaced during the interview. She felt great sympathy for the couple and believed that her child might prove the solution to their problems. The fact that the couple was related to her pastor only intensified her sense of obligation.

Sensing a serious conflict of interest, the counselor gently reminded the birth mother that her child was special in its own right. Careful not to infringe on the client's right to choose, the counselor emphasized the importance of placing the child's needs over those of the couple. Of her own accord, the birth mother chose a more suitable couple and, years later, expressed immense relief that she had done so.

MEETING WITH PROSPECTIVE COUPLES

In some adoption scenarios, a woman's social worker will select the adoptive family. Most women, however, will have the opportunity to examine profiles, collecting information ranging from the couple's financial status to where they last vacationed. Many women are able to meet the adoptive couple in person at least once.

However beneficial these meetings are, they are understandably fraught with tension. The birth mother must not only collect critical information in a short period of time, but she must also deal with her insecurities and the desire to be liked. If she chooses the couple in front of her, she knows that they too are forming an impression of her, one that will eventually be relayed to her child.

The experience is no less intimidating for the prospective couple. Their ability to make a good impression may mean the difference between parenthood and rejection. Having been selected for an interview, they may fear that a social blunder or a 'wrong' answer may close a door that they have come so close to opening.

Meetings may take place at the adoption agency or even at the Pregnancy Center. However, a birth mother can choose to meet an adoptive couple at a restaurant or another public place. Having a meal in which coffee, dinner, and dessert are served can offer helpful distractions: awkward moments or uncomfortable pauses can be averted, and the entire process of eating will offer ample time to discuss the issues at hand.

In order to relieve tension for both parties, a counselor can encourage the client to prepare a list of questions to bring to the meeting. The goal is not to interrogate the already anxious couple, but to ease them into a comfortable discussion, and to ensure that critical issues are addressed. The birth mother can begin with non-threatening, positive questions like, "So, where did you meet and was it love at first sight?", to ease the tension.

With the aid of a good counselor, a birth mother can prepare open-ended questions that will help to create a dialogue. Help the client to understand the difference between concrete, information-based questions, and open-ended, values-based questions, as the latter will give her a broader sense of the couple. For example, instead of stating, "Do you believe in spanking?", a question that will merit a specific response, a client can ask, "How do you plan to discipline your child?" Likewise, the question, "How would you describe your spiritual journey?" will promote a more in-depth discussion than, "Do you attend church?"

Depending upon the situation, a birth mother may choose to bring a friend, family member, government social worker, adoption agency worker, or peer counselor to the meeting. This person should not take control of the situation, or play an active role in the discussion. Rather, the individual should carefully listen to what is said during the meeting, as the birth mother may be too nervous to absorb the information. If she can rely on more than one memory, her ability to make an informed decision will increase. The third party can also help alleviate the discomfort a young client may feel when surrounded by adults. A fifteen-year-old who lacks the social graces of the older couple she is interviewing will be more likely to carry out a successful interview knowing that she has an advocate in the same room.

The peer counselor must always maintain her position as the birth mother's advocate. After viewing the hopes, expectations, and the tremendous capacity of a prospective couple, a counselor can become emotionally involved. If the birth mother should choose a less ideal couple, in the counselor's view, or decide to parent after promising to place, her counselor may feel tempted to advocate for the disappointed couple. However, a counselor's role is to support the birth mother in her decision, not to attempt to alter it.

After the first interview, a birth mother may meet with the adoptive couple several times before making a final decision. In some cases, women will visit the couple's home or even meet the extended family, depending on the couple's comfort level. A wise counselor will not enter into these ongoing meetings with the adoptive couple, knowing that developing any sort of relationship with them could lead to a conflict of interest.

Once each meeting is over, it is critical for the birth mother to find someone with whom to debrief. A counselor can be of tremendous help at this time, helping the woman analyze who it was that she met, process the interactions that took place, and solidify her assessment. The peer counselor can question and respond to the birth mother's observations, enabling her to see from a different perspective without offering a value judgment. Together, the birth mother and her counselor can create a list of questions for the woman to bring to her next session with the adoptive couple.

Since a birth mother will tend to focus primarily on the adoptive mother, her counselor should encourage her to take a more balanced approach, directing questions to the adoptive father as well. If one adoptive parent is more outgoing than the other, or speaks for the couple, the birth mother should direct questions to the quieter person. She may be able to make some revealing observations through this approach, understanding better the couple's relationship.

In one case, a birth mother bonded immediately to an adoptive mother, attracted by her easygoing, friendly nature. The woman's husband was nervous and quiet, and answered very few questions. Assuming that he was simply an introvert, the birth mother did not press him for more information. She chose the couple, and only during her child's first year did she recognize how controlling and condescending the man was. Although she was well aware that no parent could be perfect, the birth mother regretted not being more vigilant.

HOW TO 'COURT' A COUPLE

The meeting between a birth mother and a couple seeking to adopt is much like a blind date: both parties have been told about each other and come to the meeting with high expectations. Unlike a romantic encounter, however, both parties may decide, on the first 'date,' whether they are prepared to make a lifelong commitment to each other.

Although no match is perfect, attraction should be felt immediately. A birth mother that does not feel a 'passion' for the couple she has interviewed should not proceed with the adoption. Her child should only be entrusted to a couple she truly considers worthy—on both an intellectual level and a gut level. That said, a birth mother can expect to grow less infatuated with the couple as time progresses. By the third interview, she will begin to see the couple's blemishes, and must determine whether she can live with these faults.

Physical appearances can be misleading. As in the harsh world of dating, the physically appealing have a distinct advantage. Peer counselors should encourage birth mothers to look beyond surfaces, and to avoid selecting a couple simply because they are attractive, stylish, or obviously well-to-do. Fortunately for the adoptive couple that falls short of stunning, the saying, 'Beauty is in the eye of the beholder' often applies.

As in any relationship, honesty is essential. If a birth mother has consumed alcohol while pregnant, or has a sexually transmitted disease, the adoptive couple has the right to know. Although the truth may be embarrassing, hiding the facts can be detrimental. Adoptive parents who eventually learn that they have been deceived may no longer trust the birth mother, and may be understandably less than eager to allow her to have ongoing contact with the child.

If the truth proves too difficult for a couple, the birth mother should be reassured that her honesty was beneficial. Although she will feel rejected, she has not condemned her child to a life with parents that lack the tools, the wisdom, or the desire to cope with less than ideal circumstances. In contrast, adoptive parents who choose to take a baby despite its exposure to drugs, alcohol, or a disease will have the opportunity to educate themselves, and to seek support or medical intervention.

Dating etiquette also applies to a potential adoptive relationship. The birth mother should not give a couple false hope. During the interview, she should avoid using language that suggests that she has already chosen the couple. Instead of asking, "When you're raising our child, how will you discipline him?", for example, she should say, "If you were to raise this child, how would you discipline him?"

A birth mother is never obligated to give a couple her child, no matter how excited, hopeful, or thankful they appear. However, she does have a responsibility to treat adoptive parents with respect. She should not make commitments she is not ready to fulfill, or drag the process on if she has serious doubts. If she decides that she cannot go through with the adoption, she should inform the couple immediately, even relaying the message through an adoption agency worker if necessary.

A birth mother should also be made aware of how serious a meeting with a potential adoptive couple is. A couple who has made it to this stage will treat it like an engagement: a time of great hope and anticipation. For this reason, it is not appropriate for a birth mother to interview numerous couples at the same time, knowing that she can only choose one. Serial monogamy is acceptable in this scenario: a woman can continue to interview couples until an appropriate match is found, but she must always rule out one possibility, ending the relationship, before considering another.

Once a birth mother has selected a couple, she should treat the time before the baby arrives as an 'engagement' period. She should try to work on the relationship as much as possible before the 'marriage.' Initial meetings will be tense, but subsequent 'dates' will be more relaxed and comfortable. The more familiar both parties become, the less stressful the baby's arrival and adoption will be.

Nevertheless, a birth mother who sees any red flags during the process can change her mind—no matter how nice the couple is. She will eventually have to explain to the child why she chose its parents. Giving the child the best life possible is more important than protecting a couple from disappointment.

IN THEIR OWN WORDS

On choosing...

"The couple I chose are very much like my parents. They have similar personalities. Peter is a computer geek like my dad, and they go camping a lot—like my family did when we were kids. The way they wanted to parent was the same; my son will be raised the same way I was. And they get along with my parents. My parents' opinion was really important at the time."

—*Nicki, birth mother, age 17*

"I chose amazing parents. They're religious, which is important to me. They have a close-knit family, which was important as well. I liked their attitudes—how they talked to me and comforted me (although I suspect they had ulterior motives at times!). I'm really happy with my choice. My son is so smart! When I talk with him and see how happy he is, I know my decision was right."

—*Aurora, birth mother, age 16*

"My counselor let me know how to pick a family—what to look for. I went into this thinking, 'I just want them to love my child. That's all that matters.' I came out knowing that I wanted a two-parent family that loved animals, went to church, and lived in the same city I do."

—*Jacqueline, birth mother age 23*

"The application process sometimes makes you feel like you're marketing yourself. I don't know if that's necessarily a bad thing, but it's almost like you're bartering your skills for somebody's baby. You feel like you have to put your best foot forward and sell yourself, so this poor soul will buy in."

—*John, adoptive father*

On the first meeting...

"I met the family at the agency. I was nervous as hell. They brought a box of doughnuts and man, did I ever want to eat that whole thing! But I thought, 'I have to look pretty for them. I have to make sure that they know I'm eating properly, so they won't say they don't want my child.' So I sat there and I stared at the doughnuts the entire time.

"I think I told them too much about me. I just went, 'Blech! Here you go. Here's every single possible bad or good thing that's ever happened to me in my whole entire life. But they were nervous too, talking really fast and fidgeting."

—*Jacqueline, birth mother, age 23*

"Everything was glory, and sunshine, and rainbows everywhere after I first met the adoptive couple. These people were just sent from Heaven. I think they tried to come across that way too, because they really wanted to be chosen. Things haven't exactly gone downhill since then, but these beings that were once so heavenly in my mind are now on the earth."

—*Emily, birth mother, age 25*

CHAPTER SIX

Recovery Planning

*"Kegels! Every single girl should do Kegels! Otherwise, every time you
sneeze or cough after you've had a baby, be prepared to do laundry."*

—Jacqueline, birth mother, age 23

A birth mother's ability to follow through with her adoption plan and to successfully grieve her loss is dependent upon a component of the pre-adoption counseling called 'recovery planning.' Part of recovery planning consists of preparing the client for the stages of grief that lie ahead. A woman who does not understand the emotional upheaval involved in placing a child will likely back out of her decision shortly after the child is born. In contrast, a birth mother who is prepared for the emotional challenges she must face will be able to develop coping strategies in advance.

Along with helping the birth mother prepare for internal turmoil, a counselor should help her with the more practical obstacles she will face, including her physical recovery, disappointing or adverse reactions from others, and the need to re-establish her life goals. In order to create a comprehensive recovery plan that deals with both the physical and psychological results of placing, a counselor should provide assistance in the following ways:

Prepare the client for the physical repercussions of childbirth

Many clients have difficulty accepting the physiological changes they will experience after giving birth. For a younger woman in particular, the onslaught of fluctuating hormones, stretch marks and leaking breasts can be very distressing, especially since she has no baby at hand to serve as an explanation. A self-conscious birth mother may begin vigorous exercise or dieting to shed the unwelcome evidence of the birth. She may also choose to neglect her physical health altogether, not recognizing how serious her physical ordeal has been.

A counselor should impress upon the client the reality of the six-week recovery period following delivery. The hormones released into her body which enabled her pelvis to expand for delivery will have also loosened other ligaments, including those in her wrists, knees, elbows and ankles. A new birth mother is unusually prone to sports injuries. One client who went out for a brisk jog three weeks after delivery returned home with a knee injury that would prove chronic.

More embarrassing, birth mothers must also contend with the challenges posed by the engorgement of their breasts. The mere sound of a baby crying can lead to accidental leaks. Although pills that curb lactation are coming out of vogue in the medical community, other options, including breast binding, are available. Centers can consult prenatal instructors for alternative ideas. Some women, for example, sling bag of ice cubes over each shoulder, while others insist that placing cabbage leaves in their bras is an effective—and natural—practice. Clients should be warned against using hot compresses and taking hot showers, for heat will not only bring comfort, but an increase in milk production.

One of the most serious consequences of childbirth is postpartum depression. Although difficult to distinguish from adoption grief, depression should be suspected if the client becomes so emotionally low that she no longer functions normally. A counselor should watch for distinct changes and warn the client's family that if she appears unusually depressed at any time during the first year following the placement, she should be advised to visit her doctor immediately. (See Chapter 10 for more information on depression.)

Encourage the birth mother to take time to pamper herself

During the first three months following the placement of her child, a birth mother will become preoccupied with her loss. With her counselor, she should plan methods of alleviating the pain and averting her focus, if only temporarily, from the infant to herself. If possible, a birth mother should change her pace or place, taking a short vacation or visiting supportive relatives. Those with limited means, or with time restrictions imposed by school or work, can still enjoy 'mini' vacations, from a day trip to an afternoon in a park or a visit to a cheap movie theater. Even a bubble bath (for women who have not had surgery), a massage, or a new outfit can lift a birth mother's spirits.

Be cautious, however, not to encourage women to be too good to themselves. One well-meaning counselor unwittingly became an accomplice to a crime after insisting that a client treat herself. Dismissing the idea of a bubble bath or a quiet walk in the park, the birth mother chose instead to go on an extravagant shopping spree—using a forged cheque. Upon returning, the client was bewildered by the fuss she had created, maintaining that she was only following her counselor's orders.

Prepare the birth mother for uncomfortable reactions from others

Intrusive comments are a reality that each birth mother must contend with. Ranging from insensitive remarks made by relatives to friendly questions posed by complete strangers, these interactions can be awkward for both parties involved. Even more disconcerting to birth mothers, some individuals may avoid the subject of the birth and adoption altogether.

Advise the birth mother to share personal information only when she feels comfortable doing so. She should never feel obligated to explain her situation or to divulge any personal information. One birth mother, for example, encountered a familiar cashier at a grocery store who happily observed that she had given birth. When the cashier asked where the baby was, the birth mother simply replied, "I would prefer not to talk about it." Even though an uncomfortable pause followed, the clerk quickly recovered from the puzzling response and proceeded to chatter about other things.

A birth mother who encounters people who evade discussion about the placement can develop methods of bringing the subject into the conversation. If a woman recognizes that others are often silent simply because they do not wish to make her sad, she can put them at ease by showing a photograph of her child. Encourage the client to be bold and to express her needs, giving others permission to share her grief.

Help the birth mother establish a support system

Part of recovery planning involves identifying grief partners—two or three individuals who will actively support the birth mother as she works through her loss. Whether a close friend, a relative, a church member, or a fellow birth mother, a grief partner should be prepared to hold the woman accountable for her actions. Most birth mothers will have committed, for example, to seeing their peer counselors on a regular basis for the first year following their placements. The active presence of a grief partner may prevent the birth mother from shutting down emotionally and avoiding outside help.

A birth mother will seldom find a more apt listener than a friend made at a birth mother's support group. Here, she will no longer be isolated in her anguish. If a counselor's Center does not run a group, help the client to locate another grief group composed of women recovering from an experience similar to hers. Women who learn to mentor each other will often have some of their intimacy needs met and can uncover new coping strategies based on the experience of their peers.

Prepare the birth mother for potential difficulties surrounding physical intimacy

For women who have yet to deal fully with their grief, sexual involvement after an adoption can trigger painful memories. On one extreme, a client may avoid intimacy whenever possible, while another emotional client may rush headlong into a series of physical relationships.

For many clients, pursuing a new romance or continuing the relationship that led to the unplanned pregnancy and adoption can be detrimental. A client who becomes pregnant a second time will only compound her grief. Therefore, if a client is at all receptive, her counselor should discuss the issue of abstinence soon after the birth, helping her to determine what choices will serve in her best interest. The discussion should cover the need for intimacy and how to fulfill this need outside of sex. For many women, the pursuit of real intimacy is a novel concept.

Although a client may choose to remain sexually active, her counselor can help her become aware of what she is doing and why. The question of what she is gaining when she has sex, and whether this is what she really wants, may guide her in her future relationships.

Women in a marriage relationship should be prepared for the unique challenges they may face. One client discovered the impact that emotional baggage could have on a new marriage. Terrified of getting pregnant, she insisted on using three forms of birth control and despite these precautions, tried to remain physically unavailable to her new husband. Her fears began to take a toll on her relationship, and she went into counseling. When she recognized that entering into a new phase of life would not automatically free her from past grief, the young woman began to deal with lingering issues surrounding her adoption.

A counselor should prepare a client for the emotional reactions she may encounter when she rekindles a relationship or ventures into a marriage. Discussions may involve setting appropriate boundaries or in dealing with grief that resurfaces.

Help the client to establish long-term goals

Since a birth mother will not be investing the next twenty years of her life in raising her child, she will need to find other ways of focusing her time and energy. She should not view her decision to place as benefiting only the child; rather, she should envision the adoption as an opportunity to make positive, constructive changes in her own life. Free of the restrictions imposed by child rearing, a birth mother can pursue her education, become involved in a healthy relationship, and develop new skills and interests. She is, in essence, given a second chance.

Some birth mothers resist making progress for fear that they are behaving selfishly and somehow abandoning their children. Remind the client that becoming incapacitated does not constitute a greater love for her child than if she moves forward. A birth mother's life need not end the moment she places her child for adoption. In fact, one of the greatest gifts she can give her child is to make the adoption a turning point or a launching point in fulfilling her potential as a human being. A counselor can encourage the birth mother to become the type of person of which her child will be proud when they reunite.

Counselors should strive to ignite the woman's dreams. As new possibilities form in her mind, she can be assisted in the process of taking steps towards meeting her goals. If a birth mother longs for a more fulfilling romantic relationship, for example, she should be encouraged to examine why past attempts to find love failed. She may also need help in developing ways to resolve conflict with the birth father.

Above all, the birth mother should be warned against making any major life decisions in the year following the placement. She should be encouraged not to have a dating relationship for at least six months and be given solid reasons for avoiding immediate sexual intimacy. Many birth mothers who have received insufficient counseling get married in the first year after placing, not realizing how different their choices would be had they waited.

A counselor who is able to gently confront her client can make a significant difference, as twenty-five-year-old Emily discovered:

I started dating after I placed. Things were going fine until I went for counseling.

My counselor said, "Does he have this quality, and that quality, and all of the things you're looking for?"

I said, "He doesn't have any of that!" So right then I knew it wasn't going to work out. That was really hard for me—to go home and break up with this person.

I kept thinking, "Do I need to break up with him? No, I don't!"

Then another week would go by and I would think, "We're never going to get married. Why am I dating him?"

Emily broke up soon after, and found the experience less traumatic than she had anticipated.

While some women may be extremely vulnerable because of the adoption, others may draw from a new strength. One birth mother was casually dating a man who wanted to take the relationship to a new level. When she refused his physical advances, he grew angry and resorted to making disparaging comments about the adoption. She was incapable, he said, of taking care of her own child. Even the birth father wanted nothing to do with her. As she was kicking him out of her house, the birth mother declared, "Get out! I don't need you in my world because this is the thing that I am most proud of in my life."

Prepare the client for the isolation she may experience

The experience of bringing a human being into the world, choosing to give it the best life possible, and then grieving what feels like an insurmountable loss will inevitably alter a birth mother's perception of the world. Often the experience will be an isolating one; young women in particular tend to mature far beyond their peers. Armed with new skills, such as the ability to resolve conflict and to assert herself, a birth mother may be amazed by the comparative immaturity of her less experienced peers. As one birth mother declared, "My old friends are so silly; I have no patience with the way they talk or for what they do."

A birth mother may find relief from inane chatter or break free from harmful peer relations by temporarily changing schools or her work location. If she chooses to befriend a new set of peers, she may find that her birth mother's support group serves as a safety net. A counselor should warn the client about the temptation of reverting to old habits, since a vulnerable woman may use alcohol or drugs to numb her pain only to repeat the mistakes that led to her current predicament.

A pervading sense of isolation can also result from a lack of family support. When reflecting upon her upbringing, a client will typically harbor hope that the unplanned pregnancy and her courageous decision to place her child for adoption will change the dynamics of her family. Prepare the birth mother for disappointment; she may have to go outside of the family to find the role model or support she craves.

One birth mother longed for her own mother's involvement and support as she placed her child in an open adoption. Facing unresolved issues of her own, the mother pulled away to the extent that she ignored the adoption proceedings. When the birth mother tried to talk about her newborn son, she was harshly rebuked and told, "He's not really your child." The peer counselor gently recommended that the distraught birth mother find another grief partner.

Encourage the birth mother to share her experience at the right time

A birth mother who receives proper counseling will often become an outspoken advocate of adoption. She will typically spend several years of her life explaining to those she encounters why adoption is a positive choice. Indeed, anyone who responds to the topic by stating, "I could never give up a child," will undoubtedly be engulfed in a torrent of information. A birth mother will also encounter individuals who are resistant to the notion of open adoption, believing that access to the child will only augment a woman's sense of loss. The birth mother's testimony can be a powerful tool in this case, helping to correct misconceptions that distort the general public's views toward open adoption.

Unfortunately, a birth mother may inadvertently become an advocate long before she is ready. Recognizing an eloquent prospect, the adoption agency or Pregnancy Center may place her in the public eye when she is still consumed with grief. Since the client's needs are paramount, encourage women not to be pressured to take the stage, however compelling their stories. A stirring testimony will be no less powerful six months later.

IN THEIR OWN WORDS

On short term recovery...

"I loved being pregnant. I thought it was the best thing since sliced bread! I loved the fact that I got stretch marks on my tummy. Even labor was fantastic. I'd be a professional surrogate! I wanted to go into this with no regrets at all; I wanted to make sure I lived every single pregnancy moment I possibly could."

—*Jacqueline, birth mother, age 23*

"Recovery sucks! I thought I would be fine immediately, but I tore when I was giving birth, so that was difficult. I was really skinny before I got pregnant—a size one! It's really hard for me to see myself now with all my stretch marks and my size. Pregnancy changes your body completely. I wish I was still the tiny little girl I had been."

—*Aurora, birth mother, age 16*

"I was in a fantasy land for about three weeks. Then I had a pretty serious crash on the first night I slept alone in my apartment—a severe anxiety attack. I've only had a couple of anxiety attacks since then, but I'm able to talk myself through them. Basically, I remind myself where Kaitlyn is and why I placed her, and I think about all of the little things that confirmed my decision."

—*Chantal, birth mother, age 30*

On long term recovery...

"When I reached my three month mark, I thought, 'Oh my gosh! I have this child that I'm not raising! I'm old enough, and able—and I feel terrible!'

"So I joined a running club and decided to run a marathon. I really felt I needed to accomplish something. Reaching this goal was tremendously healing, both physically and emotionally."

—*Emily, birth mother, age 25*

"I finished my degree—one of the best things I did! I took a month off, and then I got right back into school, which was what I was supposed to be doing before I got pregnant. It was a real life-saver for me."

—*Chantal, birth mother, age 30*

CHAPTER SEVEN

"Dear Baby" Letters and Gifts

"I wrote my thoughts and dreams and hopes for my son.
It's great to look back at; it's great to go back to that time and place."

—Rosanne, birth mother, age 21

Every mother longs to give her child the best. A birth mother is no exception—a truth evident in her sacrificial decision to place her child with a stable two-parent family, giving it a life that she cannot. Many birth mothers also choose to demonstrate their love in the form of a unique gift and a "Dear Baby" letter, a love letter written to the child.

Through the process of deciding what gift to give and what words to pass on to her infant, a birth mother can begin to come to terms with the reality that she is placing her child in an adoptive home. She has the opportunity to explore multiple issues, evaluating her relationship with the child's birth father, her family history, her decisions in the past, and the question of her future. Through the process of gift giving, the birth mother's feelings are honored as she demonstrates her love for the child she has chosen to place.

The child, in turn, receives concrete evidence of its birth mother's love. Physical proof that can be seen, smelled, and touched is far more comforting to a small child than verbal reassurances from its adoptive parents about its birth mother's love. The child is also given a sense of the birth mother's personality, reflected in her unique letter and choice of gift.

"DEAR BABY" LETTERS

A "Dear Baby" letter will be the first—and undoubtedly the most compelling—love letter that an adopted child will ever receive. Contained within are the hopes and dreams of its birth mother, words of wisdom that she wishes to pass on. The letter can also provide answers to the pressing questions the child will inevitably have, including why he or she was 'given up' in the first place. In some cases, a mother may choose to write two letters: one to be given to her child when it is still small, and the other to be given during its adolescence. In addition to benefiting the child at different stages of its life, writing more than one letter can help the mother recognize that the tiny infant she holds now will grow and change as time progresses.

There are several points to consider when helping a client through this significant process:

The client should begin the grieving process as early as possible

It is often helpful to encourage a client to begin writing her Dear Baby letter while she is still pregnant. Consumed with the business of choosing the best adoptive family possible and contending with the often less than pleasant side effects of pregnancy, a woman will often neglect her own emotional needs. Writing a letter to her unborn child will help trigger the realization that she is, in fact, going to experience a significant loss through the adoptive process.

Letters should not be finalized until the birth mother has actually held her newborn

The testimony of adult adoptees who had been placed, decades earlier, through closed adoption reveals that even children who have grown into highly successful professionals are consumed by the knowledge that their birth mothers did not hold them as newborns. Since newborns are no longer immediately removed from their birth mothers—as was the procedure in the past—clients should be encouraged to tell their children what they thought as they cradled them in their arms.

A client should be strongly advised to complete her Dear Baby letter before, or shortly after, she leaves the hospital. Not only is it difficult for a birth mother to recapture the intense emotions she felt shortly before birth or the moment she held her child for the first time, but she may also become reluctant to obtain the closure the Dear Baby letter will eventually come to represent.

Life can also bring unexpected twists. One 21-year-old client was in a serious car accident a year after giving birth. Suffering from a severe head injury, she lapsed into a coma for several months, and then succumbed to her injuries. Had she not written her Dear Baby letter shortly after giving birth, this woman would have lost an invaluable opportunity.

Recognize that writing is an ongoing process

A client should be encouraged to record her feelings in a journal throughout the entire pregnancy. Excerpts from the journal—including the birth mother's thoughts when she first felt her baby kicking—can be put in a special book for the child. Not only will the mother keep in touch with her feelings throughout the pregnancy, her child will be reminded of the intensity of its birth mother's love, even when it was in utero. To ensure that her child would have no doubts whatsoever, one birth mother actually wrote four-hundred and thirty letters during her pregnancy and her daughter's first two years of life, storing them in a bin that she would eventually pass on to her child.

The birth mother may choose to rewrite her Dear Baby letter several times, from the time that she begins to bond with her baby during the pregnancy to the moment she must say goodbye. Encourage her to keep copies of these drafts, as well as a copy of the final version that she will give to her infant.

Difficult concepts should be sensitively worded

A child who is told, "I loved you so much that I gave you away," may conclude that the people who love him will also leave him. A more apt way of explaining this difficult concept to a small child would be to say, "I loved you so much that I chose two parents for you."

Encourage the client to share her letter openly

Many clients benefit from reading their Dear Baby letters aloud during counseling sessions. A letter can also be read during the entrustment ceremony.

Help clients recognize the needs of the adoptive parents

Dear Baby letters should be left unsealed to enable adoptive parents to pass them on at the appropriate time in the child's life. Parents may otherwise give the child the letter when he reaches eighteen—rather than gauging his need and maturity level earlier. It is also often helpful for the birth mother to request the adoptive parents' permission to pass on a Dear Baby letter or gift. The adoptive parents are highly unlikely to refuse her request and will appreciate the birth mother's display of confidence in their parenting skills. [Please see the appendix for samples of Dear Baby letters and a general format that can be used with clients.]

BABY GIFTS

At approximately five months into the pregnancy, a client should be encouraged to begin reflecting upon the type of gift she would like give her child. Children typically understand love in a concrete form and an adopted child will especially appreciate the opportunity to bring out the gift and reflect upon the giver.

The gift that a birth mother passes on may be, depending upon how open the adoption is, the only gift that she is able to give. Encourage the client to think of gifts with symbolic significance, rather than being primarily concerned with purchasing something expensive or elaborate.

In some instances, other family members can be encouraged to give the child a gift. By being involved in the act of gift giving, the birth father and biological grandparents can also begin to effectively deal with the pain involved in an adoption.

The following are some ideas to give a client as she searches for a tangible symbol of her love.

A family heirloom or a piece of the family tradition

A child who will not remain within its biological family can still benefit from being involved in the birth family's traditions. Whenever a grandchild was born into one family, for example, its grandmother would knit an afghan in which to wrap the newborn during its trip home from the hospital. Although one grandson was to be taken home by an adoptive couple, his biological grandmother still knit the blanket and gave it to the adoptive parents. A significant family tradition was therefore carried on even though the baby was not to be raised within the context of that family.

In another tradition, the eldest daughter in the family was given a family heirloom, a quilt that was to be passed on, in turn, to her first newborn daughter. Since the first daughter born was to be placed, her birth mother was left with a difficult decision. Finally, she chose to honor her daughter with the quilt, even though the heirloom would then leave the family.

A treasured relic from the birth mother's own childhood

If a birth mother cannot afford a new or expensive gift, assure her that cost is irrelevant.

Her child will place high value on something that she herself held and treasured as a child, such as a favorite stuffed toy or doll. Some birth mothers choose to pass on gifts they received as infants, including an engraved cup, a piece of jewelry, or a special blanket.

A gift that can be shared by the birth mother and her child

A birth mother may wish to emphasize that although she and her child have been separated through adoption, they are still two parts of a whole. A necklace with two pieces—one to be given to the baby, and the other to be kept by the birth mother—is the type of gift that vividly depicts this union. One birth mother wore a Noah's ark brooch and pinned the matching dove pin to her infant's sleeper before they parted. To her, the gift symbolized the hope that the two pieces, and people, would one day find their way back together.

A family tree or an album

Whether adopted or not, children are fascinated by their family histories and revel in hearing stories of their births. A birth mother can record information about the labor and delivery, and have the entrustment ceremony recorded on videotape. She can also create a family album or scrapbook, using copies of recent photos of herself, her family, and of the birth father, if possible, as well as snapshots from her own childhood. By creating an album, a birth mother will give the child a sense of its mother's identity that goes beyond the description offered by the adoptive parents.

One birth mother who came from a cross-cultural background created a scrapbook containing information about her parents' diverse cultures. Knowing that her child would wonder about what commonalties he shared with his birth mother, she also shared numerous details about herself, including her favorite book, hobby, color, and musical group.

Another birth mother created a family tree, using one branch to depict the child's biological family, and the other to show the adoptive family's history. She framed the diagram and at the entrustment ceremony, she asked the adoptive family's son to fill in the name of his new brother on the infant's respective leaf.

An artistic expression of the birth mother's love

A birth mother who is artistically inclined may choose a gift that reflects her abilities. One talented calligraphist copied a portion of Psalm 149 to remind her son that he was, indeed, "fearfully and wonderfully made." She made and framed two copies of the verses—one with the name she had chosen for her child, and the other with his adoptive name. "Someday my son will visit me," she explained. "The same piece of art that hung in his home as he grew up hangs on my wall as well, with a different name. He will then see that I valued him enough to give him a name that was meaningful to me."

One adopted child was given a vivid reminder of both his cultural heritage and his birth mother's love. A foreign exchange student, his mother had been sexually assaulted before leaving her home country—a country in which pregnancy out of wedlock was punishable by death. Naive, the nineteen-year-old was unaware of her condition until late in the pregnancy when she was living abroad. She decided to carry the child to term. While living with a family that offered her room and board, the woman learned how to cross-stitch. With her new skill, she created, in her language of origin, the word "life," a reminder to her son of the gift she had given him out of love. The birth mother cross-stitched an identical copy for herself to remind her of her son even when she returned home and could no longer even acknowledge his existence.

THE RESISTANT CLIENT

Some birth mothers are reluctant to give their children gifts or letters. A woman who has been raped, for example, may not recognize that she will inevitably begin to love the human being who has 'invaded' her body. Another client may have been forced—through Social Services or external pressures such as her family's wishes—to place her baby for adoption. A birth mother may also be suffering from a mental illness, or may simply be intellectually or emotionally incapable of making the decision to leave her child with a tangible symbol of her love.

Whatever the reason for the client's resistance, a counselor should strongly encourage her to write a Dear Baby letter or pass on a meaningful gift. Not only will the birth mother be empowered by doing something for her child, but the child will, in years to come, be reminded of its significance to its biological mother.

Model the gift-giving process

Even a resistant client will not feel threatened when receiving a gift that she can, in turn, pass on to her child. A counselor could, for example, give a new birth mother identical stuffed animals, encouraging her to keep one as a memento, while giving the baby the other. A birth mother will also take pride in giving a special outfit to her infant, even when she was unable to purchase the gift herself.

Use the experiences of past birth mothers

A client may be encouraged by the stories of other birth mothers who have successfully gone through the process of placing a baby for adoption. Ask former clients for permission to pass on copies of their own Dear Baby letters. To ensure their privacy, remove birth mothers' names from letters being given to new clients.

Assist the birth mother in tasks she might otherwise find intimidating

A client who is functionally illiterate or lacking in confidence will naturally have difficulty creating a Dear Baby letter. A counselor can serve as a 'secretary', transforming the birth mother's message to her baby into writing. The final letter need not capture the exact words or voice of the client so much as the expression of her heart.

The following are typical questions that will help provoke discussion and enable the counselor to capture the birth mother's individuality on paper:

How much do you love this baby?

What hopes and prayers do you have for your child?

What would you like to tell your baby about yourself?

What would you like to tell this baby about the people you've chosen as parents?

Find an alternative to the Dear Baby letter

A birth mother should be encouraged to express herself in a medium with which she is comfortable. Some women prefer recording their 'letters' on a cassette or videotape. Others may put their thoughts into a special song or poem for their children.

Recognize that the child will value any gift or token from its birth mother

If a client is unusually resistant, or incapable of giving a gift or letter, she should be encouraged to give something, however small. Even her signature on a special card that she has helped to choose or a photograph of herself will prove meaningful to her child.

Elizabeth's Story

Twenty-year-old "Elizabeth" came into the Centre consumed with a single question: What does God think of abortion? A victim of date rape, she was carrying a child through no fault of her own. After reading several scriptures related to abortion, Elizabeth found her answer. She decided to place her baby with an adoptive family. Unusually insightful and sensitive, she recognized that her daughter would eventually have questions concerning not only her birth mother, but her birth father as well. Elizabeth therefore chose to name the child 'Dominique,' meaning 'Child of God.'

"Your adoptive family may give you another name," she explained in a letter to be read by her daughter in her teen years. "I want you to know that I still chose to give you this name because you truly are a child of God."

Elizabeth carefully explained to her daughter that although she was conceived through rape, God had preserved her life. "When you want to know who your real father is, think of God," Elizabeth wrote. "You were not born out of violence, but out of love."

Wisely, Elizabeth gave the letter, along with a more standard Dear Baby letter, to her child's adoptive parents, requesting that they pass the letter on when they believed Dominique to be mature enough to deal with its contents. Despite the trauma of rape, and her initial resolve to abort, Elizabeth was able to give not only life, but a profound gift and heritage to her daughter.

IN THEIR OWN WORDS

On "Dear Baby" letters...

"I wrote a book to my son. I explained everything about my family and why I gave him up for adoption. I put in pictures of me being pregnant, and pictures of my cat and dog. I put in everything about me that I could possibly think of, because if anything ever happened to me, or if we lost contact, everything would be in the book.

—*Aurora, birth mother, age 16*

"Adoptive mothers get to see everything—the first crawl, the first step, the first tooth, the first word, everything. We don't: we get it second. I wanted my daughter to know about the very first time I saw her cry, laugh, step, and cut her first tooth, not when I heard about it over the phone, or in an email, or in a letter. So I recorded the first time I physically saw her take her first step. And every single time I visit my daughter, I write down what she wore, what happened, and how I felt. When my daughter is older, I want her to go, 'Wow! All of these things really happened.'"

—*Jacqueline, birth mother, age 23*

"I wrote a Dear Baby letter and gave a copy to the adoptive couple to give to my son when he's older. Part of me thinks that I shouldn't have, because now the control is in their hands. They can give it to him whenever they choose; the choice is no longer mine. I gave it to them out of fear. They tell you that it's an open adoption, but it's only a moral agreement. They can turn their back at any time. I gave them that letter because if they close the door at any time, my son will still be able to read it."

—*Kendra, birth mother, age 23*

On baby gifts...

"I made a quilt for Kyla over seven months of my pregnancy, even though I didn't know at the time whether I'd parent or place. The quilt—which is crib-sized and has blue teddy bears on it—became more meaningful to me the closer I came to delivery. I gave it to Dave and Angela when they left the hospital with Kyla, and they gave me a memory box made out of the same material! When my daughter grows up, the quilt will remind her that my decision to place wasn't made instantly."

—*Samantha, birth mother, age 19*

CHAPTER EIGHT

The Hospital Birth Experience and Creating Memories

"When Elizabeth came out, they placed her on my stomach. I went and touched her on the one little spot on her back that wasn't goopy. She was so soft! They make little fluffy animals that are just as soft as she was."

—Jacqueline, birth mother, age 23

Although a visit may span only hours, a birth mother's hospital experience will have a significant impact on how she feels about the adoption after the fact. A negative experience may leave her reeling with regret or destroy her confidence in her decision-making ability. A positive experience can provide her with memories of the child that will outlive the pain of loss.

In order to ensure the best experience possible, a birth mother should be encouraged to prepare for her hospital stay well in advance. Due to changes in health care policies across the United States and Canada, the length of her stay will likely be short, and time with the baby, limited. Some women remain in hospital for less than nine hours. Since the birth mother may have no other opportunity to spend time with her child, it is important that she maximize the time she does have and set boundaries to ensure that this time is of quality.

THE BIRTH MOTHER: A DISTINGUISHED GUEST

A birth mother's hospital stay will entail tremendous physical and psychological pain. Due to the nature of her sacrifice, she should be treated with special sensitivity. If possible, try to ensure that she will have a room to herself, an arrangement that can be made in advance through the adoption agency. The longer that she can stay in hospital, the better: encourage the birth mother to speak to her doctor in advance about the duration of her stay. A sympathetic physician may have the power to allow a birth mother to remain in hospital longer than the typical twenty-four hours, preventing her from feeling cheated out of time with her infant. In addition, respect the woman's wishes if she chooses to have the baby stay in the room with her.

A birth mother should be surrounded by the most supportive people possible. A birth coach is essential, as nurses may not, logistically, have the time to fully support a woman throughout the frightening process of labor. Encourage the client to choose a birth coach who will be reliable and supportive of her decision to place. The coach must also commit to being available two weeks before and after the woman's due date, as babies have little regard for their assigned due dates.

Preparations for the hospital experience should also include the birth mother's departure plan. In addition to procuring a ride to and from hospital, she should decide whether to leave before or after the baby departs, and whether to leave the child in the nursery or to place it in the arms of its new parents. She should also decide who will temporarily stay with her when she arrives home, offering physical and emotional support.

THE QUESTION OF VISITORS

A birth mother should decide in advance with whom she would like to share her child with. Although she may initially feel inclined to share her experience with everyone, the reality is that an uncontrolled parade of friends, relatives, and acquaintances through the hospital room will not only prove exhausting, but will rob her of time alone with her baby. Encourage the birth mother to place her own needs above social obligations.

The following people should be considered by the birth mother as she goes through the process of selecting visitors:

Immediate family

A birth mother will typically wish to invite supportive members of her immediate family. However, if she is estranged from her family, or if members of her family are opposed to the adoption, she should be advised to consider whether their presence will be helpful. Visits may be limited, or avoided altogether.

The birth father

However stormy the relationship between the birth parents, their child will benefit from knowing that its birth father cared enough to welcome it into the world. The birth mother will also appreciate his efforts to visit, for despite the resentment she may have for him, the couple still shares a connection through their child.

One birth mother decided that even though she had a poor relationship with the birth father, his presence at his daughter's birth was critical. Having lost her own father at an early age, she lamented the fact that she had no photograph of the two of them together. To protect her daughter from a similar loss, she ensured that photos were taken of the newborn cradled in her birth father's arms.

If a birth father is aggressive, or if he is on poor terms with the woman's family, a birth mother may specify the time he should visit, thus limiting the duration of his stay and avoiding family friction. In some cases, she may choose not to invite him at all. The birth mother should also consider whether she would like the birth father's family to see the child.

The adoptive couple

Ensure that a birth mother is aware of the multiple options she has surrounding the adoptive couple's presence, from the time of labor and delivery, to the final entrustment. Here are some of the questions she should carefully consider:

When should the adoptive couple be informed that she has gone into labor?

Should the birth mother have the honor of telling the couple that they are or will soon be parents, or should someone else perform this task?

Should the couple wait at home during the labor, or in the waiting room?

Should one or both of them actually observe the delivery?

Who should be the first to hold the child?

Although seemingly innocuous, some of these questions can have tremendous repercussions. Some birth mothers, for example, are unaware of how intimate an experience childbirth is. A woman who has granted the adoptive couple permission to view the birth may end up feeling exposed and out of control, and yet unable to retract her offer.

The question of who should hold the newborn first is especially significant. During the euphoria of childbirth, a birth mother may allow the child to be placed in the adoptive mother's arms first. However, many birth mothers express tremendous sorrow and resentment later, feeling cheated out of an experience they believe was rightfully theirs.

Gently remind the birth mother that the adoptive couple will have the child for a lifetime. The hospital experience is hers. Emphasize that she is not being selfish if she limits the adoptive couple's time with the child. A counselor should also encourage the birth mother to be the first to hold her child.

Her Pregnancy Center counselor

Since a birth mother will need to talk about her baby months, and even years, after the adoption, it is helpful for her counselor to know for whom she is grieving. Some counselors may even serve as birth coaches. Whatever the role, it is critical for the counselor to serve as an advocate for the birth mother.

An advocate should assume the following responsibilities:

Ensure that the client is given sufficient privacy

As part of the grieving process, the birth mother will need an extended period of time to be alone with her child. She may wish to speak to the infant, or to simply cry as she holds it. A counselor can ensure that the woman is kept from being interrupted by placing a "Do Not Disturb" sign on the door, requesting that nurses respect her privacy and asking them to temporarily refuse visitors.

Help hospital staff understand the situation

Because doctors and nurses have their own preconceived notions about adoption, they may, through good intentions or out of sheer carelessness, be insensitive to the birth mother. One counselor, for example, discovered that various hospital staff were trying to persuade her client to keep her baby, not recognizing that the clean-cut and "supportive" birth father was, in actuality, physically abusive. Although the birth mother had chosen adoption for good reason, the entire process was hindered because of the resulting confusion she experienced after being second-guessed by uninformed, but well-meaning staff.

Although the medical community has become increasingly sophisticated over the last decade regarding adoption, more traditional staff may still adhere to the idea that the woman should avoid bonding with her infant. Others might react to the birth mother's grief with alarm. In order to put nurses at ease, and to prevent a glut of "counselors," the woman's counselor should introduce herself and have a ready supply of business cards available.

Prepare the birth coach

A birth coach who is aware of the need to ensure that the birth mother's wishes are being respected will be an invaluable ally. The birth coach should also be prepared for the vast range of emotional responses that the birth mother will exhibit and learn how to best support the woman in her grief.

Intervene if the birth mother's needs are being compromised

On occasion, a birth mother's needs or wishes may be disregarded. Since she may lack confidence, or be too distraught to assert herself, act as her advocate. When a birth mother's family member interferes or fails to give her adequate time with the child, for example, a counselor can gently intervene and defuse a potentially harmful situation.

In one case, the birth mother was in the final stages of labor when a nurse asked if she wanted the baby to room with her. As the woman was in no condition to answer the question, her counselor stepped in, made the decision for her, and diplomatically reminded the nurse that the issue could be discussed at a more appropriate time.

Help the mother prepare alternate plans

Even the most carefully prepared plan can fall apart. If the infant ends up in intensive care or is born with abnormalities that the adoptive couple cannot deal with, the entire hospital experience or adoptive plan may go awry. The panicked birth mother will need extra support and reassurance as she forms an alternate plan.

Assure the birth mother that she can change her mind at any time

A birth mother will need to remake her decision to place once the baby is born. Encourage the client to bring her journal and decision-making paperwork to the hospital, so that she can review the concrete reasons she had when she initially decided to place. Give the woman advance warning that you will, in a private moment and place in hospital, ask her if she would still like to place her baby for adoption. Reassure her that she will be fully supported regardless of the decision she makes.

COLLECTING MEMORIES

Photographs are essential

Never tempt fate. A faulty camera or a misplaced roll of film can mean the loss of the irreplaceable. Encourage the birth mother to assign numerous "photographers" to take multiple photos of the entire hospital experience, from quirky snapshots of her protruding belly before birth to photos of the ecstatic moment she holds her child for the first time. Before and after shots, both humorous and profound, will enable the birth mother to grasp the reality of her experience even when time and a return to normalcy make this aspect of her life seem unreal.

For 30-year-old Chantal, a photo album was what pulled her through some of her loneliest hours. "Take lots of pictures!" she advised fellow birth moms. "Sometimes that's all you'll have. When I'm really missing my daughter, all I can do is bring out my photo album."

Create a memory box

Although the birth mother will leave the hospital with empty arms, she can carry powerful mementos of her baby. Encourage the client to keep tokens of her experience in hospital, including the infant's bracelet and hat, its soother, or a lock of its hair. A birth mother may also request a copy of the card with the baby's name that slips into the bassinet, and a birth certificate with the name that she has chosen for her child. An outfit worn by the baby and its blanket and can be especially meaningful; advise the mother not to wash them so that the baby's scent will linger.

If the hospital does not make prints of the baby's feet and hands, the birth mother can do so with washable tempera and special paper brought from home. A mother can also purchase a plaster of Paris kit in advance and create a wall plaque of the baby's foot and handprints. Even a record the birth mother has kept of her contractions, or a newspaper bought on the day of the child's birth, can serve as vivid reminders.

These items, along with dried flowers and cards, can be stored in a large, decorative box that a birth mother can sift through at whim. The memory box will become critically important on difficult days, such as the child's birthday and Mother's Day.

THE TURBULENT DAYS AFTER BIRTH

The physical aftermath

Few women are prepared for the physical and emotional upheaval they will experience after the ecstasy of birth has subsided. Normal hormonal fluctuations can leave them despondent. Birth mothers who have undergone C-Sections will be particularly disillusioned by how physically incapacitated they are. Therefore, warn the birth mother of what to expect, and advise her not to place the baby on the third day after delivery, as it is one of the most emotionally turbulent times.

The breastfeeding controversy

The question of whether to breastfeed or not is a controversial one. From a medical standpoint, there is legitimate concern that a mother might pass HIV to her baby through the milk.

However, many states and provinces now do HIV and AIDS testing on all expectant mothers.

The choice is usually individual. Health-conscious birth mothers often want to give their infants the benefits of the antibodies present in colostrum. Some long for the experience of nurturing their infants outside the womb. Others recognize that they may never have the opportunity to breastfeed again. Still others fear that the intimacy of nursing may create too great a bond between mother and child.

As a counselor, affirm the birth mother's choice. A birth mother's decision to breastfeed for several days will not hinder the adoptive mother's ability to bond with the child. Nor will it have any bearing on the amount of love a birth mother has for her infant. The real risk lies in taking away the birth mother's opportunity to choose whether this experience is right for her.

Saying good-bye at home

Some birth mothers choose to take their infants home from the hospital for up to a week. This choice is usually unnerving to the adoptive parents and the adoption agency, who fear that the woman will change her mind about placing. However, if a woman does eventually choose to parent, the question must be raised about whether her initial decision to place was made for the right reasons.

Often, it is women who have not had enough time to bond with their infants and grieve their losses that change their minds. Taking a newborn home from the hospital can put a woman in touch with the reality of parenting. As one exhausted birth mother eloquently exclaimed, "I didn't even have the chance to take a shower when the baby was with me!"

Make a birth mother aware, prior to the hospital experience, of her choice to take the child home briefly. If she is interested, help her procure the supplies she will need for the baby's stay. For example, the Center may be able to lend her used clothing or a baby car seat. The birth mother, in turn, should supply diapers and formula if she chooses not to breastfeed.

Aftercare

A woman who returns home without her child will face overwhelming grief and loneliness for the first forty-eight hours. She should plan carefully for this time, deciding how she will spend the time, and with whom. The birth mother should considering asking a close friend to stay with her, or to check up on her periodically.

Encourage the client to rent videos or DVDs in advance, being careful to avoid movies that are emotionally charged. The birth mother may not particularly enjoy the entertainment, but she will benefit from the distraction. If she enjoys reading, she should pick up books or magazines for the occasion. She should also plan to leave the house, taking a short walk, if her health permits, or picking up a special treat with friends. Going out will prevent her from feeling housebound, and will remind her of life outside her own grief.

If the birth mother chose to parent for the first week of her baby's life, her counselor should pick up any items that she has borrowed, such as a crib or car seat. This small favor will not only alleviate stress for the woman, but will remove blatant reminders of the child's absence.

IN THEIR OWN WORDS

On labor and delivery...

"You hear all these horror stories about labor. I kept thinking to myself, 'It's going to be short and not very painful, and it's all going to be okay.'"

—Emily, birth mother, age 25

"The one thing my counselor didn't let me know is that once your water breaks, it still comes out! I thought that it breaks, and then you're good to go. So there I was standing in the tub when I phoned the hospital. They said, 'You're going to leak until the baby comes.'

—Jacqueline, birth mother, age 23

"When she was first born, I kept saying, 'My angel is here!' It was very surreal. I've never felt so peaceful in my life."

—Chantal, birth mother, age 30

On breastfeeding...

"I would tell any birth mother that's going to give their child up for adoption to breast-feed. It helps you lose weight. It makes the baby healthier. It gives you a sense of closeness to the baby that nobody can take away from you."

—Aurora, birth mother, age 16

"I didn't want to have to go through all of this again just to know what breastfeeding feels like. So I fed her."

—Jacqueline, birth mother, age 23

"I chose not to breastfeed because I was not prepared for that kind of attachment."

—Rosanne, birth mother, age 21

On spending time with baby...

"The adoptive couple really monopolized the time I had with Robert. I was not thinking about me: I was thinking more about them and their needs. I regret not being more 'me' orientated."

—Aurora, birth mother, age 16

"The adoptive dad really, really wanted to hold Elizabeth. I thought, 'This is my time. You have the rest of your life to hold her.'"

—Jacqueline, birth mother, age 23

"Kaitlyn's adoptive mom stood in the background and just let me be Mom for two days. How hard that must have been for her since her baby girl had arrived!"

—Chantal, birth mother, age 30

On saying good-bye at home...

"I brought Robert home for seven days, which was great. I got to experience parenting: I gave him his first bath, I changed his first diaper—little firsts that are so important. I was able to make sure I was making the right decision. Yes, I loved him and yes, I could parent him, but not as well as I could now."

—*Aurora, birth mother, age 16*

"I decided against taking Elizabeth home for a week because I didn't want my house to smell like the baby. I didn't want it to look like the baby. I didn't want to pick up a book and go, 'I read that book while I held my baby.' I knew if I really wanted those memories, I could go back to the hospital."

—*Jacqueline, birth mother, age 23*

On aftercare...

"I didn't want to go back to my apartment after I left the hospital, so we went to my dad's favorite restaurant. I remember leaving the table, going to the bathroom, and crying. Then my sister came into the bathroom and actually said, 'What's wrong?'

"I should have planned where to go after: there was no privacy there. It was the worst restaurant ever!

"None of my friends were there. Kerri, who I had leaned on for everything wasn't at the restaurant, which was so hard. My mom and dad were there, but there was lots of stuff they didn't know about—things I needed Kerri for.

"The whole thing was so mumbo jumbo. I would tell other birth mothers to plan everything beforehand—the whole day, and who's going to be there. It's just too difficult otherwise."

—*Emily, birth mother, age 25*

CHAPTER NINE

The Entrustment Service

"It was like a wedding, in a sense. And it was like a funeral."

—Aurora, birth mother, age 16

The entrustment service is an important formalization of the grief process. In the act of placing her child into the hands of the adoptive couple within a ceremonial context, a birth mother will make a significant symbolic gesture. At a great cost to herself, she is entrusting her child into the care of a new set of parents, parents who are receiving both a tremendous gift and an equally formidable responsibility. In this moment, the couple's intense joy meets the birth mother's greatest sorrow.

Also commonly known as a 'placement service,' the entrustment service should focus primarily on the birth mother. Although the adoptive parents will almost always be invited to participate, they are merely guests, witnesses to the birth mother's last act on behalf of her child. Here, there is no shirking or hiding from the birth mother's pain; adoptive couples are forced to face the magnitude of her grief. Intensely sad, yet meaningful, the ceremony offers family and friends the opportunity to weep with the birth mother, recognizing her sacrifice while validating her decision to place.

There are no set rules when planning a service. The ceremony can be a non-religious occasion, or it can have a strong spiritual component. It can be held among a circle of intimate friends, or merit the presence of a hundred of the birth mother's closest acquaintances. The ceremony can be a quick, simple process held in a hospital room, or an elaborate series of readings, rituals, songs, and speeches. It may be planned and conducted entirely by the birth mother, or placed in the hands of a pastor, a Pregnancy Center staff member, a counselor, or an adoption agency worker. In short, entrustment services are as varied and unique as the women who place.

In some cases, a ceremony may actually be held in the context of a Sunday morning church service. For a woman who feels as though she has 'fallen from grace', the process of being embraced and supported by the entire church body can be tremendously healing. Both her life-affirming choice and the church's compassionate response can serve as a powerful testimony to each person attending the ceremony. For most clients, however, the thought of standing before a congregation at the best of times is mortifying. Women should therefore never be pressured to enter into a situation in which they will be made to feel uncomfortable or exceedingly vulnerable. The entrustment service is a unique expression of a birth mother's love for her child, not a performance or an obligatory task.

INTRODUCING THE SIGNIFICANCE OF CEREMONY

When first introduced to the idea of an entrustment service, many clients will respond with disbelief. The thought of sharing this painful moment of the adoption with others may very well strike a woman as absurd. However, once the significance of ceremony is explained, most clients will become receptive to the idea of planning a service of their own.

When dealing with a reluctant client, a peer counselor can discuss the role that ceremony plays in a person's life. Birth is typically celebrated with an infant baptism or a baby dedication, or in a congregation of cooing women at a baby shower. Other significant events—birthdays, graduations, marriages, anniversaries—are also recognized through elaborate rituals. The wedding analogy can be particularly striking to a client who is about to place: as in a wedding, two families will be joined by the adoption. This lifelong union, created by one new life, should merit recognition.

Should the client declare herself untraditional or unsentimental, the counselor can point out the benefits the child can reap from the ceremony. Many women have their entrustment services videotaped and pass on the memento to their children. Even though the service can be extremely painful for a birth mother, her child will be able to watch this significant moment in the years to come. A child who sees the emotion and sacrifice involved in the process of placing will never question whether it was loved.

If a client is still reluctant to plan an entrustment ceremony, she should be encouraged to speak with other birth mothers. Clients who have had an entrustment service will seldom, if ever, regret the ceremony, and will often allow other birth mothers to look at photographs or videos of their entrustment services.

If a client refuses to commemorate her placement, her wishes should be respected. However, the woman who is able to grasp the value of ceremony will have a lasting reminder of one of her most painful—and meaningful—days of her lives. The entrustment service may very well prove to be an act of closure.

LOCATION

The entrustment service can be held in a church, a chapel, a home, a quiet room in the hospital, the hospital room itself, or even a public place such as a park or a garden. In some cases, the infant can be unofficially placed in the hospital, and then formally placed at an entrustment service that is held days or weeks later. Some women may request to have the ceremony held at the Pregnancy Center.

GUESTS

A client's guest list will undoubtedly reflect her personality. A more gregarious birth mother may have no qualms about inviting dozens of guests, including the doctors, nurses, and the pregnant woman in the room next to hers. Conversely, an introverted client may cringe at the thought of being in the limelight with puffy eyes and a runny nose, and will invite only her pastor and the adoptive couple.

When composing a guest list, the birth mother should select people who care enough to share in one of her most intimate moments and who will affirm her decision to place. A grandmother who is absolutely opposed to the adoption may mar an otherwise positive experience. Likewise, if the birth mother suspects that the birth father's family might create a disturbance, she should not issue invitations. The counselor should repeatedly emphasize that the entrustment ceremony is the birth mother's event. If the presence of the birth father or even a member of her own family will upset her, it is her prerogative to limit the guest list.

However, the client should be encouraged to recognize that the adoptive parents will benefit immensely if they can invite guests of their own. In some very open adoptions, birth mothers will actually welcome the adoptive couple's extended family. Whatever her preference, the birth mother should specify how many guests would be acceptable.

ELEMENTS OF THE CEREMONY

Depending on the birth mother's wishes, the entrustment ceremony may run from ten minutes to an hour. To prepare her guests for what to expect in an unfamiliar situation, the birth mother may choose to design an order of service. As simple as an outline created on the computer, the order of service can become a lasting memento.

A typical entrustment service will contain the following elements:

A musical piece or a poem

For a birth mother, the opportunity to use her unique talents to create a song or a poem for her child can be extremely meaningful. A musical birth mother can actually write and perform a song, or record a piece of music in advance to play at the service. Likewise, a client with a natural affinity with words can write a poem to honor her child. Another woman may prefer to chose a favorite song or a reading about adoption, and then ask a close friend to perform it at the ceremony.

The birth mother's speech

The birth mother will usually either prepare a speech for her child or read her "Dear Baby" letter. It is essential that her message be written out: should she be unable to speak, a close friend, chosen ahead of time, can finish reading the message on her behalf. Similarly, a woman who plans her speech in advance will avoid saying things that may leave her feeling vulnerable and exposed later. Clients should be warned against making a spontaneous speech.

The response

The birth mother's address should be followed by a response from either one or both of the adoptive parents, or a pastor or counselor who has been asked to address the situation. It is essential that the response affirm the birth mother and pay tribute to her courage. The speaker may also have the opportunity to gently teach uninformed audience members about adoption.

For women who have incorporated a religious element into the ceremony, the response may include a devotional thought, or a prayer of blessing on the infant, its birth mother, and the adoptive couple. In one moving ceremony, the baby's birth grandfather led the prayer, passing on the family blessing to the child.

Gift giving

The entrustment service provides a meaningful occasion for the birth mother to present her child with the special gift she has prepared. The adoptive parents will often give the birth mother a gift of their own, whether it be as simple as a flower or as elaborate as a framed letter expressing their gratitude.

Vows and the signing of the covenant

More elaborate ceremonies may include spoken vows or a written covenant. The birth mother, the birth father, and the adoptive mother and father can each read vows written to the child in advance. Pledges may include the promise to always act in the best interests of the child and to remain committed in prayer.

An extension of the vows, the covenant can serve as a lasting reminder of the commitments voiced that day. The signing of the covenant should be witnessed by whomever is officiating the ceremony. Several copies (typically on decorative paper) can be made: one for each of the birth parents, and another for the adoptive couple.

The entrustment

Often the last and the most intense element of a service, the handing over of the child by the birth mother is a poignant symbolic gesture. Due to the emotional nature of this final act, the birth mother may request that everyone, except for the adoptive couple, leave the room. Then the woman and the child's new parents can exchange their final words in privacy.

The technicalities of physically passing the child over should be discussed in advance. Will the act take place on stage or among the congregation? Will the child be given to the adoptive mother or to the father? What will the birth mother do the moment her hands are empty? Who will leave first: the audience, the birth mother, or the adoptive couple? The birth mother should consider that it might be less traumatic for her to leave first and thus avoid the sight of her child being taken away.

A light lunch or tea

In some cases, the trauma of leaving the hospital after the baby is handed over can be avoided or abated by the prospect of a social gathering afterwards. As in the case of a funeral or a wedding, social mingling over food can provide a time of emotional relief after an intense ceremony.

UNIQUE ALTERNATIVES

A remarkable amount of creativity can be incorporated in to the entrustment service. Birth mothers, adoptive couples, and those officiating the proceedings will often turn a traditional ceremony into a unique, one-of-a-kind experience.

For ministers who typically officiate weddings and funerals, an entrustment ceremony may prove a refreshing challenge. In addition to affirming the birth mother's life-affirming decision on behalf of the Church, the pastor can create a unique set of vows and a covenant, and challenge the audience with an atypical devotion. In one ceremony, for example, the infant was anointed with oil. The priest then gave a liturgical blessing, leading the audience through a prayerful response.

Numerous scriptural passages can lend themselves to the occasion: in both the Old and the New Testaments, adopted children are placed in high regard. According to Old Testament accounts, parents could disown or disinherit a natural child, but could never deprive an adopted child of its inheritance. In the New Testament, Christians are likened to adoptees who have been integrated into the family of God.

Some of the most significant biblical characters were adoptees. After being set adrift in a basket, the infant Moses was raised by another family. Ironically, his birth mother continued to care for him in what was to become one of the most open adoptions conceivable. Esther, another adoptee, was raised by a member of her extended family before becoming queen and saving her people.

In some cases, participants will integrate family traditions or other symbolic rituals into the ceremony. Knowing the significance that names hold, for example, a woman might include the naming of the child in her ceremony. Typically, the child is first named by its birth mother, and then given the name chosen by the adoptive couple. In some cases, the birth mother and the couple will name the child together. In other cases, the adoptive couple will bestow a special honor on the birth mother, using her name in the child's name.

Entrustment ceremonies often provide healing in unexpected ways. In one powerful ceremony, the infant's biological grandmother paid a tribute that her daughter would never forget. Although she had been opposed to adoption throughout the entire process, the woman stood up and read a letter to her daughter. Without even mentioning the baby, the client's mother praised her for the courage it took to make a selfless decision even at the risk of losing her family's approval. She then declared that she had never been as proud of her daughter as she was that day. The birth mother, who had believed that she had only brought shame to her family, broke down and wept. Both women then embraced, their relationship restored.

The healing process was even more widespread at an elaborate ceremony devised by a twenty-year-old birth mother. Everyone who was involved in the adoption process sat in a circle. The pastor who was officiating the ceremony then asked each person to express her feelings about the adoption. A close friend of the birth mother began, candidly admitting that she had first thought that the birth mother was selfish, passing her responsibility over to a pair of strangers. After seeing the adoption process and the intricate plans that the birth mother had made, she explained, she was left with nothing but respect for her friend.

Each person spoke, affirming both the birth mother and the adoptive couple. The adoptive parents spoke last. They described how they had initially felt very reluctant to pursue an open adoption. After becoming part of the adoptive process and hearing the affirmation that came from each person within the circle, they explained, they were left with one thought. Turning to the birth mother, they said, "After all of this, how could we not involve you in our lives?"

PREPARING THE ADOPTIVE COUPLE

During the entrustment service, the adoptive parents will come face-to-face with the birth mother's grief. In an intensely uncomfortable moment, they will be unable to escape the fact that as their dream is coming true, someone else's dream is dying. Because an entrustment service is such an unusual ceremony, adoptive parents may have little idea how to act or what to expect. With the birth mother's permission, a peer counselor or another Pregnancy Center worker can meet with the couple to prepare them in advance.

The peer counselor should emphasize that the entrustment service is held to honor the birth mother. The adoptive parents should not avert the focus to their new infant. Most importantly, they should not be pushy or assertive, but respectfully give the birth mother time and space. During one entrustment service, the birth mother had great difficulty placing her child in the hands of its new parents. Rather than leaning over and extending her hands, the adoptive mother backed off entirely until the woman could regain her composure. Then, after the service was over, the adoptive mother handed the baby back to the birth mother with a warm bottle. Her thoughtful gesture conveyed the message that she would not abandon the birth mother and that the relationship would not end.

The adoptive couple should be encouraged to bring a gift to present to the birth mother. Even something as simple as a card will be meaningful, as people seldom receive written blessings. The adoptive parents will be given a priceless gift on the day of the entrustment service. By being supportive and sensitive, they can acknowledge this gift, inhibiting their joy in order to experience a small part of the birth mother's pain.

IN THEIR OWN WORDS

"I walked into the ceremony with my baby. I left without him. It was like I was missing something when I left. I would not wish that feeling upon anybody, ever. That was one of the hardest things I've ever had to feel."

—*Aurora, birth mother, age 16*

"Diane was bustling around, getting everything cleaned up. There was nothing to clean up! There was nothing there, but she was all nervous. Her husband said, 'Hold the baby.' She said, 'Oh, no. I can hold her later.' He was like, 'Hold her.'

"That was it. Waterworks! She was crying. As soon as he placed Elizabeth in her arms she couldn't control herself. She was saying, 'Thank-you so much. This is the best day. Blah, blah, blah, blah.'

"That was my favorite day. My most favorite day. I made them so happy. I made a family."

—*Jacqueline, birth mother, age 23*

"I was aching, but it was a joyful pain. It was something that was meant to happen. I was supposed to be placing my baby, but that didn't mean it didn't hurt."

—*Chantal, birth mother, age 30*

"It's not easy emotionally for an adoptive parent either. Part of you wants that baby so badly you would do anything. But part of you thinks, 'What am I doing? I couldn't possibly walk out of here with that baby!'

"We put the baby back into her parents' arms and said, 'Take her home.' They said, 'No. This is what we want. We're just grieving.' It was a hugely emotional thing that went on and on and on.

"When people say to us, 'You did it the easy way,' we just smile at them. If only they knew."

—*Linda, adoptive mother*

CHAPTER TEN

Adoption Grief

"With that six pound, five ounce miracle came the highest and lowest emotions I've ever felt so far in my life."

—Erin, birth mother, age 17

While Pregnancy Centers view adoption as a positive, life-affirming option, they are often not as present or consistent in walking a client through her grief process as they are in helping a woman who has had an abortion. This oversight is tragic: upon finding no support, women who have placed for adoption will often delay their grief, a grief that becomes increasingly complicated as time passes. There is not a Pregnancy Center director or speaker on the planet who has spoken about crisis pregnancy issues without being approached afterwards by a gray-haired lady who discloses that she placed a baby for adoption fifty years ago, and is still haunted by her grief. Centers must begin to recognize that adoption grief is a unique, isolating grief that is under-supported and seldom understood.

Grief is easy to ignore. A counselor can easily become caught up in the excitement of an adoption, seeing the joy that a new life brings to a childless couple, and recognizing the benefits that both birth mother and child will reap from the decision to place. The birth mother herself will often insist that all is well and that she has no regrets. The overwhelming positives of adoption can enable a counselor to avoid delving into the pain that lies beneath the surface.

However solid her decision was to place, a woman will inevitably encounter intense, and often confusing, grief. She has experienced the intense emotions involved in bringing a human being into existence, and the high of giving an adoptive couple an unparalleled gift. At the same time, she will become consumed with the instinctive need to mother a child who is now gone. A woman who has lost a spouse will describe the strange sensation of not having her partner next to her in bed and the need to leave his pillowcase unwashed to preserve his scent. Similarly, a woman who has carried a baby to term and roomed with it in hospital, holding it constantly, will feel a disconcerting physical sense of loss. At a time when she should be consumed with meeting the needs of her infant, she will instead have excess time on her hands.

Her need to physically recover will limit her ability to distract herself. Coping mechanisms usually used to deal with stress and emotional upset—such as engaging in vigorous exercise or aggressive sports—may not be available.

Most women find that they are supported in the first three weeks after they place their babies. However, in a misguided effort to be sensitive, those who care for these women stop talking about the loss she has experienced. At this point, more than ever, a woman needs to be sincerely asked how she is feeling. A counselor who understands the grieving process can offer support when others, out of ignorance or a desire to avoid pain, fail to do so.

A GRIEF TIMELINE

Although each woman has unique issues surrounding her pregnancy and will use her individual coping mechanisms to deal with pain, there are some basic markers in the grieving process. The majority of women, when properly counseled, will experience predictable responses during the following stages of their pregnancy and placement:

The third trimester

At approximately seven months a woman will start to recognize that the pregnancy she thought would last forever will soon end. At the same time, the growing child that she is carrying will begin to seem like a real baby rather than an abstract concept. A woman will experience some intense grief during this bittersweet time when she physically longs for the pregnancy to end, but emotionally wishes to delay the inevitable separation from her child.

Those who encounter the birth mother at this stage will frequently view her grief as an indication that she should not be placing. In reality, a woman who begins to grieve before the pregnancy ends will be more likely to follow through with her plan to place. The grief to come will be lessened, while a woman who remains in denial at this point will have a greater emotional obstacle to surmount.

An effective counselor will use this time to inform the client about the entire grief process, as the woman will be less emotional than she soon will be. A picture of what grief looks like should be regularly impressed upon her and she should be encouraged to develop strategies to deal with the upcoming upheaval. If friends and work colleagues are unaware of her decision to place, the birth mother should warn them in advance. She should also be given permission to be proud of her pregnancy, as birth mothers often feel that they have no right to feel this way because they will not be parenting.

Delivery

Immediately after birth, a woman will experience a surge of adrenaline and a feeling of euphoria. At this point, her plans to place may no longer make sense. If she has no doubt, on the other hand, she will likely see no need to grieve. Her high may convince her that she has mastered the situation and her emotions, and that her noble act could have no downside.

A counselor should warn the client that an extremely low point will soon follow her emotional high. She should also be given permission to crash when the euphoria passes. If a woman has been told how well she is doing and praised during her high period, she may feel obliged to manufacture a high after the authentic feeling has passed. If she has been encouraged to face her pain, however blunt, a woman will be more likely to experience a successful recovery.

Three days postpartum

Three days after delivery, a woman may experience an intense negative physical and emotional reaction. This feeling of being completely overwhelmed can last up to three weeks. A client should be warned in advance that her counselor will be a consistent presence at this time and will almost become a nuisance should the client avoid calls or break appointments. This message can be conveyed in a humorous manner, as long as the underlying show of support is obvious.

Grieving is essential at this stage. A counselor is by no means a masochist who wants her client to endure pain for pain's sake. However, the only way to maneuver through grief is to directly face the pain; there are no shortcuts around it. Grief cannot be put off indefinitely; it must be dealt with. Perhaps the most effective way of encouraging a birth mother to grieve is to lead by example, sharing the client's pain. A counselor who sees and holds the new infant will better understand the birth mother's sacrifice—the person that she is letting go. Counselors need not strive to remain emotionally collected, or act strong for the client's sake, but can allow themselves to cry alongside the woman they are counseling. It is crucial, however, to continue to offer hope—hope that grief will subside and that pain will lead to growth.

One practical way that a birth mother can begin to deal with her pain is to tell her birth story. Engaging in a practice that spans cultures, women have always shared, in vivid detail, both the glorious and gruesome aspects of childbirth. Any man would feel faint after overhearing an explicit discussion about what medical interventions were necessary; how many hours of labor each woman had to endure and how much it hurt; the extent of the tearing; which nurses were angelic and which were woefully incompetent; and the trials and tribulations of a woman's first attempts to breastfeed. Indulging in these tales of war and heroism help women overcome the trauma of giving birth. The fact that a woman has placed her baby for adoption should not deprive her of involvement in this universal ritual.

When groups of women converge and the topic turns to childbirth, birth mothers often do not feel entitled to join in the conversation. A woman who is aware that she can legitimately be called a mother can preface her comments with a statement such as, "When I had Daniel, the child I placed for adoption, I felt the same way about my doctor!" If she can deliver this line smoothly, there will either hardly be a pause in the conversation, or she will be asked about the adoption process (questions for which she can be prepared). She need not ever pretend that she has not had a child!

Three to six months

At this stage in the grieving process, most women will notice a startling change: they are no longer consumed with thoughts of their babies. Up to this point, almost every waking minute will have been spent thinking about the child or the delivery, especially since the physical recovery served as an unavoidable reminder of both. A birth mother will go from wondering if she will ever last an entire morning without thinking of her child to actually experiencing this respite. Ironically, however, her initial reaction will not be relief, but an intense guilt. She will fear that she no longer loves her baby.

This first marker of grief recovery should be a cause to celebrate, not a reason to feel despondent. Birth mothers' groups can be an excellent place for women to proudly declare that they went an entire morning, or even a day, without fixating upon the adoption. Counselors must be careful, however, to discern between clients who have made a monumental step in recovery, and those who have simply avoided grieving altogether. A woman who has worked or studied obsessively, avoiding thought of her child through frantic activity, is, in actuality, making little progress.

At this stage in the grief process, a peer counselor can begin to draw out the client's dreams for the future. By the third month, a birth mother should have started to overcome the lethargy created by her physical recovery and grief. If she is not beginning to resume a normal life, working and becoming involved in social activities, her counselor can begin to encourage her in this direction. By identifying her goals, the client can regain a sense of hope and start living again.

Clients should be strongly advised not to fill their empty arms again by becoming involved in romantic relationships. Sensing a birth mother's vulnerability, unsuitable men may be drawn to her. She may end up with a 'rescuer,' a man who relates best to women who are dependent upon him. If involved in an unhealthy relationship—or even a positive one—a woman will push aside her grief to give full attention to her romantic feelings. In order to combat this problem, one counselor consistently challenged her clients to wait an entire year before becoming involved in a one-on-one relationship. Whenever a client would protest that she had met 'Mr. Right,' the counselor would remind her that the said gentleman would not be deterred by a delayed relationship. Indeed, maintaining a platonic relationship and dealing with her grief would bode well for her future.

Six months to one year

For many women, this stage is primarily a positive one. A birth mother will begin to recognize how the experience of having and placing a child has changed her. She will be able to identify growth within herself and to name some of her character strengths. If she has been dealing with her grief, she will be able to claim a new identity, an identity she owns because of the experience of adoption.

Along with the recognition that some remarkable changes have taken place comes a new type of grief. In this stage, birth mothers will not only grieve the loss of their children, but the loss of the children they once were. Having understood pain, they will perceive the world through different eyes. Friendships, once significant, may now strike them as shallow. One exasperated client complained to her counselor, "My friends are boring! All they want to do is go to the bar and talk about silly things!"

A peer counselor should affirm the growth she sees in a client, cheering her on through this stage. Specific signs of maturation can be pointed out, and if a woman has dropped bad habits, she should be commended. She should also be prepared for the next stage to come.

Baby's first birthday

The child's birthday, and the days leading up to it, is a time of significant pain. The intensity of emotion a birth mother will feel may convince her that she is backsliding, falling back into the intense grief she felt during the first three months after placing. At the same time, the client will also begin to recognize some of the difficulties she will face as she inevitably moves forward. Part of the transition involves becoming more than a birth mother, an identity that she has clung to over the past year. Instead of developing character through grief, she must now mature with no such catalyst for growth. The mundane reality of normal life, in other words, will begin to set in.

At this stage in the grief process, a birth mother should be reminded that emotional fluctuations are normal. She should also be assured that her identity does not rest solely on her position as a birth mother; she has a personhood and personality apart from the adoption.

The second year and beyond

The grieving process typically lasts for a minimum of two years. Bittersweet memories linger much longer. However, a woman who is dealing with her grief will come to a point in her journey when the adoption becomes cause for celebration, rather than sadness. One birth mother sent her counselor a compelling letter when her child turned five. "Her fifth birthday has come and gone," she wrote. "On that day, I took out my photos and my video of her and spoke with her on the phone. But this year, instead of crying, I smiled. Not because I didn't want to feel pain, but simply for the fact that there was really none left. All my years of grieving the loss of my little girl and the loss of my 'motherhood' have passed. I am simply truly happy for the little girl in my life."

As a woman comes to a state of resolution, her counselor's presence can begin to wane. As time progresses, the counselor can encourage her client to come in for an occasional "tune-up," rather than keeping regularly scheduled appointments. Although the relationship can go on for years, especially when subsequent pregnancies stir up old emotions, it will inevitably change. A counselor can become like an old friend, and the client, a peer.

THE FIVE FACES OF GRIEF

Current research has offered various models that depict the range of emotions that a grieving individual may experience. The following section will be based on one of the more traditional grief models because of its simplicity. According to this model, grief is expressed in five basic ways: denial, bargaining, anger, depression, and acceptance.

A woman may experience these stages of grief in a random order, moving back and forth between them. A peer counselor may be perplexed to discover that a client who has reached a stage of acceptance one day will lapse back into denial the next. However, these transitions will be less disconcerting once they are recognized and understood. In order to help a client process her emotions, a peer counselor should examine several grief models, gathering as much information as possible.

Denial

A birth mother who is in the denial stage can easily dupe an unwary counselor. She will openly declare that adoption is wonderful and that every woman in her child bearing years should consider placing an infant. Acting as the 'good girl,' a client will insist that all is well, and repeatedly praise the child and its adoptive family. In other words, the world the birth mother verbally creates is a utopia, a flawless place that is inconsistent with reality.

A peer counselor may face the temptation to take the woman's words at face value, especially if the client gives God credit for the good things in her life. Joy is, after all, much easier to bear than raw grief. Adoption agency workers and family members will often support a woman's denial, affirming her decision and strength of character while carefully avoiding raising questions that might burst the bubble.

Denial has other guises as well. A woman may approach life at a frantic pace, exhibiting a ferocious work ethic or making huge life changes. Two months after placing, for example, one client signed up to do relief and development work in Africa. Her counselor confronted her, warning her that living in an impoverished village on another continent and watching people die of AIDS would not be conducive to her own grieving process. The client reluctantly admitted that her motives were not merely altruistic: she was trying to avoid the trauma involved in placing.

Other women escape grief by using alcohol, drugs, or the party scene to dull their emotions. The results can be devastating: some birth mothers become pregnant a second time. Ironically, family members often encourage this behavior, believing the birth mother deserving of 'fun.' One birth mother informed her counselor that her mother and stepfather were planning to get her drunk on her eighteenth birthday, though she had only placed a month before. Another client became pregnant three times after repeatedly returning to a wild social life. Unable to deal with the placement of her first child, she kept her second, and aborted her third. Today, she claims that most of her pain stems from the abortion, a choice that she would never have made had she confronted her adoption grief much sooner.

Denial can begin well before the baby is even born. One woman entered a Center for a pregnancy test—even though she was visibly seven months pregnant! When her counselor inquired whether she felt any movement in her belly, the client casually stated, "No, it's more like kicking." Nevertheless, a pregnancy test was still carried out.

A counselor should not strive to break a birth mother's denial, but should gently probe when the woman pretends that all is well. The client needs to be reminded that there will be sad times ahead, and that feeling unhappy is natural and necessary, however uncomfortable it makes others. If a birth mother is engaged in destructive behavior, however, she should be warned of the dangers inherent in her behavior.

Bargaining

A woman who is in the bargaining stage will create fantastic scenarios, envisioning the return of her child through miraculous circumstances. She may anticipate the death of the adoptive couple in a car crash. She may place her hope on the lottery, believing that although she is virtually penniless and stuck in a dead-end job, she will soon have the means to care for her child. A birth mother may see potential in a boyfriend who has abandoned her, or believe that a miraculous transformation will quell his abusive tendencies. Basically, she will hope against all odds that she will be reunited with her child to form a harmonious family.

Bargaining is typically tied in to a woman's legal reality—where her adoption is in terms of the legal process. She may return to the bargaining stage as long as there is a slim chance that her decision to place can be altered. "Erin," a 17-year old birth mother, vividly described her transition from denial to bargaining:

"I went through the classic 'honeymoon phase' where I just thought the adoptive couple was perfect and that I was a saint for making them a family. Reality hit me at about three and a half months after my daughter's birth. It suddenly sank in that

this was permanent and that she was no longer mine. I had a bit of a 'freak out' and even went as far as phoning a lawyer and several single mother support services to try to get her back. I never did make any attempts, but it hit me really hard when my denial phase ended."

A counselor can support a birth mother during the bargaining stage by helping her to perceive her situation realistically. If she is preparing to take drastic or irrational actions to get her baby back, she should be strongly advised to review her original reasons for placing, and to assess if, and how, her situation has changed. Her baby's welfare should be brought up repeatedly. If she placed in order to give her child the benefits of a two-parent family, for example, she may need to be reminded that she is still single, or dating a man who is either unfit to be a father, or has yet to prove himself worthy. Finally, the agitated birth mother should be encouraged not to make a rash decision, but to allow a certain period of time to pass before taking action. Even twenty-four hours may bring her to a calm enough state to rationally consider her options.

If she is legally able to change her mind and appears rationale, the client should be asked if she is seriously considering parenting. In some cases, she may simply miss her child and eventually recognize that does not really want to become its full-time mother. However, if a woman is convinced that her decision to place was a serious mistake, her counselor must offer full emotional support and initial guidance, helping her to work through the decision of whether to ask the adoptive couple to return her child.

It is imperative that the birth mother be the one to approach the couple, to seek legal and professional help, and to deal with the ramifications of her decision. If she does not have the skills to get out of the adoption, it is unlikely that she will have the skills needed to be an effective parent.

After a lengthy discussion with a client who was seriously reconsidering her decision to place, one counselor gave her a list of ten things she needed to do immediately. The tasks were complex, but the woman returned the next day having completed each one. Recognizing that the client was willing to do what it took to back out of the adoption, the counselor celebrated her decision with her and began a crash course on parenting. She continued to emphasize that the client could change her mind again—even after parenting for a period of time. However, the counselor made it clear that the adoptive couple may be unwilling to adopt her child because of the emotional upheaval of having already lost that child. The client recognized that if she should change her mind again, she faced the possibility of having to select a new couple.

.Anger

Anger is the easiest form of grief to identify: its intensity and authenticity is unmistakable. It can also be the most perplexing emotion, as it is often irrational or triggered by the slightest irritation. One client became furious after the adoptive couple sent her a photograph of her two-month-old infant. She shoved the photo into her peer counselor's face, expecting a similar reaction. When the counselor looked perplexed, the birth mother explained that the infant was not on sucking the pacifier that she had specifically given him at the hospital. Furthermore, he was placed next to a teddy bear other than the one she had provided. Eventually, both client and counselor would laugh about the incident.

Anger is frequently directed at the adoptive mother as she is perceived to be the birth mother's replacement and the most significant source of competition. Adoption workers may also bear the brunt of a woman's emotion, as they are facilitating the adoption that is the source of her tremendous pain. A worker who was well received initially can suddenly become a villain, in the birth mother's mind, an enemy whose every move or gesture is misinterpreted. Even Pregnancy Center workers may not escape the birth mother's critical eye during the anger stage. A peer counselor's failure to call at the correct time may be perceived as blatant insensitivity.

Birth fathers, of course, seldom escape their partners' indignation. After birth, a woman's anger towards a man who was not present will escalate, even if the relationship ended before the pregnancy was discovered. If a couple has remained together, the birth mother may still resent her partner, feeling acute irritation over the fact that he is not grieving in the same way she is.

Although anger is normal and healthy, a client should be warned that what she does with it can permanently color the adoption process. If she composes a scathing letter to the adoptive couple, denounces a long-time friend, or isolates a supportive birth father, she will reap the consequences of her actions. A birth mother may be wise to bring any letters that she has written to her counselor before sending them. Though heavy editing may be in order, her final product will be a productive expression of her emotions, not an embittered diatribe that will alienate the recipient.

When dealing with her anger toward the birth father, a client should be reminded that grief is individual. The man will mourn the loss of his child in his own way and may find his partner's grief perplexing. The birth mother cannot expect the father of her child to also assume the role of her girlfriend.

If a birth mother seeks closure to a relationship that ended under unpleasant circumstances, she should be encouraged to examine her motives. Is she seeking revenge, affirmation, or authentic closure? Women who confront a former boyfriend for the wrong reasons are often hurt again. The chance that a man will repent of his past deeds, praise a woman for her strength of character, and stroll with her off into the sunset with baby in tow is obviously unlikely.

Birth mothers can also be given ways to physically vent their anger. One client who had the strength to pound holes into the walls of her apartment found that pounding a plastic baseball bat into her bed brought the same relief. Another found great comfort in running up a hill and screaming at the top of her lungs. Her counselor had to persuade the woman's horrified family that her uncivilized antics were actually a healthy expression of her grief and not a symptom of mental derangement.

Depression

If a client suddenly disappears for weeks on end, her counselor can reasonably assume that she has entered a depressive state. She may plummet emotionally, eating little or excessively, exhibiting erratic sleep patterns, and suffering from lethargy. She may put little energy into maintaining her appearance and may refer to herself in condescending terms. A birth mother can also be prone to wallowing in her misery, talking about the adoption and nothing else.

A counselor should carefully observe a client during this stage, being present despite the woman's attempts to avoid her. If a birth mother slips from normal grief into what appears to be postpartum depression for an extended period following birth, medical intervention may be required. Some women suffering from severe postpartum depression can actually suffer bouts of paranoia, hearing voices or harboring bizarre suspicions.

To support a client in this difficult stage of grief, a counselor can assume a motherly role. Questions involving the birth mother's health will serve as a reminder to take care of herself. She should be asked whether she is eating properly (getting sufficient protein instead of carbo-loading on fast foods), drinking enough water, taking daily walks for exercise, and leaving the house on a regular basis. Even styling her hair and putting on make-up can give a woman a small boost.

In cases of severe depression, a birth mother's counselor has a responsibility to send her to a doctor. If she refuses, walking out of the Center after threatening suicide, she should be accompanied to the hospital. If, by chance, she continues to resist, threaten to call the police. A woman will seldom resist some form of help, as she too will be concerned about herself.

Acceptance

A client has reached acceptance when she can express her love and happiness for her child, while investing time and energy into her own life. She will be able to be objective, identifying things that she did not like about the adoption process, but confirming that she made the right decision. Although she may waver, revisiting her grief during stressful periods of her life, her grief will have come full circle.

A woman's entrance into this stage should be celebrated. A counselor can gradually begin to change the tone of the relationship, moving meetings from the confines of the Center to a restaurant or a coffee shop. The client's role will change as well, for she can begin to act as a mentor to other birth mothers. Birth mothers often have the makings of exceptional peer counselors.

After reaching the acceptance stage, one client had an unusual opportunity to help another woman begin a journey through grief. After placing her child for adoption and processing her grief, "Erin" spoke openly about her experience. When she became engaged to an adoptee, and grew closer to his extended family, her future mother-in-law pulled her aside and disclosed that she had also placed a child for adoption when she was a teen. Neither her natural children nor her adopted son—the client's fiancé—knew about their sibling. Only through a young woman's candidness did a long-kept secret emerge and the healing process begin.

IN THEIR OWN WORDS

Julie's Story

"I come from a single-parent family where communication is not a priority. My mother comes from a very religious background and she's heavily involved in the church. My pregnancy was really embarrassing for her.

"I immediately decided to place for adoption because I had nothing going for me. I was living with my mom and I was working in a coffee shop, making nothing for money. It wasn't fair to bring a child into the world and care for it under these circumstances.

"The original plan was that my best friend would be with me during the delivery. My mom ended up being there as well. At first I didn't want her to be involved at all, but when it came down to the crunch, I wanted my mom there. She found it pretty hard, sitting there watching me go through all this, knowing what would happen in the end.

"The day I was being released, I changed my mind. I was laying on my bed crying, and the nurse came in and asked me what was wrong. I told her that I was thinking about changing my mind. She called in a doctor, who was also a member of my mother's church. He came in and basically told me that I was being stupid. 'Stupid' was his exact word. He said that if I kept this baby, I would become just another statistic. He pounded me into the ground, making me feel inadequate. So I listened to him.

"My mom drove me home that day and we never even talked about the adoption. I remember sitting there eating lunch when I just lost it. I cried for five minutes. And that was that.

"Ten days later, I moved to a different city and started college. I had a brand new life. I didn't give myself the chance to grieve. I didn't even know that I was allowed to, because that's how my family deals with things. We usually get over it and move on.

"But I couldn't get over it. I vented and dealt with it the wrong way. I got in with the wrong crowd, drank a lot, was promiscuous, did drugs here and there, and partied a lot. And I ended up right back where I started—pregnant again!

"The day I found out I was pregnant again, I knew I had to talk to somebody. I didn't have that opportunity the last pregnancy. I remember going through the phone book, looking through shrinks and counselors. I kept coming across the Pregnancy Care Centre. I thought, 'No way! It's a Christian organization. I don't want that.' But I kept coming across it.

"I started counseling. I honestly can't remember anything from that time. (Sometimes I can remember, and sometimes I can't.) What I do know is that I decided to place this child with the same family that adopted my first. I didn't want an entrustment service. It was basically, 'Here you go, have a nice day!' I went home and was going to be fine.

"Two weeks later, I wanted my daughter back. I went to pick her up and spent two or three days with her. I kept the baby. And that was that.

"I kept her for three weeks. By the end, I had had enough. I phoned Social Services and my daughter was placed in foster care. Then I placed her with a different family, one that lived closer.

"This time I went through a grief process. I ended up in hospital a couple of times, but I did it. The difference is that I had professional counseling, whereas the first time I only had my mother who prayed for me.

Nicki's Story

"I was five months along before I admitted to myself and everyone else that I was pregnant. I had just denied it at first. I was almost at the point where I thought I had ovarian cancer. There was no way I was pregnant! I even thought I had gas, though I could sometimes see my stomach moving. My mom had to finally sit me down and tell me.

"After that, I thought of the baby as an 'it.' It was never a 'he,' or a 'she,' or a 'person.' It was just this 'thing' that was happening to me.

"My mom encouraged me to come to the Centre. I wasn't dragged; she wanted me to come and I agreed. It was a good experience. I could say whatever I needed to say. I really liked the feeling of not being judged. I felt like I could air my dirty laundry without feeling like it was going to get back to anyone or hurt anyone's feelings.

"I always felt that adoption was the right thing to do. Still, I didn't deal with my emotions, or my grief, or anything until I got pregnant again. I was back at work two weeks after I delivered my first baby. I got really involved in life, working, mainly, and just doing lots of 'stuff'—nothing in particular, just stuff.

"I couldn't let myself feel anything. I never really felt an attachment to my son. Even now, I look at him and he's not my son—he's Jeff and Amy's son. I know I gave birth to him, but he's almost like a friend's kid.

"Everyone kept telling me that I was supposed to grieve and have finality. I just kept wishing my son was dead because then I could have a funeral. I could go to a grave and that's where he would be, and I would know that he was gone. Everyone could understand how I was feeling because there was a death. As it was, people were trying to understand, but couldn't.

"There was no finality to it. It kept going. I kept going and seeing him, and I would get to a point where I couldn't see him for a couple of months, or hear from the adoptive couple, or see pictures. I needed the finality, and I never got that.

"I stayed with my boyfriend, which was a big mistake. He didn't encourage me to get help. He needed me to keep grieving so that I would stay with him. He didn't want a girlfriend: he wanted a mother. Being in that relationship was easy because I didn't have to deal with anything and I could mother him, getting those emotions and needs out.

"At that stage in my life I was rebelling against my parents, rebelling against the church, rebelling against everyone and everything around me. So I did not turn to the people closest to me for support. There were definitely people who tried to reach out, but I didn't reach back out to them. I was on my independence kick. I didn't realize I needed anyone and I didn't want anyone's help.

"Despite everything, I went to the birth mom's group. Some days I went home and felt like I had been so fake that it was just pointless for me to go. I came, and put on a front, and pretended everything was fine. I thought everyone believed me. Why wouldn't they? There was nothing wrong! I sort of faked going through the emotions. I kind of went through them, and kind of didn't, and I thought things were okay.

"After my son's first birthday I thought, 'This is too much!' I realized I had to do something, but at that point it was way too big for me to face head on. I had let it fester too long to do anything about it. I decided I didn't want to see my son, and I didn't see him for six months. On his second birthday I didn't even send him a card.

"I was so angry. I was very angry at my boyfriend. I felt he had pressured me into placing. He didn't, but I felt he did. I had major anger towards the adoption agency, since they were the people who did the adoption. I was mad at my godparents, because they had adopted a little boy. And, my word, was I angry at Jeff and Amy!

"I was angry at God, of course, and the church, and my youth pastor. I wondered why God would let this happen to me. I felt like my youth pastor didn't care. I felt like I couldn't go back to church, because everyone would look at me and know, and I would be so judged. It was a good experience going back when I finally did, but I was scared out of my mind!

"Sometimes I wanted the adoptive couple to go away! But they didn't let go. They realized that I would come back in my own time. They wanted my son to know me and to ask questions when he needed to.

"My second pregnancy was a replacement pregnancy. I desperately wanted another baby, but I didn't want to admit that to anyone else. But when I found out I was pregnant, I was horrified! I was like, 'No, not again. How could I make the same mistake?' I didn't tell anyone for a month. But this time I let myself feel. I was excited about this pregnancy after the initial shock wore off.

"When my daughter came, I started to recognize my responsibility to Benjamin. I realized that I had to get my act together so that I could be there for him. I felt really guilty about the fact that he might ask me why I had placed him and not Meghan. My life situation hadn't changed, so I couldn't use that for a reason. I had to understand myself why I had placed him, and why I hadn't placed Meg, and why I avoided seeing him. I needed answers. In searching for answers I was able to begin to grieve.

"It's so much better now! I'm back at church, which is the biggest thing. Jeff and Amy have become my family. I've grown up a lot. Every time I step back and look at my life, I say 'Wow!', because the way people have come into my life and touched me is really cool."

CHAPTER ELEVEN

Special Days

"Every day leading up to the court date I thought I was going to die of depression."

—Emily, birth mother, age 25

When dealing with clients, peer counselors must recognize that some days are particularly challenging for birth mothers, while others are especially joyful. Mother's Day, Father's Day, Christmas, and baby's first birthday may trigger complicated emotions—sometimes involving both the adoption and the client's own childhood. Dates specific to the adoption, including the day of placement, the days leading up to the finalization of the adoption, and the court date itself may be especially painful. Even seemingly innocuous times, such as Thanksgiving or birthday celebrations held in honor of nieces and nephews, may cause an unexpected reaction. Rather than simply accepting a client's mood swings, the counselor should prepare the woman for difficult days and celebrate with her during meaningful times.

'Special' days are individual: each client will attach a different meaning to an event. Rather than finding Christmas or her baby's birthday especially difficult, for example, one client felt the most intense grief on Thanksgiving. Once her favorite family time because of the overabundance of food, laughter, and camaraderie, Thanksgiving became the occasion in which her child's absence was most obvious.

Clients who can identify that some days are more difficult than others can devise strategies to cope with their grief. For some women, setting aside time to sift through their memory boxes can prove healing; others may prefer to go to a park and journal. Clients should be encouraged to do something for themselves to commemorate special events. A woman should not be ashamed to buy herself flowers, for example, or to purchase something that specifically reminds her of her child. She should strive to celebrate the day, rather than viewing it solely as a day of mourning.

The following events are some of the most common days of grief and joy for birth mothers:

The Finalization of the Adoption

For some birth mothers, the court date—the day the adoption becomes legal—is one of the most significant times of grief. Others may focus on the actual signing the adoption papers, or on the final hours and minutes leading to the moment when their decision will become irrevocable. Each woman is individual: a significant date that unleashes a torrent of emotion in one may pass by another unobserved.

The finalization of the adoption, however anticipated, is usually an anti-climactic end to an emotionally intense experience. What began as a crisis pregnancy quickly turned into the all-consuming experience of carrying a child, and then the ecstatic moment of meeting this person for the first time. The entrustment ceremony and the placement also presented unique joys and challenges. During each of these experiences, the birth mother was in a position of power and at the center of attention. On the court date, however, everything changes: she will lose her legal leverage; she may find herself marginalized; and she will no longer have any big events to plan or anticipate. Her identity, once centered on the adoption, will need to be reconstructed.

If a woman wishes to attend court, she should be encouraged to do so, provided the legislation in her particular region will permit her presence. The adoptive couple should be warned in advance so that the birth mother's presence does not create fear that she has changed her mind. In some open adoption scenarios, the adoptive parents and the birth mother will actually celebrate the event together afterwards, going to a restaurant or spending time with the child in its new home.

Clients should be prepared for the actual court experience: if a woman is prepared for an emotional letdown, she will find the ordeal less traumatic. While she may envision a long, drawn-out process, the finalization of the adoption is usually just a mere legal technicality that takes minutes to complete. Women often enter the courtroom and leave shortly after, disillusioned and displaced. Since a birth mother may feel abandoned at this stage, the counselor should repeatedly clarify that although her contact with the adoption agency may end at this point, the Pregnancy Center will continue to affirm and support her.

Birth Mother's Day

Birth Mother's Day, held on the Saturday before Mother's Day, has yet to become widely recognized. Pregnancy Centers should therefore promote the occasion, recognizing birth mothers as mothers and celebrating the positive nature of adoption. In some cases, Centers may even have the opportunity to educate the public about adoption, as the local media may wish to cover the event.

For many birth mothers, the simple act of acknowledging their motherhood will go a long way. The experience of bearing a child transforms a woman's identity, giving her an awareness of her innate power expressed through her ability to carry a life. To pretend that a birth mother is not a mother is to deprive her of her new identity and to deny that she has gone through a significant rite of passage. The fact that a birth mother has given birth and, in a loving and responsible way, chosen parents for her child means that she is qualified to be called a mother.

Whether insensitive or ignorant, some people will openly question a birth mother's status. One client came to the Center incensed because her mother's friend had declared that she was not a 'real' mother. The counselor's response was simple. 'Did you give birth to a child?' she asked. The birth mother nodded. 'What do you call a woman who has given birth to a child?' The answer was obvious, and the client knew that she would ask that very question if confronted again.

Birth Mother's Day is typically celebrated by Birth Mothers' Groups. There are no hard and fast rules governing the affair; some groups may have lunches or brunches in honor of birth moms, while others may bring adoptive couples and birth mothers together to celebrate. After holding a light lunch, one Birth Mothers' group asked a group of people, including a birth mother, a birth father, an adoptive mother and father, an adoptee, and a birth grandparent to speak about adoption. As each part of the adoption constellation spoke, the audience was given a striking picture of what adoption could look like. For many of the women at the beginning of their journeys, the sadness of the day was replaced with hope for the future.

While Birth Mother's Day may be a cause for celebration among those for whom adoption was a good and healthy choice, others may view it as a day of mourning. For women of closed adoptions, those forced to relinquish their children, or women who did not receive good counseling prior to and after their adoptions, the day may prove solemn and grim. Peer counselors must be sensitive to the needs of these women and allow them to express their grief.

However, counselors can also help women move forward in positive ways by empowering them to see the positive in even the most negative situations. Although a woman who had no choice but to place may have lost her child, for example, she did choose to give this child life. Even though she may be suffering, the birth mother has created a child that may impact many lives in positive ways. Considerable good might come from an undesirable situation and the birth mother, however sad, should be honored for her contribution.

Mother's Day

Mother's Day can be an alienating time: while women who are not actively parenting may not feel entitled to think of themselves as 'mothers,' adoptive mothers share a similar sense of inadequacy, this time based on their inability to carry a child to term. For birth mothers, bridge-building may alleviate some of the sorrow that this day brings. A woman can send the adoptive mother a card thanking her for raising the child and affirming her ability as a mother.

One birth mother went a step further in acknowledging her child's parents. For Mother's Day, she enlarged and framed an original photo of the bald baby laughing with its mouth wide open, and delivered it, along with a card. On Father's Day she put a matching photo—this time with the baby pouting fiercely—in a matching frame and wrote a letter in honor of the adoptive father.

Women of a religious persuasion should be warned that their churches may celebrate traditional mothers and the nuclear family, and fail to acknowledge birth mothers. If attending church that day will only drag her spirits down, a woman can choose an alternative, perhaps going on a day trip with a friend instead.

Since most people will not think to acknowledge the birth mother on this day, a peer counselor can send a Mother's Day card to each of her clients. The Center can also celebrate the occasion by holding a potluck dinner during the Birth Mothers' meeting closest to that date, or by giving each woman a rose.

Father's Day

Father's Day has a tendency to stir up multiple issues. For some women, this annual celebration of fathers brings to light their own fathers' deficiencies. Some women will have placed for this very reason: lacking a positive father figure while growing up, a woman may have engaged in early sexual activity and, upon becoming pregnant, placed to prevent her child from a similar upbringing. Although a birth mother can ensure that her child will have a father, this fact may do little to assuage her own sorrow.

Birth fathers, in turn, are seldom celebrated on this auspicious occasion. Many a birth mother once entertained a 'Cinderella' fantasy, believing, against the odds, that her handsome prince would declare her unplanned pregnancy a stroke of luck, and whisk her off to his castle—or, at least, to his luxurious condo in the Bahamas. In reality, many birth mothers are abandoned during this vulnerable period and are forced to contend with the unpleasant reality that their supposed knight in shining armor is anything but. For women whose partners may qualify for the lesser position of 'squire,' disappointment may still be a reality. Clients often lament that the birth father has no interest in the wonderful child he has helped to create.

If a woman's relationship with the birth father has been remotely positive, she can be encouraged to send him a Father's Day card. She can also acknowledge the adoptive father. If anything, the birth mother should be prepared for a sad and reflective day, taking time to write in her journal or to engage in comforting activities.

Christmas

Christmas, in our society, is centered on children and the family. For those who are isolated or who have suffered a loss, the pressure to celebrate may only exacerbate feelings of inadequacy, loneliness, and grief. Understanding this reality, a counselor should give the birth mother permission not to be totally joyful during the Christmas season. When the absence of her child overwhelms her, she need not feel ashamed of leaving her family or friends temporarily to spend time alone.

While giving voice to her grief, the client should also find ways of celebrating the season. One birth mother chose to commemorate her son every year by purchasing a Christmas tree ornament. Each ornament reflected the boy's age—from a sleepy ceramic infant in a cradle inscribed with the words, "Baby's First Christmas"; to a pajama-clad toddler nestled in a pale yellow moon; to a miniature train bearing intricate, tiny gifts. Every year, a new ornament was added to a small tree set aside for that purpose.

If an adoption is relatively closed, or if gift-giving is not an option, a client can devise creative options. One twenty-year-old client, for whom gifts were extremely significant, selected a gift for her child each year. Although she had not seen her child in six years, she wrapped her newest acquisitions, wrote and dated a thoughtful note, and placed them in a large box. If she was ever reunited with her son, she reasoned, she would give him the gifts that had compiled over the years.

Another client tackled her Christmas blues by contributing to a campaign geared to helping underprivileged children. Every year following the placement, she went to the agency's Christmas tree, which was decorated with the names and ages of needy children across the city. Each time the client selected a little girl the same age as her daughter.

For a woman facing Christmas alone, or with an unsupportive family, the idea of investing herself in a worthwhile cause may be especially fitting. One birth mother who did not have the funds to fly home for the holidays decided to travel in a more unique way. Joining a busload of volunteers dressed as elves, the client helped distribute gifts to needy children across the city. A potentially disastrous holiday alone was transformed into a meaningful, memorable time simply because the birth mother was able to step into a world outside of herself.

If a client will be alone at Christmas, her peer counselor should try to find a volunteer or a mentor with whom the birth mother can spend Christmas Day. If the woman is part of a church, families or groups of singles may be happy to include another person at the table. It is essential that a grieving birth mother—especially one who is facing her first Christmas without her baby—find some place to go.

For some women, the prospect of spending Christmas with their families may be as disconcerting as spending the holiday alone. Expectations about the holidays should be discussed in advance, either at a Birth Mothers' Group or during a private counseling session. Unrealistic perceptions should be challenged. A birth mother may be unaware, for example, that there are other people who find the holidays extremely trying. Despair is widespread: ironically, suicide rates rise during this festive occasion. If a woman is aware that statistically, many people have no place to go at Christmas, she will not feel so alone.

A birth mother may also harbor the false hope that her pregnancy and placement may alter her family's irksome habits during the season. She must be gently warned that although her own perceptions and values may have been transformed through the adoption experience, her family may very well carry on its disagreeable traditions. If her family is prone to fighting or excessive drinking, for example, the probability that tempers will flare or that groggy people will emerge with hangovers the next morning is high. Rather than hoping for the best, the birth mother should be prepared to deal with the worst, and to develop strategies to improve the holiday.

The Pregnancy Center can honor women in every way possible. Counselors can hold a Christmas party for birth mothers, giving each one a gift that has been donated by local churches or benefactors. One church created quilted Christmas stockings each year for the women. 'You do so much for us,' one birth mother observed after receiving the simple but meaningful gift.

Baby's Birthday

Of all the occasions, the one that a birth mother will never fail to celebrate is her child's birthday. For birth mothers included in the festivities of the day, baby's birthday can be a memorable event. Unfortunately, some adoptive families fail to recognize how significant this date is to birth mothers.

If a birth mother is not included, or is intentionally excluded from the day's proceedings, her counselor can encourage her to celebrate the event separately. For example, she could bake a cake and bring it in to work, honoring the day regardless of whether she provides her co-workers with an explanation.

Peer counselors should keep careful records of each child's birthday and send a card or a gift every year. Counselors who have contact with birth families can advise them to honor the birth mother on her child's birthday instead of allowing the day to pass without acknowledgment. One counselor surprised her Birth Mothers' Group by baking a cake and writing the name of each child in blue or pink icing. Each woman, she observed, strategically ate the piece bearing her baby's name.

Family Reunions

Gatherings are, for dysfunctional families, typically complicated affairs. Adding a recent adoption to the event will only further complicate the situation. If a birth mother has discussed the placement with her immediate family and most intimate relatives, she may feel awkward around distant relations who are unaware that she was even pregnant. Even worse, her new identity as a birth mother and her child may be ignored altogether if her relatives feel too awkward to approach the subject. At the celebration held for one birth mother's grandparents, a huge collage of all the children and grandchildren had been painstakingly constructed. Her child, the birth mother discovered while scanning the collage, was the only person not included.

Knowing the potential for hurt feelings and dashed expectations, a peer counselor should prepare the client in advance. Several questions may need to be addressed. Which family members, for example, will know about the adoption? Will the birth mother inform those who do not know? What type of responses can she expect? Would it be best to avoid the family reunion altogether? Clients should also evaluate their family's unwritten policy around frank discussions: if a woman upsets the order of how a family functions, speaking boldly when others expect her to be silent, she should be prepared for the repercussions. Is breaking the family silence worth the grief that might result?

In most cases, concealing the adoption will be detrimental. If only one other person is aware of the placement, the secret may come out. In the case of one client, it was the birth father that broke the silence. Upset by his partner's refusal to tell her family about the adoption, the birth father actually phoned one of her relatives and explained the entire situation. Chaos ensued, but in the end, the woman expressed relief that she no longer had to conceal her secret.

---

11 In Alberta, where this interview took place, there is a ten day waiting period after a birth signs her consent to release, during which time she is free to change her mind and parent without question from the agency or the couple.

IN THEIR OWN WORDS

"Even now, the ten days are hard.[11] Some days I'm upset when I wake up in the morning. Then I look at the date and I realize what day it is—the day the adoption was finalized. It's been, what, two years and I still have a hard time facing that day."

—Aurora, birth mother, age 16

"The tenth day is really horrible for me. It was the worst day of my life."

—Nicki, birth mother, age 17

"The ten days came and went. For me, the court date was the hardest. It was then that Jeremy's identity changed forever. He was never going to be my son in anyone's eyes ever again—not on paper. In the eyes of the law, it was like he was born to the adoptive couple."

—Kendra, birth mother, age 23

"I hate Christmas with a passion. My family knows what it's like for me at Christmas and, of course, they avoid it big time. They do the whole, 'We're a happy family' thing."

—Julie, birth mother, age 21

"Her first birthday was the hardest—I bawled. I had a pity party. It wasn't so much about Kaitlyn. It was more that I wasn't in the place where I could have her, or be a wife and a mom."

—Chantal, birth mother, age 30

"I saw Elizabeth on her first birthday. At first I wasn't supposed to: her parents wanted me to come the next day, or the following week. I had specifically said to them, 'I don't care if I see her on any other day. If you can only give me one day a year, it has to be her birthday. I don't want to see her on the day before, or the day after.'

They had forgotten how much it meant to me, obviously, because they said they were too busy on her birthday. I thought, 'I can't be upset about this,' but I was very upset.

When they called me and said, 'We've had a cancellation. Is there any way you can come on her birthday?', I said 'Yes!' I had plans: we were supposed to go to a wedding and do a million other things that day, but I canceled every single thing I had to do so that I could see her. She walked right up to me, her hair all wild, and I said, 'Oh hello! Happy birthday!'

"It was probably one of my most memorable moments."

—Jacqueline, birth mother, age 23

CHAPTER TWELVE

Familial Reactions

*"My mother is still grieving. My father has a new family—he doesn't need us anymore.
My grandmother said, 'Suck it up, it's okay. Everything will be fine, so get over it.' "*

—Aurora, birth mother, age 16

The influence of a birth mother's family on the adoption process should never be underestimated. Even a family that is estranged from a client can wield tremendous power, pressuring a woman to place or to dismantle a solid adoption plan.

One peer counselor was shocked by the influence her client's estranged mother held. Struggling to raise a toddler, the pregnant twenty-year-old recognized that a second child would stretch her beyond her capacity. After extensive counseling, she chose an engaging family and stated that despite her pain, she had no doubt about the wisdom of her decision to place. Shortly after giving birth, the client contacted her family, whose connections she had all but severed several years prior. She became distressed when her mother—who was residing in a psychiatric ward in another city—accused her of making a foolish and selfish decision. Within a couple of days, the woman changed her mind and the infant was returned to her. Ironically, she then received no support whatsoever from her family.

If a counselor can draw a family into the adoption process, the birth mother, her child, and her loved ones will reap the benefits. When a woman's parents and siblings learn that adoption grief is real and significant, they will be less apt to minimize her pain. Furthermore, they can learn to identify their own reactions to the loss. A family can be so conscious of the birth mother's pain that it neglects its own needs, failing to understand the unique grief process of each member. Ironically, when a birth mother longs for others to enter her grief, her loved ones may try to protect her by concealing their emotions.

One birth mother came into the Centre shortly after Christmas and declared, with a bright smile, that her father had broken down and wept on Christmas day. Her family tradition, she explained, was to have a photo taken of all the daughters and granddaughters with Santa Claus. As a gift to her father, she had arranged to have her birth daughter included. When her dad opened his present on Christmas morning, he went from being stern and composed to openly revealing his love for his grandchild. The incident marked one of the most significant moments of the birth mother's grief process.

Recognizing both the impact that family members can have on the adoption decision, and the emotional benefits reaped by an informed family, a counselor should address issues that surface at the following stages of the adoption process:

The Decision-Making Stage

If a client is even remotely interested in the adoption option, her counselor should encourage her to consider the significant members of her family. How would they react to the possibility of placing? In what ways might they try to influence her decision?

If the client has already approached her family, her counselor can help interpret their responses. A woman may not understand why a family member has reacted in a particular way. She may also be unable to distinguish between a verbal affirmation of her decision and the 'real' message, a negative response conveyed through body language or subtle verbal cues.

If a woman is seriously contemplating adoption, she should consider inviting her family members to attend a counseling session. Participants, whether parents or siblings, can be educated around the adoption process and assured that procedures are in place to ensure that the infant is put in a safe, nurturing home. They can also be prepared for the birth mother's reactions to the adoption.

More importantly, a counselor can emphasize the importance of taking a hands-off approach. Parents must allow their daughter to make the adoption plan. If a woman is pressured during her family's attempts to be supportive, she may regret the placement and blame her loved ones in her grief.

One seventeen-year-old who wanted to place, but who also longed to please her family, brought her parents to the Pregnancy Care Centre for several counseling sessions. Her counselor quickly discovered that although the client's mother was somewhat receptive to the idea of adoption, her father was adamantly opposed. How much better, he openly argued, to raise the child himself. A contentious situation was avoided when the father was warned that he might have to choose between his daughter and his grandchild: in depriving his daughter of her choice, he was taking the risk of alienating her. He decided that the potential cost was too dear.

Even if parents are pro-adoption, they should be encouraged to allow their daughter to reach her own conclusion. By maintaining some distance, and allowing the counselor to be the one to discuss some of the harsh realities of parenting, a woman's parents will stand a better chance of maintaining a solid relationship with their child under the pressure of adoption grief.

The parents of younger clients in particular will benefit from counseling sessions. If a woman is financially dependent, she may carry unspoken assumptions about how much support she will receive should she parent. It is not unusual for a fourteen or fifteen-year-old client to assume that her mother will quit work to become the child's full-time nanny. She may anticipate leaving her baby at home on weekends while she dates and socializes. In discussions mediated by the counselor, parents can clarify, in concrete terms, how they envision their supportive role.

Although parents are often reluctant to set boundaries, doing so is advantageous. If a woman is given specific guidelines, she can plan her future accordingly. One set of parents may define 'support' as a promise to allow the birth mother to live in their home, using one bedroom for herself and another for her child, and to baby-sit one night a week and three weekends a year. Their daughter, in turn, may be expected to buy the baby's essentials, including diapers, formula, and clothing. Another set of parents may agree to offer only what they would have had the child been born under more favorable circumstances. The child, in other words, would be treated no differently from the other grandchildren.

If parents intend to raise the child as their own, they should be warned of the risks involved. If they assume too much responsibility, they risk setting themselves up for substantial pain when their daughter becomes independent. She may return for the child or move to a place of her own, 'robbing' her family of a person with whom they had bonded. The woman, in turn, may resent their input and over-involvement.

Before becoming engaged in peer counseling a family, it is absolutely imperative that a peer counselor clarify, to the client, that she is her counselor. The counselor is seeing her family for her benefit, and will not betray her confidentiality, especially when she is not present. To maintain trust, a counselor can discuss, with the client, what issues will be addressed in a counseling session. And in complicated or volatile situations, a separate counselor should be assigned to the family. Extreme care must be taken to protect the birth mother's interests and confidentiality.

One Month Prior to the Delivery Date

Shortly before the baby's arrival, a woman's family should meet for another counseling session to prepare for the hospital experience. Various issues should be addressed, including the birth mother's need for time alone with her child, the importance of taking photographs of the infant with its birth family, and the question of which family members will be personally involved in the entrustment service.

The family can also be reminded of how the birth mother's grief will manifest itself in the weeks and months to follow. They should expect that on special dates, such as the finalization of the adoption—ten days, three months, six months or even two years after delivery, depending on the location—the birth mother might exhibit behavior typical of a person under immense stress. She may, for example, become extremely irritable or reckless. Families should be encouraged to be sensitive to the birth mother's needs, reaching out through a phone call or an invitation to supper, or through the simple remark that she is a wonderful mother. Family members should also be taught how to recognize the symptoms of postpartum depression and be encouraged to seek medical intervention if necessary.

Several weeks after delivery

A meeting held after the baby is placed can be useful. From anywhere between several weeks to several months, family life will have resumed its former pace. Members may be lulled into believing that everything has returned to normal—that everyone, including the birth mother, has overcome the emotional ordeal of placing. A reminder of the value of grieving, and of the ways in which grief is expressed, may prevent the family from repressing healthy emotions.

One counselor received a frantic call late at night from a client who had placed her baby four months earlier and then moved to a different city. Her family, the woman sobbed, had told her that since she was in a new situation and had enrolled in a new school, there was no point in mentioning the adoption to anyone. Although she had done a great thing by placing her child, her parents reasoned, she was young and needed to move on with her life. Over the next hour, the counselor assured the agitated birth mother that her parents' advice was wrong: moving on could only be accomplished by sharing her adoption story and taking time to grieve. Had this otherwise supportive family been counseled previously, they may have avoided inadvertently wounding the young woman.

In an effort to be sensitive, some families may remove all reminders of the child from their home. Their attempts to protect, however, will only shame the birth mother. Her desire to talk about her child should not be discouraged. Photos should be plastered on the refrigerator for all to see. The embarrassment of an unplanned pregnancy should not hinder a family from discussing the child with guests if questions arise. Indeed, the fewer secrets a family has, the healthier it will be.

In many cases, birth mothers have families that are too disconnected or dysfunctional to be supportive. Although not necessarily opposed to her decision, a woman's family may be incapable of entering the emotional journey of adoption. Some parents have never been emotionally supportive, and respond to the adoption as familial practices would dictate. In such cases, counseling, if it takes place at all, may have little or no effect. The peer counselor's only response in these circumstances can be to commiserate with the client and to discuss alternate means of finding emotional support. A client may actually benefit from recognizing a parent's inability to be present and from examining the ways in which the parent is offering support, however insufficient.

In some cases, adoption grief will serve as a catalyst for family growth. One client had lost her father to cancer four years prior to her unplanned pregnancy. When she placed her daughter—the first grandchild in the family—the resulting grief triggered emotions long submerged. In the process of resolving adoption grief, each family member was also able to address unresolved feelings associated with the father's tragic death.

Unfortunately, grief from other losses can occasionally subvert the adoption process. After deciding to place, one client backed out, unable to deal with the emotional repercussions. When her counselor gently probed, the sixteen-year-old revealed that her sister had been killed in a car accident two years earlier. Although adoption was clearly the best alternative for her, the woman explained, another loss would be unbearable.

COPING AT SCHOOL AND AT WORK

The Perils of the Classroom

A client who has yet to finish junior high or high school should be strongly encouraged to complete her education. A variety of options may await her. In some school divisions, a pregnant teen can study on-line or through private home tutoring. These alternatives can be attractive to a client in a hostile school environment.

However, the isolation of independent study may leave a birth mother disheartened. She must have enough discipline to succeed: if a woman had difficulty focusing on her studies before the pregnancy, independent learning during this stressful period might prove daunting. A woman's success may hinge on whether the program includes regular visits with an in-school mentor, or whether she has an outside source of encouragement and accountability.

Some jurisdictions offer educational programs for pregnant and parenting teenagers. The quality of these programs differs in each community. Unfortunately, these programs frequently hold a bias against teens choosing to place: because they are geared towards keeping adolescent parents in school, the peer pressure to parent may be overwhelming.

Another option is for the client to continue attending her current school. Her counselor should warn her of the difficulties that may arise. The school, she must understand, has a responsibility to meet the needs of two constituencies: the individual student and the larger school body. Some school administrators believe that the removal of a pregnant teenager will serve in the best interests of the majority. Pregnancy is sometimes viewed as contagious: if a pregnant student wanders the halls, according to this perception, her peers will assume that her condition is acceptable. Rather than assuming this risk, schools may choose to send the woman to another educational institution.

If a client expresses interest in remaining in her current school, the counselor should first help her determine whether she has the physical and emotional stamina needed to succeed academically while facing the possibility of being socially ostracized. Gossip is inevitable: although no one escapes life without being the target of a malicious discussion, a pregnant teenager will receive more than her fair share of spite. Speculation may arise about her sexual history. She may also receive negative feedback about her adoption decision from her peers and teachers, being viewed as irresponsible or heartless by those with no conception of her reality.

A peer counselor can be instrumental in preparing the client for the challenges that await. She can help the young woman develop answers to use in potential confrontations, responses that will not only give her dignity, but will put others in their place. Should a fellow student accuse her of 'giving her baby away,' for example, the client could respond: "It's obvious that you have limited information about the subject. From the extensive research I've done, I've learned that adoption is a loving and responsible choice. Maybe you should get more informed before you share your opinion."

If a young woman can learn to create clearly stated boundaries, speaking to an issue in a powerful way without being derogatory, she will attain a valuable life skill. The ability to be positive and pro-active will also continue to serve her well. For example, a client may consider approaching her individual teachers. The student can explain that she is pregnant (before the information is spread through gossip), and that she is receiving counseling (which will reassure a teacher who might otherwise feel responsible for her wellbeing). Then, after clarifying that she is not seeking preferential treatment, the client should ask the teacher to support her attempts to remain in school. It is unlikely that teachers will reject a student who approaches them in this way.

In some cases, a teacher will criticize a pregnant student by using her as an example in class, or by making disparaging comments directly. The client should be encouraged to respond in a respectful, but assertive manner. 'I feel' statements can be effective. For example, the student might state, "I feel hurt and disrespected when you make comments about me in class. Many of my peers are sexually active, so why should I be singled out?" Few teachers can argue with this type of statement.

One unusually outspoken sixteen-year-old was insulted when she heard that her life skills and human sexuality teacher had used her as an example in another class. After discussing the situation with her peer counselor, she approached the teacher and said, "I heard that you've been using me as a teaching opportunity. Wouldn't it be better if you actually invited me into your class and let me speak for myself?" Taken aback, the teacher agreed, and the fiery student was given the opportunity to publicly defend herself and to teach her peers about adoption.

Humor is another method clients can use to deflect criticism or diffuse an awkward situation. The client should be aware that even her well-intentioned peers could be awkward, thoughtless, or unaware that she is even pregnant. Even experts have been known to miss the obvious: one pregnancy counselor who visited a high school to give an abstinence presentation inadvertently selected a pregnant student during a role-playing illustration about pregnancy. Ironically, of the four students selected, this pregnant teen was the one to escape pregnancy in the illustration! Fortunately, the entire classroom—the pregnant teen included—had a good laugh at the sheepish counselor's expense.

If a client is prepared for the challenges that await her, she can successfully continue with her studies despite her unplanned pregnancy. She will undoubtedly develop many new skills as she maneuvers around obstacles, including teachers, classmates, and administrators who will question her integrity and her decision to place. The client may even change the hearts and minds of others as she advocates for adoption and educates those around her—people who might otherwise have little exposure to the issue.

Allie's Story

Allie was fifteen when she became pregnant. Unable to stomach the thought of an abortion, she decided to place instead. Hoping to complete the tenth grade despite her pregnancy, Allie and her mother made an appointment with the school principal. The principal, although compassionate, could make no promises: this was a Christian school, where premarital sex was considered a serious offense. An emergency meeting was held to discuss the matter.

The school administration was left in a difficult position. If Allie was allowed to continue to attend class, several board members argued, pregnancy might be viewed by other students as glamorous, or as a means of securing special attention. To send her away, however, would not only show a lack of forgiveness, but would prevent Allie's peers from seeing the consequences of sexual activity outside of marriage. The administration chose a compromise: Allie could attend the school, but could not talk about the pregnancy.

Three years later, Allie came to the Pregnancy Care Center for the first time with a friend who was four months pregnant. The meeting reopened old wounds, and Allie soon returned for her own counseling session. She spoke of what it felt like to be fifteen and unable to defend herself: when other students noticed the obvious, they questioned her decision to place. The reality that many of her peers had also been sexually active made Allie's mandatory silence even more difficult to bear.

"I was fifteen years old and as big as a house!" she told her peer counselor. "Why they would think that other kids would want to be pregnant and look like that is beyond me."

Had Allie received peer counseling at the time of her pregnancy, her experience could have been different—or, at the very least, she may have found it easier to cope. It is unlikely that a single, pregnant teenager will change an administrative bureaucracy. Even a particularly strong woman may only see small changes in the system during her pregnancy. However, some clients will return several years after their pregnancy and, by speaking from a place of maturity and wholeness, give significant feedback about their experience.

With the permission of the student, Pregnancy Centers can offer to educate the administration about teen pregnancy and adoption. Christian administrations need to be challenged on the impact their decisions can have. In the recent past, for example, bible colleges and other post-secondary Christian institutions inadvertently contributed to an increase in abortion rates among their students, simply by expelling unmarried women who became pregnant.

When helping a student in Allie's position, it is essential that Pregnancy Centers give advice only where it is welcome. The Center can offer to educate school staff, but must never force this information upon unwilling recipients.

Coping in a work environment

One of a client's greatest challenges in the workplace is to discuss her pregnancy at the right time. When she divulges the information to her employer, she risks having her hours cut back or being indirectly terminated. Conversely, if she fails to discuss the issue until the end of the pregnancy, she may jeopardize her future with the company over the long term.

Once a client has made a solid adoption plan, she should decide how to approach her boss. Prior research is essential. If she has been employed for a reasonable amount of time, what maternity benefits are available? Are these benefits different for a person who is placing? What national policies will affect her employment situation? Are there nationally funded leave programs, such as the employment insurance leave program that is available to Canadian women? What are the state or provincial policies? A Pregnancy Center counselor can help the client sort through the information and identify the resources available in her community and situation.

The client should also evaluate her current work environment. Are there environmental hazards that could affect the pregnancy? Will she be required to do physical labor? Is the workplace safe, or should she seek a leave of absence? What policies does her company have in terms of pregnancy? What sort of relationship does she have with her immediate supervisor?

Although a woman is under no legal obligation to inform her boss of the pregnancy, she should do so in order to procure whatever assistance and support may be offered. A boss will be understandably perturbed by an employee who gives insufficient notice. The same employer may be quite accommodating if told, in advance, of the situation, and the fact that the client's absence from work will be limited. Although the woman will require some additional kindness when she returns, there is almost no chance that she will take leave and then resign—a risk associated with women who are parenting.

Employment standards vary across North America, but in the majority of cases, it is illegal to terminate a job due to pregnancy. Some companies will end a job by finding an excuse, claiming, for example, that a worker has requested too much time off for doctor's appointments. Other companies may reduce the client's hours until she can no longer afford to work there. In other cases, however, the woman's decision to place may be met with respect from her employer and colleagues, mature adults who have a concept of the sacrifice she is making.

Clients can be certain of one thing: any information disclosed to one colleague may soon be known by all. Offices are often hotbeds for gossip, and an unplanned pregnancy can spark many a lively discussion around the water cooler. A client should decide in advance how much information she wishes to disclose, knowing that these facts will be known by all. If a client is dreading the prospect of informing her co-workers of her situation, she might consider identifying the most outspoken gossip in the group, and allowing this person to speak for her. Having been chosen as a confidant, this individual will likely be more protective of the woman and less malicious.

Although the client's decision to be place will be supported by many of her co-workers, she may encounter some opposition. In one case, a co-worker actually tried to help the client keep the baby, locating a free crib, baby furniture, diapers, and clothing. In this sort of scenario, a client should express appreciation for the help that is being offered, but emphasize that the issue is not whether she can or cannot parent, but whether this choice would be in the best interests of herself and her child. She can tell any overly 'helpful' colleagues that should she change her mind about placing, they would be the first to know. She should also clarify that she is receiving counseling, so that colleagues will not feel obligated to question whether she has thought through her decision.

A peer counselor should warn the client to resist the temptation to place her baby with a co-worker, or a colleague's relative or friend. One client placed her baby with a co-worker's infertile brother and sister-in-law. It was only when the birth mother decided to parent at the last minute that she recognized her predicament: she would have to deal, on a daily basis, with a co-worker whose family had been devastated by her decision. Another birth mother placed her daughter with a favorite colleague who promised that the adoption would only improve their friendship. When the adoptive mother could not deal with the birth mother's close involvement, however, the birth mother lost both her friend and contact with her child.

Returning to school or work

A client who returns to school or work after placing her child should prepare a standard speech for her peers and co-workers. Her explanation can be simple: "I had a healthy baby boy, and I placed him with a wonderful couple. My child has a great home, and although I miss him, I will be okay."

The majority of the people the birth mother encounters will be genuinely curious about open adoption. If she feels empowered by the process of educating others, the birth mother should answer the assortment of questions that will come her way. Knowing more about a subject than the general public can build a woman's confidence. However, if she feels overwhelmed or awkward, she can simply say, "There's more information on the Internet than I could ever give you," and suggest a website. She can always share her experience at a later date.

Through role-playing exercises, a peer counselor can model responses to inappropriate questions. Responses can be bold. When asked an invasive question, for example, the birth mother might retort, "Now why would you ask that question?" When a question is rude, she can respond, "I'm not comfortable answering that question," leaving the other person to apologize or walk away. Or she can allow the other person to save face by simply ignoring the question and asking another unrelated question back.

IN THEIR OWN WORDS

"My mother was very adoption-oriented. She hates children! My father wanted me to give the child up—to him. I wouldn't do that. I didn't enjoy my childhood, so why force that upon someone else?"

—*Aurora, birth mother, age 16*

"It seemed more about them than it was about me. It was about how they were going to feel—the fact that I was placing their grandson for adoption. It wasn't just my son: they thought I should have realized the pain this was going to cause my entire family. It still makes me cry now. I hurt every day after I placed my son for adoption. I didn't need the fact that I had placed their grandson thrown in my face."

—*Kendra, birth mother, age 25*

"I was treated like an AIDS victim. My mom was a big member of the church and everyone thought, 'Oh, poor Sherri!' I can remember my mom saying those exact words when another girl in the church got pregnant several years ago. My mom actually told me one day that I had completely humiliated her.

—*Julie, birth mother, age 21*

"I didn't really have any family support. I have three older brothers and they don't talk about it. They don't ask; they don't care. I try to talk to my youngest brother once in a while, but he just shoves it off. He couldn't be bothered."

—*Jamie, birth mother, age 19*

"My dad went to the adoption agency with me. We never talked about 'it'—the pregnancy. (He's the strong, silent type.) He came, though, which was so important to me."

—*Nicki, birth mother, age 17*

"My family was one hundred percent supportive—all of them. I was petrified about telling my dad, because losing my relationship with him would have killed me. Knowing that he was still proud of me made all the difference."

—*Chantal, birth mother, age 30*

Aurora's Story

"I was in a top A school—one of the best schools in the city—when I found out I was pregnant. They had an image to maintain, so they tried to kick me out. They said (in their words), 'There are other places that have more resources than we do.' I went to the school that they recommended, and they didn't have any education programs that I could take. They had knitting! How does knitting help me? So I stayed right where I was.

"I was harassed a lot. I was called names and pushed around. I was the first pregnant girl in years. There were whispers all around the school and I was used as an example in classes. My sister was in a CALM [Career and Life Management] class and the teacher said, 'Have you seen that pregnant girl walking around the school? That's what happens when you don't use birth control.' My psychology teacher said that adoption screws up everyone and that pregnancies ruins teenagers' lives. I just sat there in class feeling devastated. I even had teachers yell at me.

"I had a couple of good friends. One was seen with me, I think, because he thought it was cool. My other friends didn't know how to handle all of the criticism. They really backed off and we ate lunch in the band room so that no one would see us together.

"I put up a big wall: I was nasty. If anybody said anything to me I would snap back. If somebody bumped into me, I would blow off the handle. I had to put up that wall of anger and become a bully just so I could protect myself and my child. When you're upset and there's nobody there to hold your hair back when you're in the student washroom throwing up, you don't have much choice but to lash out.

"Yes, I got pregnant, but that doesn't mean that I'm a slut. Just because I made one mistake doesn't mean that I was sleeping around with everyone in the entire school and that I don't know who my child's father is!

"After I had my son, coming back to school was hard. I was still known as 'the pregnant girl.' All of my friends were really happy to see me, but other people didn't talk to me anymore. Even some of the teachers that didn't know that I was the one who had had the baby still talked about me in their classes. There I was, basically being insulted to my face without them knowing it.

"Many of the students didn't know it was me either because the school was so big. I walked into my Social class after I had just come back. One girl said, 'Have you seen that girl that was walking around pregnant? What an idiot!'

"I said, 'Excuse me, you think I'm an idiot?' You should have seen the look on her face!

"It was hard being different from the way everybody remembered me. I was bigger and graduation was coming up. All of my friends were getting ready to go to grad, and there I was trying to fit into a grad dress. Getting back into study mode was also difficult. I was trying to grieve giving up my child for adoption, while worrying about the fact that I only had two months before my final exams.

"I'm stronger because of my experience. I can handle anything that gets thrown at me. I go after what I want; I don't shy away from things anymore. I'm more open to people, and friendlier. And if I see somebody who is pregnant on the bus, I will give her my seat, no matter how young she is!"

CHAPTER THIRTEEN

Dealing with the Birth Father

"He's so not who I thought he was!"

—Chantal, birth mother, age 30

Women will often dismiss the idea of adoption for fear that the birth father will interfere in the process, preventing the adoption from taking place. A birth father may, in fact, use the adoption issue to manipulate his partner, maintaining contact and influence even when the relationship has spiraled out of control. In the majority of cases, however, he will not stop the adoption from taking place.

In some cases, birth fathers will actually initiate a discussion about adoption, encouraging the birth mother to place and then supporting her through the process. Rather than being seen as evading a long-term responsibility, these men should be recognized for their desire to act in the best interests of the child.

Even when a birth father is uninvolved, unaware, or disinterested in what happens to his child, he should never be taken lightly. A birth mother who discounts her partner's rights or denies his input can imperil the adoption process. Today, many provincial and state courts are giving more credence to the man's rights. In some states, a birth father must be notified about the placement; in other states, his signature is required before the adoption can proceed. Most jurisdictions extend rights to men who have played no part in the child's conception: a man who is legally married is considered the father of his wife's child, even if the infant is not biologically his. A woman who has been estranged from her husband for five years and becomes pregnant by another man, in other words, may actually be giving birth to her husband's child in the eyes of the law. It is therefore imperative that both client and counselor understand the laws of their individual state or province.

There are, of course, other reasons for not dismissing the birth father. However angry the birth mother, the man with whom she has conceived is her baby's father. His active involvement can be extremely meaningful, giving the child a sense of its full heritage. If the father supports the adoption, or is at least willing to give a medical history, the child will benefit.

Fathers—birth fathers included—are important and their role must be recognized. Although they express grief and exhibit love differently than women, their needs and contributions should be acknowledged. If a birth father can be brought on side, even through a third party like a Pregnancy Center worker, the birth mother will seldom resent his support throughout the adoption process. If his individual role is affirmed, he has the potential to become a consistent, loving figure in his child's life.

OPENING THE DOOR TO MEN

Part of a birth father's reluctance to become involved in the pregnancy and placement can stem from the stigma attached to his position. Although birth mothers bear the brunt of society's judgment, birth fathers are often perceived as culprits who are not 'man' enough to provide the basic necessities for their offspring. They may be ashamed that adoption is even being considered, believing that it highlights their failure to provide and protect. Fearing that he will be deemed irresponsible or inadequate, a birth father may think twice before entering a Center or an adoption agency—places staffed primarily with females.

Considering the psychological obstacles facing men, a Pregnancy Center that focuses solely on the rights and needs of women will do a great disservice to both sexes. Something as seemingly innocuous as decorating a Center with bows and fluffy feminine fixtures, or providing magazines geared only to women in the waiting room, can make a man feel alienated and ill at ease. Centers must recognize that every man that walks through the door has the potential to be receptive to counseling and to assist his partner in the adoption process. His very presence is a sign of character and he should be warmly acknowledged.

At the same time, the peer counselor must clarify that the Center's mandate is, first and foremost, to care for birth mothers. The Center can work with a man only to the extent that his partner is willing.

As part of a ministry to men, larger Centers should consider starting a birth fathers' group. Although attendance may be sparse, the men who participate can learn how to deal with their conflicted feelings. They will also appreciate having their partners' emotions explained: most birth fathers will attest to the difficulty of understanding the elusive, complex, and ever-changing emotions of the female.

A birth father's group may also attract men who have become involved with a birth mother. Since the child placed was not his own, a boyfriend, fiancé, or husband may struggle to understand his partner's experience. Hearing an explanation of her grief through a counselor or a group of men can be enlightening. Furthermore, the man will be more likely to support her in her grief than to demand that she move on before she is ready.

HELPING BIRTH FATHERS COPE WITH ADOPTION

When a male agrees to have his child placed for adoption, his decision will be typically based on a logical assessment of the situation. Whereas the birth mother bonds with the child while it is still in her womb, the birth father will usually view his baby as an abstract entity throughout the pregnancy. It is typically when a man physically encounters his newborn for the first time that the baby will move from being a concept to a person. At this point, the birth father will have his first glimpse of the grief that awaits him.

Not surprisingly, many birth fathers begin to seriously question the decision to place shortly after the baby is born. If the birth mother does not understand the dynamic behind his doubt and indecision, she may find her partner's intense reaction perplexing. She should be warned that he was an awkward bystander during the pregnancy. Now, as he holds his child and recognizes his own traits reflected in the infant, he too may become emotionally involved and fiercely protective.

Because of his tendency to view the unborn child as an abstract concept, a man may initially try to coerce the birth mother into placing. His reasoning will be logically sound: if there is no way to parent and the woman is opposed to abortion, the third option is the rationale one. In some cases, the birth father may perceive the baby as a financial liability, one for which he is unprepared. He may be receptive to the idea of being a father, but only after he has completed his education and found the 'right' woman. Other men may be genuinely concerned that the woman carrying the child will make an unfit parent. Whatever his reasons, the man's right-brained thinking may appear heartless to his partner, who will likely feel a stronger bond to the child during the pregnancy.

Some birth mothers will lament their partners' apparent indifference to the situation at hand. Rather than writing a man off, however, both the birth mother and the counselor should recognize denial's role in his grief process. One of his strongest protective mechanisms, denial is most evident when a birth father involved in a long-term, monogamous relationship questions paternity. It is also evident when a man divides his life into tidy compartments, keeping his relationship separate from his career, hobbies, and social activities. Or, if a man is estranged from the birth mother, he may fail to inform his colleagues, friends, and family members of the pregnancy and birth.

In some cases, a birth father will avoid discussing the pregnancy at all costs, even with his partner. One exasperated client lamented that her common-law husband had acquired a sudden obsession with computer games. When she confronted him, he indignantly denied trying to evade the issue at hand. Nevertheless, he still refused to discuss the adoption, claiming that it was all that his partner ever thought about.

If a birth father is to be drawn further into the adoptive process, his unique abilities must be affirmed. Men respond to the role of protector and provider. If a birth father recognizes that he can fulfill his role as protector by helping his partner choose adoptive parents and screen out poor prospects, he will be more apt to be present. In fact, his right-brain orientation and ability to distance himself emotionally may prove highly useful in selecting an adoptive couple.

A man's natural inclination to provide can also be nurtured. He can meet his child's needs during the pregnancy by caring for the birth mother in practical ways such as buying maternity clothes, attending prenatal classes, or helping to cover her expenses. Remind him that however difficult dealing the birth mother may be, he will look back at his actions in ten years' time and feel no shame.

It is essential that the counselor affirm the birth father's courage to stay with his partner throughout the adoption process and offer his wisdom, insight, and discernment. He must also be called to consistency and given concrete ways to support both mother and child. For example, he should be challenged to seriously consider what role he will play once the baby is born. During the decision-making process, a man may generously state that he will support his partner in whatever choice she makes. In reality, he is evading responsibility, leaving the woman with both the decision and the blame, should her choice prove faulty. Similarly, a birth father who states that he will be as involved in his child's life as the birth mother wants him to be is really avoiding commitment.

Above all, the birth mother needs to know the level of support that she can realistically expect from him. A counselor should encourage the birth father to consider how he would respond if the woman reneged on her decision to place. Would he pay child support, and how much could he contribute? How often would he see his child? Would he be willing to baby-sit on a regular basis? These questions require much thought, and promises will be difficult to fulfill. However, if he is a man of his word, and can envision his degree of involvement, his partner will be able to prepare accordingly.

Since he will likely be a target for the birth mother's anger, the birth father should be prepared for the intense emotional reactions of his partner. If he can understand the birth mother's grief, and the fact that her hormones have gone awry, a man will be less likely to take her rage personally. Even if he is being accused of wrongs both real and imagined, a counselor should assure the birth father that his partner really longs for his support. Even if unacknowledged, his honesty and presence will be appreciated. Furthermore, the birth father should be informed of his right to express his feelings, even in difficult situations.

If a birth mother's anger is so scathing that the birth father feels that his presence will serve no purpose, assure him that some adoptive couples are willing to grant separate visitation to each of the child's biological parents. As in a divorce situation, the child will benefit more from his involvement than from his absence. Both he and the birth mother should be warned, however, that to openly attack or belittle the other birth parent will damage the child's self-esteem. The birth father can be challenged to recall what attracted him to the birth mother in the first place, for no human is devoid of virtue, and to speak graciously of her in the child's presence.

Despite the apparent odds against a workable relationship, disputes can be resolved and ill feelings dealt with. One former client, who had placed her daughter six years earlier, invited her counselor to a picnic. When she arrived at the park, the counselor was amazed to see not only the child, the birth mother, and the birth father, but the birth mother's fiancé as well. The little girl was in her glory, proudly declaring that in addition to having two adoptive parents, she had a birth mother, a birth father, and "a fiancé."

Birth fathers frequently struggle with the belief that they might become too involved in the adoption process, a fear is augmented by the fact that they seldom exercise any control over the situation. Emotionally involved, and yet powerless, men may choose to leave rather than to become vulnerable. In this sense, the adoption process is more difficult for the birth father than it is for the birth mother. During counseling, the birth father should be encouraged to vent his feelings of frustration and be reminded that he will never regret any time that he invests in his child.

If a couple is estranged and at odds, both parties can still remain involved in planning the child's future. In such cases, a two-counselor model is imperative. The birth father should have his own counselor—preferably male—and have at least a few individual sessions. Both parties, and their respective counselors, can occasionally meet, if desired. The confidentiality of both parties must always be respected. Counselors should seek to facilitate dialogue during these meetings instead of divulging information disclosed in private sessions. Counselors should also exercise great care when case conferencing. When discussing the situation, neither the man's counselor nor the woman's should address information that was not discussed in the presence of both birth parents.

Counselors should be cautious in how they affirm and support their clients. In a private, heated discussion with the birth father, a client may weave her counselor's words into her invectives, using the personal affirmation she received to strengthen her verbal attacks. The wounded recipient may then feel personally affronted by the Center, believing that his partners' counselor has been unjustly critical. Both parties should be warned, in advance, that like a lawyer, a counselor is expected to take her client's side. Given a one-sided account, a counselor will have limited information about the situation, and may have an impression that is not really reflective of her client's partner.

Above all, a birth father should be encouraged to participate in long-term counseling. Although men process grief differently than women, the process of dealing with an adoption is one that no person, male or female, should have to face alone.

THE ABUSIVE BIRTH FATHER

A counselor is typically first introduced to a birth father through an embittered birth mom who has lost a child, a relationship, and the dream of beginning a family. Obviously, the client's ability to be objective in the face of such losses will be undermined. In some cases, however, her complaints about the birth father may go beyond his betrayal and irresponsible behavior: he may be an actual threat to her safety.

When suspicions are raised, a counselor must first determine whether the birth mother is involved in a conflicted relationship—one in which the couple is in constant strife over seemingly irresolvable issues—or in an abusive relationship. This process can be difficult: a birth mother may have become so accustomed to abuse that she may not identify it as such; likewise, a woman who is in a rocky relationship may be open to the suggestion that she is being abused. [For more information on abuse, please consult the appendix.]

If the birth father is identified as an abuser, the peer counselor must acknowledge that the situation is beyond her skill level. In other words, she must not facilitate joint sessions or attempt to counsel the birth father. The Center must have no ongoing contact whatsoever with the birth father.

The Center should direct the woman to outside help if she needs to obtain a restraining order or to seek temporary refuge in a shelter. The Center must also immediately notify the adoption agency, which should, in turn, apprise the adoptive couple of the situation. Any contact made with the birth father must be arranged through the adoption agency only.

If a woman who has left an abusive relationship seeks counseling, her counselor should be aware of how complex her decision to place will be. Overwhelmed by the trauma of the abuse, fear of the birth father, and feelings of hopelessness and inadequacy, a birth mother may have difficulty assessing her real feeling about adoption.

Her fear of the birth father should not be the primary reason she places. Although her desire to sever all ties with the child's father and to protect her baby from abuse is legitimate, she must ask herself if there are other reasons she wishes to place. If not, she may regret her decision once she manages to fully extricate herself from a relationship with the abuser.

IN THEIR OWN WORDS

On Birth Fathers...

"We talked about marriage and raising a child together, but he just wasn't the guy I wanted to marry. I decided that adoption was the better choice, but he was really against it. He was very bad for my thought process—he would drink a lot and call in the middle of the night. He was not a bad person, or evil in any way. He was just irresponsible.

"We decided to go our separate ways. Later on, he took the easy way out by trying to deny paternity. Now he's out of the picture and he hasn't contacted me since."

—*Emily, birth mother, age 25*

"He was the man! He was the man! Getting a girl pregnant was proof that he got 'laid,' as they call it. His friends were like, 'Oh yeah, man, you're lucky! We're sorry you're having a baby, but she's giving it up for adoption—so you're the man! He was never criticized the way I was."

—*Aurora, birth mother, age 16*

"I was seeing a man that was twice my age. I was with him for about a year and a half when we got pregnant. He was pretty much going to force me to have an abortion. He was literally at my house ready to drag me out—he actually had me by the arm. We argued and fought, and he left. And that was that."

—*Julie, birth mother, age 21*

"My boyfriend was scared when we found out I was pregnant. He said, 'Whatever's easiest, do it.'"

—*Jacqueline, birth mother, age 23*

"The father of one of our adopted daughters is apparently a cocaine dealer with two other children. We offered to meet him in a neutral place to get a medical history and to ask him to write a letter to his child. That's never happened and he's never shown any interest.

"The birth father of our second daughter tried to sue us for custody. We met him at the hospital and he was rude and arrogant. He's known to be abusive and violent, and to abuse alcohol—certainly not qualities that we want our kids exposed to. But if he were to prove himself to be a decent person, we would allow some contact, though under very controlled circumstances.

"We're not at all closed to a relationship with either man, but neither has demonstrated the kind of character that would make us want to pursue a lot. I'm not sure either one is functional enough to even have a clue of what it means to build a relationship."

—*John, adoptive father*

Erin's Story

"Our situation was a bit weird because the birth father and I had broken up, and he had a new girlfriend at the time we conceived. When I found out I was pregnant, I called Michael up. He accused me of lying—of being desperate to break up his new relationship. I suggested he come to the ultrasound appointment to see that this was no hoax.

"After seeing the baby on screen, he seemed to smile at me and I thought things would be okay. Once we got into the car, though, things were the opposite. He told me he wanted nothing to do with me or the baby. The only time I would hear from him, or his lawyers, would be when the paternity test was done, or if he was forced to pay child support.

"I think we were both blown away by the pregnancy. However, at the beginning, Michael could walk away from things, whereas I couldn't. I'll admit there was a lot of pressure on him. He came from a very 'high-society' type of family, and his parents forbade him to ever see me again.

"My own mom booted me out of the house. I ended up living in a maternity home and the two girls there before me had placed their babies for adoption. Everyone was so proud of them. Michael knew that he was not ready to parent and was one hundred percent for adoption. My dad also thought it was a good idea, as he still wanted me to have the opportunity to go to school and do other things that 16-year-olds do, without having the stress of parenting as well. I felt like I really didn't have much choice.

"The pressure can be summed up in one feeling: if I don't give the baby up, no one will be there for me at all, no one will help me financially or give me a place to live, and no one will help me take care of the baby. I knew I couldn't do it on my own.

"I don't know what decision I would have made if there was no pressure. I know the chances are very good that I would have kept, because at sixteen, my motives would have been more selfish. I would not have wanted the pain of losing the child.

"About three months into the pregnancy, Michael came around and was completely supportive. I was grateful for his complete attitude turn-around, and for his support during the last half of the pregnancy especially. I was hospitalized several times with pre-term labor and bleeding, and he was there constantly, except to go home and sleep. He was also there during my entire labor and delivery, and was with me and the baby from early in the morning to last thing at night.

"Michael also supported me the whole way through the adoption process, from selecting and interviewing the adoptive couple to visiting the baby. Even when the baby was placed with her new family, he still stuck around to support me and to see her. He had no obligations to us anymore. He could have taken off, but he didn't. I've always appreciated that! Even today, Michael is still involved in Sarah's life through pictures and visits. He always intends to be, so long as the opportunity is there.

"Still, I've felt a lot of anger. At first I wasn't angry at anyone because I knew they were trying to do what was best and I was quite high from being the hero who helped complete a family. However, once the honeymoon phase ended and reality set in, so did a lot of anger. I blamed everyone except myself. My boyfriend, parents, counselors, the family I lived with, the girls who had placed before me, anyone who had anything, even remotely, to do with the fact I wasn't with my child.

"I think my angriest time was about seven weeks after placing Sarah up for adoption. Both Michael and my father told me they would have supported me in any decision I would have made. This really made things worse because I was devastated that they had 'lied' to me, making me feel as though I had no choice.

"Still, I don't know if there was exactly a point where I regretted my decision. I know there were several occasions where I wished she was still with me, but she was adopted into the most amazing family and I couldn't imagine any other life for her. I also think of how my life would be if I had decided to parent. I know I wouldn't be married to the wonderful husband I have now and I probably would not be going back to school.

"Don't get me wrong. I would have laid down my life for Sarah, but God had bigger plans for the two of us. After nearly eight years, we still have a very open and wonderful adoption. She is very aware of who I am and the role I play in her life, and I can't imagine our lives any other way."

Michael's Story

"I was seventeen when Erin found out that she was pregnant; she was sixteen. I just about had a heart attack! At the time, we weren't even dating anymore. We had been dating on and off for three years, and we were in the 'off' stage.

"She phoned me up and at first I didn't believe her. Part of that was not wanting it to be true. It wasn't something I wanted to do, or something I was ready for. I come from a family that has high expectations, and being a teenage father didn't fit into that at all. I had a set plan for where I was going in life—one that didn't involve flipping burgers and being a parent at seventeen.

"At the start of things, Erin was pretty intent on keeping Sarah. I wasn't. I put my energy into convincing her that adoption would be best for everyone involved. I knew that it was her decision—one hundred percent. Women give you the whole, 'I want your input; I want you to be part of this.' Yet if you want something that they don't, they'll do what they want and you get to pay for it.

"It really was up to me to persuade her and I did it the only way I could: I basically gave her an ultimatum. I said, 'If you want to do this, you're doing it alone. I'm not going to be part of it and I'm going to do everything I can to make it miserable for you.'

"It took three or four months before she was even open to the idea of adoption. Her parents were leaning that way and she knew what my desires were. I don't think that adoption was something that she really wanted to do, and I think that's why she had such a hard time after. I don't know whether she perceived how much influence I had over her decision. I did try to be relatively subtle, knowing that she's the type of person who would say the sky is green just to start an argument!

"I think the first time Erin ever really got keen on the adoption idea was when we got to see profiles of families that were looking for a little girl to make really lucky. Our worker at the adoption agency was fantastic. We gave her a list of the things that were important in parents for us.

"We looked through two dozen files and narrowed it down to three. We were going to meet with all three, but after we met with Tom and Terry, we made up our minds. They were such a warm, caring, outgoing, friendly, genuinely good people. They answered all of the questions we had for them exactly the way we wanted them answered, from religion to education. They even looked like us!

"It was very late in the pregnancy before I told my family. Not being pregnant myself, I could pretend it wasn't happening. My mom didn't speak to me for a month. My sister was delighted—a typical little 10-year-old girl reaction. My brother was pleased, I think, because I had always been 'the good child.' Finally I was the one to make a big mistake!

"I'll admit it is significantly easier for a man to detach himself from the situation. It is our child, but we didn't give birth to it. It's a foreign concept until it's born. We see these little ultrasounds and it's this black and white thing on the screen. It's not real.

"I didn't receive any counseling through the process. I'm not the counseling type. Most of my emotional support came from Erin. If she was crying, I cried with her. I sought some legal counsel, though, just to know what my options and responsibilities were. Knowing that yes, I was going to be responsible if she decided to keep the child, had a positive impact on the way I treated the situation.

"Because Sarah was early, Erin and I didn't make it to many birthing classes. We got a crash course one afternoon because Erin was having false labors. It was a quick birth. Doctors were flying in and out, the adoptive parents were there, as well as Erin's family and some of our friends: it was a three-ring circus! When Sarah came out, she looked like a little blue gremlin!

"There were two really big emotional moments for me. The first was seeing Sarah born— a life-altering experience. The second was the day we gave her up for adoption. However, I never ever considered keeping Sarah. It would have been terribly unfair to her. I think that adoption is the best thing we could have done.

"I see her three, maybe four times a year. Could I do with less? Yeah, probably. I tend not to think about her as much as I did before. During the first year, I thought about her every day. As she grows up, and I know how well she's doing, I think of her less frequently.

"Every time we see her, she grows a little bit more. I get flash frames of time. It's a bit sad that I only get to see the little bits and pieces of her life, and I don't get to be there. But all the time I balance that off knowing that she wouldn't be where she is today if we had kept her. She wouldn't be the same person.

"I don't feel like her 'dad.' I never have. It was never a role I sought or wanted. Sarah is more like a favorite little cousin who's a blast to play with.

"I think that I supported Erin because I've always loved her—she was really the first girl I ever loved. I wanted to be there for her and help her through it.

"Your first reaction is always to run: 'It's not my problem. You deal with it.' But it is your problem. Whether you like it or not, if you don't do something about it, you'll get a knock on your door nine months down the road. It will be someone serving a summons. You can't hide! And do you really want your child to grow up hating you because you're a deadbeat dad? You did this. It's not a one-person show. Buck up and take responsibility. If you do the right thing now, there's a chance that the situation will end up being positive for everybody."

CHAPTER FOURTEEN

Birth Mothers' Support Groups

"It was extremely valuable getting together with people who had made the same choices I did and seeing how much we valued our decisions. I needed that affirmation because you don't get that from the world."

—Sandra, birth mother, now age 38

The birth mothers' support group is a vital part of helping women grieve. The potential intimacy, community, and empathy a birth mother can find among her peers is unequaled. No one, including her peer counselor, will understand her pain as fully as those who have also placed a child. Ideally, a birth mother will find respite from the judgment and ignorance of the outside world, being unconditionally supported through the most difficult parts of the adoption process.

Group has the potential to create bonds between women regardless of age, cultural background, or education. Since birth mothers are familiar with feelings of ostracism and shame, they are often willing to accept differences, and to learn from others. One facilitator was concerned about a mentally challenged woman who had joined the group, but was having difficulty understanding the discussion. The leader was amazed when the woman made one of the most profound insights of the evening. "I know adoption was the right thing for my son," she told the group. "I know it in my head. But the problem is, my heart doesn't know it."

A Pregnancy Center should consider starting a group when several conditions can be met. First, the Center must have two potential facilitators—women with some training around adoption and experience in counseling birth mothers. Facilitators should be passionate, empathetic, and mature. Life experience is a necessity. More than one facilitator is crucial because the group will be ensured of some long-term consistency even if one leader moves on, and each leader will have some legal protection and a witness should an unpleasant situation occur. Furthermore, a co-facilitator can take an emotional birth mother aside, if necessary, offering her support while the larger group continues its discussion.

Secondly, a group should not begin until at least three birth mothers are willing to commit to attending the group on a regular basis. These women should be reliable and mature enough to follow through with their commitments. Finally, a consistent location and time should be established.

Before setting up a group, the facilitator should research what support services are already available in the community. Networking can prove useful: adoption agencies are often helpful, offering information and support, and even referring clients to the group. Larger events, including Birth Mother's Day celebrations, can be planned with the surrounding adoption community. By participating with local groups, Pregnancy Centers can complement the work done by other agencies.

Each birth mother who enters the group should be asked to sign a waiver form that explains the limitations of the services being offered. Women must recognize that they are participating in a peer support group, not in professional counseling. Furthermore, group members must agree that what is said during the group must remain within the group. Confidentiality is critical. If someone wishes to share information outside of the group, she should have a clear purpose for doing so and speak generally—unless she has obtained written permission from the group member involved.

Since grief does not rest during the holidays, birth mothers' support groups should meet on a regular basis, including the summer holidays. Sessions should generally last for two hours, at which point the women can share pictures of their children, socialize, or approach the facilitator with questions that were not answered during the discussion.

It is essential that each group member has the opportunity to speak. Groups should therefore contain no more than fourteen members, and preferably fewer than twelve. If a group grows too large, all of the birth mothers can meet for the introduction and icebreaker, and then split off into two smaller groups for discussion, with a facilitator leading each. By maintaining a larger group for the more sociable time of the evening, the facilitator will not completely separate birth mothers who established close connections when the group was smaller.

Participation should be mandatory; birth mothers must be committed to attending group whenever possible and to making a contribution. However, a woman who is too shy or too broken to speak should not be pressed. In one case, a birth mother came to each session and sat with her head down, refusing to make eye contact and crying throughout the entire discussion. The facilitator recognized that although this particularly fragile woman said nothing, she was able to benefit from Group by releasing emotion and hearing other women's stories. Although perplexed by the woman's emotional condition, the other group members gave her written notes of affirmation, gently drawing her into their circle.

Tears are another essential element of Group. Women should be allowed to weep, and open displays of emotion should not be checked or glossed over. A birth mother who can allow herself to be vulnerable should be commended. The facilitator can ease the situation through humor, stating that she has succeeded when women cry, and failed when a session has left the participants dry-eyed.

GROUP FORMAT

How Group is run will depend largely upon the facilitator's interests and abilities. An artistic facilitator, for example, can incorporate visual and tactile techniques, helping women to express their pain through drawing or painting. A facilitator with a dramatic flair could encourage role-playing, placing a chair in the center of the room, for instance, and asking women to pretend that the birth father is seated among them and is a captive listener to what they wish to say. If a group is receptive, the variety may help birth mothers find alternate means of expressing themselves.

The facilitator should pay careful attention to ambiance. Chairs placed in a circle can help create a sense of intimacy, as can candles and dim lighting. A vase of flowers can bring color to an otherwise stark room, while balloons can be used to create a celebratory mood for special occasions. Above all, the atmosphere should be inviting and fun, even though the discussion may be serious.

Refreshments are another important element of creating a hospitable atmosphere. For a birth mother who is feeling uncomfortable or emotional, the act of refilling a cup of coffee or taking another serving of dessert can help her survive a socially awkward moment.

Sessions should begin with an ice-breaker, one that will put new members at ease and stimulate discussion. The birth mothers can be invited to draw humorous or thought-provoking questions out of a hat, or to answer a question directed to the entire group. Women could be asked to share humorous memories, such as their most embarrassing date; fond memories, such as a favorite family vacation; or more serious things, such as the most important thing learned from a parent.

The group facilitator can then set the tone by sharing a reading that relates to the topic at hand. Topics should be planned ahead of time and introduced at the beginning of each session. Birth mothers can be given some ownership over what is discussed, as the ideas that they suggest will usually be relevant, pressing, and unique.

Themes can also correspond to the calendar. Issues pertaining to romantic relationships and birth fathers might be discussed around Valentine's Day, for example, with snacks and decorations planned accordingly. The session held closest to New Year's Day can focus on new beginnings—the hopes and dreams that women have for the upcoming year. During occasions that may prove painful, such as Mother's Day and Christmas, the facilitator should be sure to inject some positive, happy associations.

Facilitators can also plan according to significant events in the group members' lives. If a birth mother has repeatedly mentioned that her court date or her baby's first birthday is approaching, the group can discuss related issues at that time. Individual women should be given special attention during these stressful events, receiving a phone call from the facilitator or another birth mother, and being asked to share what has happened.

Once a topic has been introduced, the facilitator can begin a discussion by asking a question, and then responding herself. She might use a story about the experience of an unidentified birth mother she has worked with in the past, or, if appropriate, relate a story from her own life. For example, if the theme involves women's relationships with their mothers, the facilitator may share one of her own significant childhood memories of her mother, reflecting upon how this experience has shaped her life. Other women, particularly the more confident women in the group, will usually follow suit.

The facilitator should plan an entire line of questions and be willing to change directions should a question fall flat or evoke uninspired, one-word answers. If the conversation begins to go in an unplanned, but healthy direction, or if one question elicits a strong response, the facilitator should allow the conversation to continue uninterrupted. It is often in these unexpected moments that women share profound ideas, speaking, from experience, into the lives of other birth mothers.

A facilitator who has peer counseled or birth coached a birth mother in the group, and assumes she knows every detail about her grief, may find Group eye-opening. During a session on family relationships, for example, a normally stable woman, who had finished most of her grief work years ago, suddenly left the group, sobbing. When the concerned facilitator was finally able to reach her by phone several days later, the woman disclosed that another birth mother's comment had triggered the realization that she too still had issues with her mother. Eventually, this woman went on to confront her parent, seeking closure and repairing the broken relationship.

While being flexible, a facilitator must ensure that the discussion does not go off onto an irrelevant tangent or center primarily on one birth mother. In some cases, a needier birth mother may try to monopolize the conversation; in other cases, a woman may avoid dealing with her own issues by counseling other women or averting a painful question by leading the group on a series of rabbit trails.

If a woman is monopolizing the conversation, the facilitator should thank her for her input and direct a question to another group member. If she persists, the group leader should speak to her privately afterwards, encouraging her to come in for more one-to-one counseling sessions. In the worst case scenario, she should be gently told that Group is probably not conducive to her healing process, and be given the attention she craves in a private counseling session. If the screening process is done properly before women are invited to join a support group, however, the latter scenario will rarely occur.

Should a birth mother assume the role of a counselor, confronting another woman or routinely offering an assessment of another birth mother's problems, she should also be pulled aside. The woman should be thanked for her insight and input, but told that the other woman may not be ready to confront her issues. If she can be brought on side and subtly nudged in the direction of addressing her own problems, an overly 'helpful' birth mother will not feel that her opinions are being dismissed.

One healthy way in which women can speak into each others' lives without being intrusive is to speak from their own experience. Rather than telling another woman what she should do, a birth mother can relate a time when she was in a similar situation, describing how she handled the challenge, and what the outcome was.

At the end of each session, women should be given several minutes to write in their response journals—coil binders in which they can write questions, comments, and feelings about the session. These journals, which will be read by the facilitator, can give valuable feedback. Birth mothers may make comments that they were too shy to make in front of others, and a facilitator who believes that a session made no impact at all may be pleasantly surprised. Facilitators should respond, in a sentence or two, to each entry, encouraging each birth mother individually.

At the end of session, the birth mothers should be free to socialize. Since a typical group will only meet once a month, women can be encouraged to keep in contact with each other. Those who are open to ongoing communication can be given a list of phone numbers, and then talk to each other or meet for coffee during the weeks to come. If a birth mother is having difficulty making friends, the facilitator can approach a reliable, longer-term group member and ask her to go out of her way to make the new member more comfortable.

WELCOMING THE NEW MEMBER

Since a grieving woman's natural tendency can be to withdraw, the facilitator should make special efforts to draw her into a group of her peers. The following suggestions can be used to ease a birth mother into the group setting:

Interview a woman before inviting her to participate in Group

A group facilitator should determine whether a woman will benefit from the group experience. If a woman does not appear ready to participate, or if she is abrasive, confrontational, or uncontrollable in social situations, she should be gently told that she would probably benefit more from individual counseling at this stage in her grief process. When informed in a loving way, a woman will not feel that a door has been slammed shut, but will recognize that group participation would not benefit her at this time.

This process of carefully screening participants is crucial. Women with untreated mental health issues, personality disorders, or issues related to drug and alcohol abuse will usually benefit more from one-to-one counseling. In one situation, a woman with a bipolar disorder joined a group after recently placing her son for adoption. Because she was not medicated and was in the manic phase of her illness, the woman monopolized the group, interrupting other birth mothers when they tried to speak and sharing explicit details about her life. The facilitator's attempts to rein her in proved futile: the woman repeatedly brought the discussion back to her own situation or onto irrelevant tangents.

Encourage a client to attend at least one group

Many women are reluctant to join a group of women they have never met before, baring their souls in front of strangers. The first session is particularly awkward: even the thought of entering a room and finding a seat may intimidate a client. It is therefore essential for a facilitator to be as non-threatening as possible. When inviting a woman to attend Group, she should encourage her to listen in on one session. If the client is convinced that Group is not for her, she is under no obligation to join.

If the client has not met the group facilitator, she should be introduced in advance: it is much easier to enter a room when there is at least one familiar face waiting. A counselor can even come to the group before the session starts and introduce the new member. Although the counselor cannot stay for the session, she will have eased her client into the new setting.

Enlist the help of the co-facilitator

The co-facilitator can be a valuable asset to Group. She can sit beside the new member, ensure that she is comfortable, and speak with her in the socially awkward moments when the session is over.

If the facilitator leading the group is too focused on the material and the task at hand to observe the larger group dynamic, the co-facilitator can intervene. If a woman is agitated, fidgety, or obviously wanting to speak, the co-facilitator can ask her to give her opinion. Similarly, if a woman who attends Group regularly is avoiding eye contact during a specific discussion, a perceptive co-facilitator can gently tease her about it and ask about her thoughts regarding the topic. The co-facilitator's goal should not be to put a woman on the spot, but to encourage a more shy or pensive woman to speak.

Create a safe, predictable atmosphere

A facilitator must be protective of each group member, recognizing that a birth mother's pain must never be put on display. For this reason, no observers should be allowed: the group should be open only to birth mothers, women who are seriously considering placing, and committed facilitators.

Nothing should be done without the birth mothers' permission. A special speaker may be invited in, but only with the group's consensus. Every person in the group must be prepared, in advance, for the speaker's arrival, and informed, upon arrival, what has been planned for the session. Care must be taken to avoid any surprises. If a birth mother feels uncomfortable, she should feel no pressure to participate that day.

Respect a birth mother's boundaries

Each woman has the right to politely refuse to answer a question, or to choose to answer a question later. She has the right to be in denial, to pretend that she has gone through the stages of grief when she clearly has not, and to claim that her life could not be better. Although others may gently question her claims, no one has the right to aggressively confront her or to force her to face her grief.

In one group, a woman repeatedly insisted that the birth father was conscientiously striving to be a better person, one that would soon completely support her in the adoption process. All of the birth mothers in the group were visibly skeptical, recognizing that their peer was in denial and clinging to a hopeless relationship. No one, however, stated the obvious. When the woman finally announced, one session, that she had ended the relationship upon realizing that her boyfriend would never be supportive, the entire group cheered. Then each birth mother shared what she had seen earlier, affirming the woman's decision.

Allow a woman to return in her own time

In some cases, the issues brought up in group may be too difficult for a birth mother to deal with in her present condition. If she is a new member, she may not return, while a long-term member may suddenly cut off all contact with the group and the Pregnancy Center. It is crucial, at this stage, to avoid pushing the birth mother to return, yet to clearly indicate that she will be welcome when she does.

When a new member joins Group, the facilitator should debrief with her after the woman's first few sessions, ensuring that she has felt comfortable. Should the birth mother fail to return, the facilitator should call her two or three times, inviting her back in a warm, non-threatening fashion. If a birth mother is connected with another group member, the facilitator can also encourage the woman's friend to invite her back. If she chooses not to return, her decision should be respected.

A birth mother may rejoin Group when she is ready to continue grieving, or if her fellow friends convince her to return. In one case, a nineteen-year-old discovered that she was pregnant again and because she was so ashamed, she avoided both the group and her facilitator's calls. Other group members encountered her over the next few months and, each time, encouraged her to return. After giving birth, she returned, ready to grieve and feeling overcome by the warmth of those who continued to care for her despite her lengthy, unexplained absence.

The Makings of a Facilitator

A poor facilitator can impede a group's progress or even cause it to disintegrate. For this reason, the executive director of the Pregnancy Center must choose new facilitators with caution, observing their strengths before inviting them to consider leading Group. The following qualities are essential to an effective facilitator:

The ability to affirm

The facilitator's most critical role is to affirm women in a genuine, truthful manner. Most birth mothers are ashamed of the adoption and crave respect, but seldom receive affirmation among the general population, which neither recognizes nor understands the sacrifice they have made. Group is one of the few places where birth mothers are reminded of how courageous they have been.

Commitment

The stakes are high for a leader: group members may lose interest if her efforts are half-hearted, or may have difficulty trusting her enough to confide within the group context. Since trust takes so long to build, a new facilitator or co-facilitator must become as involved as possible. She must also show a readiness to learn, reading every book on adoption available to her and doing extensive research on the tried and true methods of running a group.

Transparency

Even if she is not a birth mother, a facilitator must be willing to tell the group about her own experiences with grief. If she is unable to be transparent or vulnerable, she cannot expect birth mothers to expose themselves emotionally.

When she introduces herself for the first time, a new facilitator should tell the group about herself, perhaps relating an event from childhood, or talking about an unhealthy relationship in which she was once involved and what need she was attempting to meet. Appropriate self-disclosure is judged by whether it will help individual group members, or the group as a whole, grow. One facilitator shared some of the events leading up to her divorce, for example, and gained acceptance because the birth mothers saw that their leader was not infallible.

A group leader should not hide her emotions. She should openly express her anger when a birth mother describes a time when she was mistreated, or cry when a story moves her. She should also be willing to laugh at herself.

Respect

The women who enter Group will have a variety of beliefs. A facilitator should never preach about abstinence or religion, as group members may feel pushed or judged, or resent their leader for promoting an agenda. If a contentious issue is raised—especially one relating to sexuality or spirituality—the facilitator should avoid immediately sharing her opinion on the subject. Instead, she should ask other birth mothers to address the question at hand. Birth mothers may very well share their faith in a relational way or promote abstinence, and these discussions should be allowed to occur naturally.

Diplomacy

Support groups can be extremely political. A facilitator who has privately counseled someone within the group will often be closely 'guarded' by the birth mother who views the leader as 'her person.' An effective facilitator must be able to affirm women with whom she has a close relationship, while letting the other group members know that they are equally important to her. Strategies can include sitting next to a less familiar woman in session, or phoning a well-known birth mother—an affirmation that will not be observed by the other group members.

Tips for Preventing Burn-Out

Facilitating Group can be a tremendously rewarding—and exhausting—experience. The following tips can be used to prevent burn-out:

Avoid holding weekly group meetings

Group should typically be held once a month. If desired, facilitators and group members can keep in contact by phone or email.

Make use of co-facilitators and facilitators-in-training

A group facilitator must be able to take a month off occasionally, or to pass on the responsibility of leading in times of stress or illness. For this reason, it is crucial to have both a reliable co-facilitator, and an individual training to be a facilitator, one who can step in when need arises.

Always debrief after group

The facilitator should have someone with whom to plan and debrief. Both individuals should pray together before each group session, and then meet afterwards.

The Story of a Group

Eight women ambled into the meeting room of the Pregnancy Care Centre. Some were curious; others were visibly awkward. The woman who took her place at the front was probably the most nervous of all: this was her first time leading a birth mothers' support group.

With her encouragement and direction, the birth mothers began to share their adoption stories, and continued to share each time the group met over the next three months. The descriptions were powerful and poignant: even the shyest woman was able to describe what it felt like to hold her baby for the first time, and to then hand this child over to its new parents. A couple of the more colorful characters in the group provided comic relief, sharing—at times in detail that made the leader cringe—what they had learned about labor and birth, birth fathers, and men in general.

By the end of the third month, however, the group facilitator observed that the women's enthusiasm for group was waning. The colorful characters had difficulty concealing their growing boredom, and stories that had once moved people to tears were now quietly endured. The facilitator realized that her group was at risk of collapsing—like many of the groups started by other Pregnancy Centers and adoption agencies. Phoning other leaders, she discovered a troubling commonality in birth mothers' groups: members would only remain in group for a short period of time, and when they left, the cohesive group would inevitably disintegrate.

After much thought, the facilitator finally recognized that no one in the group was moving forward emotionally or spiritually. Once a birth mother had told her story several times, she became bored with the angle. Some women even seemed to resent their identity as birth mothers: because they were stuck in their grief, their adoption stories had also become their life stories.

Hoping to salvage the group, the facilitator added a teaching component to each session, following a different theme each night. Rather than merely recounting their stories, women were asked to explore specific topics, such as maintaining a solid relationship with the adoptive mother or improving relationships with their own mothers. On special occasions, guest speakers were agreed upon and invited to address the group. One session even consisted of the birth mothers discussing open adoption with an adoptive couple.

The group leader also began to emphasize the fact that being a birth mother was only one part of each woman's identity. Group members who had worked through their grief were applauded for pursuing other challenges in life, whether academic, career-oriented, athletic, or social. The skills they learned in group were gradually applied elsewhere, and the women became more assertive, making positive changes to their own family dynamics, in some cases, or successfully dealing with problematic employers or teachers.

One of the most successful innovations was the open-door policy. New birth mothers and women who were contemplating adoption were invited to attend Group. These women could see, through their peers, what adoption looked like three months, three years, and even five years after placement. Seeing that the grief was overwhelming at the beginning, but changed as time progressed, prepared women for the challenges—and hope—ahead of them.

The facilitator had not anticipated how much impact the new group members would have. When a new woman arrived, the more established birth mothers took ownership of helping her overcome her grief. Rather than establishing cliques, they welcomed newcomers and even monitored their progress, expressing concern when a peer failed to show up to a meeting or was spotted in an unsavory environment.

Using their experience to nurture other birth mothers gave women a sense of purpose and pride. They were also able to revisit their own grief in a new way. Rather than being told that she was in denial, for example, a birth mother could recognize the symptoms in herself through the process of watching others struggle. Even the most confident and capable members identified sore points that they had previously neglected.

Birth mothers were strongly encouraged to be proactive rather than assuming the role of victim. Many expressed the desire to use their experiences to advocate for adoption. Several of the women regularly wrote letters to newspapers or agencies when adoption was portrayed in a negative or misinformed way. Two of the birth mothers had their stories printed in a local newspaper.

As time passed, the birth mother's group continued to grow, branching off into two separate groups. When asked to pinpoint how the group had sustained itself, the facilitator responded without hesitation. They key to a successful group, she said, was hope: the belief that grief could be overcome and that the process of adoption could make women stronger, wiser, and more competent to deal with anything that life would throw at them.

IN THEIR OWN WORDS

"It was good to see what everyone else was going through. From the people who had gone through it I saw where I might go and where my relationship [with the adoptive parents and my child] might end up. From the people that came behind me, I saw what I went through (or should have gone through). It was peer support—just being in a room with people who have done the same things. You could say things that you knew no one outside the group would really understand."

—Nicki, birth mother, age 17

"It gets us all into the talking mode. We get angry, we get happy, and we cry. We yell at the ex-boyfriend, and get mad at the birth father and the adoptive parents. Everything just gets out in the open, which is very therapeutic. You can say, 'Okay, I'm not the only one feeling this way. Everybody else feels this way, so I can move on and just get every-thing out.'"

—Aurora, birth mother, age 16

"I'd now say that the birth mom's group was the most valuable thing to me. I don't know if that was the case back then. I was really angry at things and all of a sudden I would blow up, fiercely angry, and I had no idea why. I know now: I hadn't grieved properly after having the baby."

—Sandra, birth mother, now age 38

CHAPTER FIFTEEN

Managing Open Adoption Long Term

"I invited her to participate in the birth of my child. She didn't invite me to her first birthday."

—Emily, birth mother, age 25

"It's gut-wrenching when you realize these young women almost give up their very soul. If we want to take the baby and run, nobody wins."

—John and Mary, adoptive parents

In the new millennium, the term "open adoption" has come to signify not only the placement of a child in a home selected by its birth mother, but the establishment of an ongoing relationship between the woman and the adoptive family. Sometimes called "kinship adoption," open adoption today broadens families, integrating birth mothers into an intimate social unit.

Although detractors of open adoption fear that such familiarity may create confusion in the children involved, open adoption advocates believe that there is far more potential harm in keeping secrets. According to an old adage in family therapy, the more secrets a family has, the unhealthier it is. The closed adoptions of the past, open adoption proponents would argue, were riddled with secrets. Attempts were made to conceal the birth mother's pregnancy. The adoptive couple, whose infertility was well known, though never spoken of, typically pretended that they had conceived and given birth to the infant. The child, though suspicious, would maintain the silence, seldom daring to raise the forbidden subject.

Secrets, in the new adoption scenario, are viewed as destructive. A birth mother who is asked to deny the existence of her child will be unable to grieve her loss. A child who is asked to deny the existence of its birth mother will struggle with issues of identity and rejection. An adoptive couple who are asked to pretend that the child is their own flesh and blood will never come to terms with their infertility.

Whatever a Pregnancy Center worker's views may be on adoption, the reality is that the open adoption cannot be ignored. For many women, the fear of secrets—of not knowing what has become of their children—would make the possibility of placing in a closed adoption scenario inconceivable. As one twenty-three-year-old birth mother explained: "I couldn't bear the thought of not knowing where my child was. I want to know that she's okay and that she's healthy. If I didn't have that choice, there's no way I would have placed."

As the face of adoption changes, Pregnancy Centers must meet the challenge of fostering healthy relationships between clients and adoptive families. Several questions must be carefully examined: What factors should be considered at the onset of a client's open adoption? How can a woman establish and manage a relationship when she knows of no one who has been in her situation? What boundaries must be put in place to ensure that her experience is positive, and the relationship, respectful? How can a Center support a client whose relationship with the adoptive family is in jeopardy?

As an advocate for the birth mother, a Center must first prepare clients for the potential challenges—and joys—that await.

PREPARING CLIENTS FOR OPEN ADOPTION

Predelivery

A woman who is considering open adoption is beginning a relationship, one that will evolve over time. As with any relationship, certain tensions exist. The birth mother must allow herself to be vulnerable, while exercising caution; show enthusiasm, while trying not to be overbearing; assert herself, while not exhibiting aggression; and be flexible, yet unwilling to allow herself to be trampled upon.

For women who find 'normal' relationships difficult, the power differential in an adoptive relationship can be daunting. A younger client whose social network consists primarily of her junior high school comrades will be out of her element when connecting with an older, wiser pair of strangers who appear to hold all of the cards. A client in her mid-twenties or thirties will have unique challenges of her own: she must relinquish her parental authority to a couple that may not be much older than herself.

One of the foundational principles that a client must grasp about the adoptive relationship is that she is allowed access to her child only at the will of the adoptive parents. She must treat them with respect, or risk finding herself in a closed adoption scenario. Even if a birth mother disagrees with how the child is being parented, for example, she must let her grievances go. Like a wise grandparent, she should offer no advice or criticism concerning her 'grandchild's' parenting—unless she is asked directly.

A birth mother has one major card to play: the choice of who will parent her child. Subsequent decisions belong almost exclusively to the adoptive couple. The counselor should warn the client, at the decision-making stage, that the adoptive parents she selects could potentially choose to move to the other side of the globe. The couple has the right to close the adoption for any reason, whether the decision is in the best interest of the child or merely rooted in insecurity and fear. Some couples, the client should understand, may be unable to resist family pressures, ending an adoptive relationship simply because relatives perceive the birth mother as a threat, not as the giver of a remarkable gift.

Even though a client should be candidly warned of potential losses, she should also be reassured that the majority of birth mothers have some degree of success in their open adoptions. Many couples deliberately seek to maintain an open relationship, recognizing the benefits to their children. The ideal is attainable, especially when the adoptive relationship is carefully nurtured.

For some clients, of course, an open relationship is neither desirable nor feasible. A woman with significant mental health issues or lifestyle patterns, such as drug addiction or prostitution, may be living too dangerous a life to connect with her child. She should be prepared for the reality that the adoptive parents may be willing to adopt her child, but unwilling to give her their home address. In some scenarios, an adoptive couple will consider bringing the child to picnics hosted by the adoption agency or attending meetings facilitated by a third party; other couples may close the adoption entirely due to anxiety about how the birth mother's instability will affect the child.

When a more stable client is in the initial stages of planning an adoption, she may lean towards creating a relatively closed adoption, one in which contact is limited to the exchange of letters and pictures. The counselor should challenge the client at this point. What a woman wants during her pregnancy, and what she will want after she has grieved the loss of her child, may be radically different. Her initial instinct will be to avoid pain—and its source, her child. However, if she closes the adoption during the negotiation process, she will have little chance of having access to her child should she eventually long for contact.

A wise client will ask for an adoption that is more open than she desires. Should the scenario prove uncomfortable, she can always reduce contact in the early stages of the relationship, especially since the infant will not yet be aware of her presence. To open a closed relationship is far more difficult, not to mention unfair to the couple who had anticipated a closed adoption, only to encounter an unhappy birth mother.

After delivery

Both the birth mother and the adoptive couple will go through a highly stressful adjustment period when the baby is born. In the months preceding delivery, the birth mother may find the openness of the adoptive relationship irksome. She may complain that she feels judged—that her every move is being evaluated. She may believe that the adoptive mother is critically eyeing her selection of lunch, and may resent the couple's anxiety concerning her health and lifestyle choices. Indeed, the adoptive parents may not be subtle or mindful of appropriate boundaries. In their eagerness to secure a healthy baby, they may become too invasive.

The tables often turn during the initial period after delivery. Consumed with meeting the demands of an infant, the couple may view the birth mother's mere presence as intrusive. Many couples, especially those who are preparing to raise their first child, will discredit the amount of adjustment that is required to accommodate a new baby, especially since a physical recovery from childbirth is not a factor. Studies have shown, however, that infants require ten hours of care every day. To an adoptive mother who is accustomed to a forty hour work week, the additional thirty hours of work—plus the time needed to complete normal household tasks—can prove overwhelming.

To complicate matters, the adoptive parents must bond with the little stranger that has entered their lives and work to establish a family identity. While being grateful to the birth mother, they may simultaneously long to separate from her. The adoptive couple's most joyful experience is the birth mother's most devastating, and the two opposing spectrums of emotion can be unsettling. By pulling away, the adoptive couple can temporarily alleviate any feelings of guilt they have about the fact that their joy has come at a great cost.

When managing an open adoption, it is crucial for a counselor to help both parties establish, in advance, what the relationship will look like during the first few months after delivery. The birth mother will benefit from knowing that she will see her baby at a specific time, whether it be a week, a month, or two months after the placement. The duration of the visit should also be established, be it a one hour, two hour, or five hour stay.

Part of the peer counselor's role is to help the birth mother empathize with the adoptive couple, thereby setting realistic expectations. Although she may desire to see her baby every day, for example, she should recognize the strain that her constant presence will put on the adoptive relationship. At the same time, a birth mother who is so eager to please that she neglects her own needs can be given permission to approach the adoptive couple with reasonable requests.

Another issue that should be discussed in advance is the question of how the adoptive couple and the birth mother will explain their relationship to other people. Being proud of what they have done, birth mothers will often provide a detailed explanation to anyone that asks—or to anyone, period. Adoptive mothers are typically more reluctant to make a public announcement, perhaps fearing, in part, that the adoption will play too large a part in the child's identity. They may even wish to avoid appearing in public altogether. A frank discussion is therefore necessary. Will meetings be held in the privacy of the couple's home? If both parties are comfortable with meeting in public places, how will they introduce each other to friends, acquaintances, and strangers? How will they address each other in front of the child?

The long-term relationship

Once the adoptive relationship moves past the awkward stage of fumbling introductions, and through the intense roller coaster of emotions surrounding the child's birth and placement, it will enter another stage entirely. Pre-adoption promises will have been tested, and both the birth mother and the adoptive couple's preconceptions and impressions will have been replaced with a more holistic sense of the situation.

In order to determine what the adoptive relationship should look like over the long term, the 'second year rule' can be applied. By the time the child has reached its 'second' birthday, according to the rule, both parties should have come to terms with what openness entails. They will have gauged their compatibility and, in some cases, settled into a mutually satisfying arrangement. From the second year on, then, both parties should strive to remain consistent, recognizing that as the child matures, inconsistency can be perceived as rejection. If the birth mother would like to give her child a birthday present, for example, she should continue to do so every year.

The birth mother should be reminded that maintaining consistency is not only the duty of the adoptive couple. If she has promised to be present, she has the responsibility to avoid entering in and out of her child's life. Even if the birth mother marries and begins her own family, she must recognize her child's ongoing need for affirmation. A sensitive child may actually need additional reassurance to be convinced that it is not being replaced, but still holds a significant place in its birth mother's life.

There are several issues that will arise in a long-term adoptive relationship, creating considerable tension if not anticipated and addressed. One involves the question of significant others. When the birth mother becomes involved in a romantic relationship, she will naturally want her new suitor to meet the child. If she is an avid dater, however, the adoptive parents may not wish to open their home to a parade of men. The birth mother and the adoptive couple should determine at what point in a romantic relationship a significant other can be introduced. The child, the peer counselor can point out, can be adversely affected if too many people become part of its life, only to disappear as soon as the romance dissipates.

The extended birth family may also create tension in the adoptive relationship. The question of what role the child's biological family should play in its life should therefore be addressed as soon as possible. An outgoing adoptive couple may be comfortable with having an open door policy, inviting the child's biological grandparents, aunts, uncles, siblings, and the family pet over for a barbecue. A more private couple, in contrast, may wish to limit visits with extended family to once a year, or to allow only the birth parents to see the child. In some cases, the relationship may be limited to the birth mother's family; in other situations, the birth father and his extended family can be incorporated into the adoptive family's social sphere.

Before the extended family becomes involved, the issue of gift-giving should be openly discussed. When is gift-giving appropriate, and what limits should be set on the number of gifts a child receives? If the child has siblings, how can rivalry or jealousy be avoided? What steps can be taken to prevent the adopted child from anticipating the arrival of the gift, rather than the giver? Will the generous birth family become the 'good guys' in the child's mind, while the adoptive couple becomes 'bad' the moment boundaries are put in place?

One adopted child quickly found himself the envy of his peers: in addition to having a large and more than generous extended adoptive family, he was also regularly bestowed with gifts from the relatives of both his birth mother and birth father. Visits with his birth family typically coincided with major holidays, which equated to a staggering number of gifts. To his chagrin, however, his adoptive parents quickly curbed the flood of presents by appraising the well-intentioned birth family of the situation.

TEN TIPS FOR BIRTH MOTHERS

A significant part of a counselor's role over the long term is in helping the client adjust to the idiosyncrasies she now sees in the strangers she chose to parent her child. As the birth mother and the adoptive parents become increasingly familiar, the strengths and deficits of each will become evident to all. Time will reveal traits that an adoptive profile or an interview cannot. A birth mother may be pleased to discover that the adoptive father is not as shy as he appeared during the interview, and that behind his reserved demeanor lies an offbeat sense of humor. Conversely, she may realize that the couple's financial stability, an attractive feature initially, is coupled with a materialistic attitude that she overlooked.

A peer counselor can be a supportive listener when a birth mother expresses her disappointments and frustrations. However, the client should be advised that she cannot expect or demand change from the adoptive couple. Certain issues can be addressed, of course, and misunderstandings put to rest. Neither the birth mother nor the couple will be involved enough, though, to expect one another to make changes in character. Each person must be accepted as a package, virtues and vices included.

That said, there are ways in which a birth mother can alleviate tensions and foster a good adoptive relationship. The following ten suggestions can help a birth mother maintain a rewarding open adoption:

Take a team approach

However different their personalities, the birth mother and the adoptive parents share one mutual passion: the child. If a birth mother exhibits a willingness to pursue the child's best interest, regarding her own needs as secondary, the adoptive couple can be brought on side and may even be more willing to take risks. By uniting in a common purpose—to protect, love, and nurture the child—the birth mother and the adoptive couple can become allies, rather than adversaries.

Make a game plan

Children are notoriously adept at asking difficult questions. They will ponder everything, from sexual matters to the peculiar growth on a stranger's face. An inquisitive child may ask, for example, why his birth mother would 'make' a baby if she was unable to raise it by herself. Another child may question, in the middle of a family dinner, why her birth mother is slim, while her adoptive mother is decidedly not. As a team, the birth mother and the adoptive couple can prepare a response to the few questions that can be anticipated.

There are several serious issues that should be addressed. For example, what will the adoptive parents and the birth mother call each other in front of the child? What aspects of the birth mother's past are open to discussion? If the adopted child is an adolescent, how should his birth mother handle questions relating to sexual morality or spirituality?

Develop a relationship with the adoptive couple outside of the child

A birth mother who focuses solely on her child during visits can unwittingly create awkwardness and tension in the adoptive relationship. If she shows a sincere interest in the couple and the child's siblings, however, she will become less of a threat or an imposition. Finding a common ground and engaging in adult conversation can have other benefits as well. Depending upon what stage the child is at, the arrival of its birth mother—one more boring adult—may not be particularly alluring, especially when a bin of Lego or a rambunctious sibling awaits. If the birth mother is temporarily abandoned because of her child's previous appointment with a jury of stuffed animals, her ability to carry on a comfortable conversation with the other dull adults in the child's life may salvage an otherwise disappointing visit.

Some birth mothers take additional steps to building a good rapport with the adoptive couple. A client can ask the adoptive mother to lunch without the child, for example, or send the adoptive father a humorous card on his birthday.

Ask permission whenever possible

In order to put the adoptive parents at ease and to gain trust, a birth mother can involve them in minor matters. If she would like to buy the child a special videotape, for example, she can ask the couple beforehand if they would consider the movie appropriate. If she wishes to purchase a special treat for her toddler, the birth mother can ask the adoptive mother if the child is allowed to have candy. By extending a certain degree of courtesy, a birth mother can affirm the couple's position as parents. The couple, in turn, will likely respond in an equally courteous manner.

Be prepared to contribute more than the adoptive couple

The need for a birth mother to give more and to work harder is inevitable in a relationship where she is not in control. If she pushes her needs and desires, she may very well push herself out of the picture as well. In contrast, if she acts in a respectful manner even when she feels herself being disrespected, or if she continues to make special efforts even when the adoptive couple fails to return or acknowledge the favor, a birth mother can maintain a peaceful relationship. In the long term, her needs will be better served, for her efforts may preserve the relationship with her child.

Affirm who the 'real' parents are

An adoptive relationship can run into difficulties when an astute child recognizes its unique position and attempts to play one party against the other. If a headstrong adolescent is furious with his parents for imposing a rule he wholeheartedly disagrees with, for example, he may declare his intentions to move in with his birth mother. Another child might conclude that since her adoptive mother is not her 'real' mother, her authority is also 'unreal.'

A birth mother can reduce friction by affirming, throughout the child's life, the authority that the adoptive parents hold. When a child is young, the birth mother can openly reinforce the adoptive parents' decisions whenever the opportunity presents itself. In early adolescence, the birth mother may very well have to state, during a candid conversation with her child, that there is no possibility that her son or daughter can move in with her. Humor can often be used to diffuse unpleasant situations. As one birth mother responded to her disgruntled daughter, "If you think your parents' rules are tough, be thankful you're not living with mine!"

One of the greatest affirmations a birth mother can give is to describe the adoptive mother as the "real mother" in the presence of the child and other people. This statement will solidify the open adoption arrangement in a profound way: while it does not diminish the birth mother's role, it acknowledges the day-in-day-out sacrifice made by the adoptive mother.

Keep the lines of communication open

In any relationship, especially those fraught with emotion, misunderstandings will inevitably arise. Body language will be misinterpreted and flippant comments imbued with significance. It is therefore crucial for both parties to address issues when they arise, preventing otherwise innocuous comments or actions from being grossly misinterpreted, especially since the offender may be completely unaware of the crime that was unwittingly committed.

When dealing with an issue, the birth mother should first carefully contemplate her position. A hasty or embittered confrontation can destroy the adoptive relationship. Should she decide to write a letter to the adoptive couple, she should analyze a rough draft with her peer counselor before mailing the final copy. The peer counselor can also encourage the client to do role playing, rehearsing the discussion she will initiate with the adoptive parents. When handled properly, misunderstandings can usually be dealt with, and the adoptive relationship strengthened.

If an issue is particularly serious or complicated, the peer counselor should, with the permission of the birth mother, contact the adoption agency. Because the agency deals with both the birth mother and the adoptive family, it is in a position to facilitate a positive understanding between the two parties. The peer counselor, however, should never get in the middle of a conflict. Her role is to coach the birth mother, giving her the tools needed to develop life skills and to resolve conflict, not to fight her battles for her.

Keep gift-giving to a minimum

For many birth mothers, giving presents is a tangible expression of their love for their children. However, excessive giving can be harmful to the child, taxing to the birth mother, and exasperating to the adoptive couple who cannot help but feel competitive. A birth mother can choose, instead, to give sentimental gifts or to bring small, inexpensive gifts that foster the child's creativity. A pack of stickers, crayons, or a book can be much more useful than the latest, loudest, trendiest toy.

Birth mothers should also be sensitive to the needs of the child's siblings, giving them each a little gift as well. One sensitive birth mother would periodically mail her child's sibling a little card with stickers enclosed to ensure that the seven-year-old would not conclude that he was valued only during holidays or in the presence of his adopted brother.

The gift giving habit can also be avoided altogether. One birth mother, who did not want to earn the title of 'the present fairy,' chose instead to store the presents and letters in a large bin, one that would be presented on her daughter's eighteenth birthday. To every gift she attached a note, explaining its significance and her feelings for her daughter on the day the present was purchased.

Avoid harboring fantasies

A perceptive client may come to the realization that there is a possibility that the adoptive couple will predecease the child before it is fully grown. As with any parents, adoptive couples are not impervious to accidents or illness, and may be even more so, depending upon the age at which they adopt. The birth mother may therefore fantasize about this scenario, envisioning the return of her child to her.

If a tragedy does occur, however, returning the child to its birth mother may be one of the most devastating events of its life. Not only will it have lost its parents, but the child may be robbed of its extended adoptive family and siblings. Unless the birth mother is in an exceptional circumstance, she should not expect to ever parent the child, nor should she resent the adoptive couple if she is not named the child's legal guardian in their will.

Respect the boundaries set by the adoptive couple

Even if a birth mother does not agree with a boundary, and has sound reasons for disagreeing, she should respect the adoptive couple's wishes nonetheless. All parents are entitled to make mistakes; adoptive parents are no different. A birth mother can respectfully ask questions concerning why the boundary has been set, but must then accept it. To respond to the couple's request in anything less than a totally respectful manner will put stress on the adoption.

In one case, a birth mother was invited to attend a variety of functions, including her child's birthday parties, violin recitals, and soccer games. At these functions, she proudly took initiative and identified herself as the little boy's biological mother—to virtually everyone. When the adoptive couple asked her to stop openly identifying herself as the child's birth mother, the client was deeply hurt. She believed that the couple was ashamed of her and the fact that their son was adopted.

After discussing the issue with her peer counselor, however, she realized that the couple was not being territorial, but were concerned about the child's well-being. Her need to publicly claim him was making the boy stand out among his peers and question whether he really belonged to his adoptive parents. By backing off, the birth mother allowed her son to be a child, and saved the adoptive relationship from unnecessary strain.

IN THEIR OWN WORDS

"I'm pretty lucky. You listen to some of the other birth moms, and it's like, 'I'm so sorry for you. I'm fortunate that I picked this family and that I didn't pick your family.' It's mean to say that, but it's very true."

—Jacqueline, birth mother, age 23

Emily's Story

"There's not really anything terrible about the couple I chose, but I think my daughter's adoptive mom has some security issues. I'm twenty-nine now and she probably sees that I could have raised Laura on my own, which makes her insecure.

"Kristina was really good at the beginning. She said that I could come to the city anytime I wanted to see Laura. I took her up on that a few times. When I was there, Laura's adoptive dad always said, 'Here, hold her! Feed her! Play with her!' But Kristina was more reserved and I had to assert myself.

"By the end of the first year, she started to back off. We do a family portrait every Christmas and we thought that Laura should be in it. Kristina came to the studio at the mall and was quite stressed out about passing Laura over for the photograph. I think that's where everything started.

"The following year, she decided that Laura would not be allowed to be in the picture. She said that her family had its 'own traditions.' I thought that she was being unfair, but I let it go.

"I asked to come to Laura's birthday two months later, but Kristina said that she had a full day that day and couldn't accommodate me. I think that Laura's birthday is a very hard day for her. Still, if there's any day a birth mom should see her child, it's on its birthday. I wasn't asking for time alone or anything. I just wanted to be included.

"Kristina definitely has an issue with me having photographs taken with Laura—just the two of us. One day, when the family was visiting, Laura started crying. I picked her up and was walking around with her, and my sister followed me onto the patio and snapped a picture of us. After they had gone home, Kristina called and said she didn't like the fact that there was a photo session going on on the patio. She made it sound as if there were flash bulbs and white lights, when in reality, my sister had just snapped off one photograph. That photo meant a lot to me: it was the first picture Laura and I had taken together since the hospital, when I looked yucky and she looked like an alien.

"Now Kristina is sort of okay as long as she's taking the photo. I think her problem was that both Laura and I were out of her sight. Maybe pictures aren't even the issue.

"She's just very uptight and high-strung generally. At a community barbecue, for example, she wouldn't let Laura pick up a dirty ball and throw it around. I thought, 'She's a kid. It's a picnic. Let her get dirty!'

I wonder if Kristina was putting on a show for me. Was she trying to show me she could raise Laura? Did she think, 'Emily has put all this trust in me. I'd better keep Laura clean and make sure that not a grain of dirt goes into her mouth!'?

"When confronting Kristina, I state my case, but I think a lot before I say anything that's going to be damaging. Even if it means backing down, it's better than saying something that will make her even more insecure, or that I'll regret for the rest of my life.

"It's very difficult, though. Kristina had originally agreed to let me see Laura once a month. By the end of the first year, she said, 'I think we're going to cut back to three times a year.' I pointed out that we had agreed to meet once every month. She said that she had other plans and people to see, and so I let her win that battle.

"At some level, I think that Kristina thinks I'm going to take Laura away. I'm not! It's not so much that it's the wrong thing to do, but that I don't want to raise a child by myself. Laura has her own family now, and I would never take that away from her.

"I see other adoptive moms giving a lot to birth moms who don't even have it together. They even give alone time, which Kristina shies away from. I had envisioned, when I was pregnant, getting on a plane with Laura and taking her home to see my mom and dad. But Kristina doesn't want Laura and me to have any time alone together. She says she's not ready for that.

"I don't know if she'll ever be ready."

Julie's Story

"I don't regret placing. I don't think I would be where I am right now if I had been a single mom. My one regret, though, would be placing with the Kreugers.

"When I first met them, they were open and very friendly. They had a little boy that they had adopted previously, and things were going really well. They did a lot of promising: 'You can come visit him whenever you want.' I thought, 'Great!'

"We did some visits after Benton was born. Then they went to Arizona. They had originally planned to stay a month or two. That was four years ago.

"I felt really burned and very angry. I don't know the adoptive father well, and I don't think he had much input. But I would have things to say to the adoptive mom. She stripped me of my title of being a mom, and I would like to say to her, 'What makes you think you're so worthy of having my child and doing this to me? Does it make you feel good? It doesn't matter how far away you keep him from me. That little personality of his—that's mine. Those big blue eyes that you look into every day—they're mine.'

"They sent me a letter at Christmas. It wasn't personal. It was one of those letters that you do up for the whole family and send out to a gazillion people.

"Even now, when I get pictures of Benton, it's just like looking at pictures of somebody else's kid. It's been so long since I've seen him."

Jacob and Linda's Story

"When we adopted Jasmine eleven years ago, we were a little freaked out by the idea of open adoption. We decided, along with her birth parents, that we didn't want to keep in contact after she was born. Instead, we planned to do letters and pictures.

"After a year, we decided that this just wasn't good enough for us. We contacted Jasmine's birth parents, who were still together at the time, and they agreed to meet her. They saw Jasmine when she was sixteen months old and then requested again not to have contact with us physically—to continue with letters and pictures.

"Our son Chase is six and half now. His adoption was open from the very beginning. We see his birth mother a lot and have a great friendship, as well as a relationship through our son.

"Initially, we planned to keep his adoption open for up to two years, but to close it off when Chase was able to start asking questions. We believed the argument that open adoption is confusing for the kids. We were also reluctant to keep the adoption open because Jasmine's was so closed. So when Chase was two, we sat his birth mom Amber down and told her that we would like to begin to close the adoption because he was becoming aware of her presence.

"In the following six months, our hearts changed. We realized that this is who our kids are and that we cannot, in good conscience, deny this part of them. We went back to Amber and asked her to be a permanent part of our lives. We also decided to push the envelope a little bit for Jasmine's sake and for the sake of her birth mom. We knew that they would both eventually want to explore a relationship, so we contacted her birth mother and began to open the adoption.

"Since then, the relationship with Chase's birth mom has really evolved. It has worked, in part, because Amber is very sensitive to Jasmine. When she comes over, it's not like she comes over to hang out with Chase. She's just as much with us and with Jasmine as she is with her son.

"This is not to say that there hasn't been tension. The last time Chase's birth mom was over, we noticed some very subtle behavior changes. Jasmine and Chase were having trouble getting along. By the end of the day, we sat Jasmine down and said, 'What's going on?' She came up with this and that.

"Finally, we just said, 'How do you feel about yesterday? How do you feel about Amber being here?' She started to cry. It came out that she feels, very deeply, that when Amber is here, she's Chase's birth mom and not hers.

"We worked through all of that. We worked through the question, 'Why is it?' and 'How does it make you feel?'

"A couple of days later, Jasmine spoke to her birth mom on the phone. We were upstairs tucking Chase in and Jasmine was already in bed. Jasmine ran to answer the phone.

"Her birth mom made a decision, right there, not to hang up. When Jasmine said, 'This is Jasmine speaking,' there was a long silence. Jasmine's birth mother tends to be a little bit fearful, but she made the courageous decision not to hang up.

"After Jasmine got off the phone, she was just bouncing, she was so excited. The way the conversation ended was, 'I love you too.' She was just so excited.

"That was huge for her. It took all those feelings that were boiling up and put them to rest because she had that connection again. Every few months she needs that connection.

"For Jasmine, her adoption is an extremely important part of her life. She's a very sensitive child. We knew from very early on that she would be the kind of child who would ask questions and search very deeply for who she is.

"Early on, we told Jasmine that everyone has a 'differentness' about them. One of my 'differentnesses' is that I can't grow a baby in my tummy, so that makes people ask me weird questions and look at me strangely sometimes. But that's just my difference. We all have them, and for her to get hung up on that 'differentness' about her is pinning her whole identity on her adoption. We don't want her to be an adopted person, but to be a person who experienced adoption.

"Jasmine's birth mom got married, and she had a little girl three years ago. We told Jasmine about her birth family. Having a half sister out there somewhere was a huge connecting point with her. She was eight years old at the time and in the romantic phase of her life, dreaming about everything. When Jasmine heard that her birth mom was pregnant, she kept saying, 'I hope it's a girl! I hope it's a girl!' She wanted to connect with a little sister, and when the baby was born, she was thrilled.

"Several issues came up with that. Jasmine didn't come right out and ask, but she sort of referred to the question, 'Does this mean I go back there now that my birth mom is ready to have a baby.'

"We had always told her that the reason behind her adoption was that, at the time, her birth mother did not feel ready to parent for various reasons. So in a child's mind, the question, 'Oh! She's ready to parent. Where does that leave me?' was raised.

"We used that time to confirm in her mind that we're a forever family: that we believe that there was a plan for her life all along. Before she was even born or conceived, she was meant to be a part of our family. That's not something that's going to end at any point.

"We also affirmed her birth mom's desire and need to go on and have a family. Some day, Jasmine will connect with these people, people who are probably very much like her in a lot of ways.

"For us, it was a process of letting go of a dream, of saying: 'Our family was built in a different way. I never dreamed that it would be built this way, but I'm going to accept that. I'm going to embrace who my children are, and not live in denial.'

John and Mary's Story

"We got married late: John was forty-three and I was thirty-nine. We thought of adoption right away, knowing that at our age, it's a lot more difficult to conceive. We did, indeed, soon find out that we could not have kids.

"We didn't suffer from the infertility trauma that most couples experience. The biggest reason is that we did get married later. Neither one of us had been married before, so we had all of those years to grieve. You grow up through the process of realizing that you might not meet somebody you want to spend the rest of your life with. By the time you actually do get married, you have already dealt with the possibility of never having children.

"We had a friend who'd released a child for adoption in her youth. She was married and had left her husband because he was abusive. Then she found out she was pregnant. She was nineteen and had no way to support a baby, so she released the baby for adoption, back when everything was closed. She was told that the adoptive parents were both schoolteachers and wonderful Christians. None of this was true. She didn't know for twenty-two years whether her son was alive. It just ate her up inside, this black hole in her life.

"When she found her son, he wasn't with an ideal family. He may have well done better if he had stayed with her.

"Having heard that story, from the birth mom's side, we realized that the adoptive parents are not the only ones in the equation that matter. The birth mother very much matters.

"In December, we got a call saying that a birth mom wanted to meet us. It was nerve-wracking! She had the advantage: she'd seen our album, read the home study, knew all about us—and we knew nothing about her. We were meeting her in a restaurant and we didn't even know who she was.

"Shauna turned out to be a teeny, tiny little thing—two foot nothing and seven months pregnant. Even so, it was intimidating! Once we got chatting, we could see that she was very interested in us and asked a lot of good questions. What really impressed us was that from the moment she found out she was pregnant, Shauna quit drinking and started taking good care of herself. And when it came time to choose a family, she took it very seriously.

"We met with her six times before Thea was born. The entrustment ceremony was so emotional! Shauna had just given birth two days before, and she could hardly walk. We were both filled with wonder that someone could be strong enough to place her baby for adoption. We felt guilty too. You think, 'How can I do this to somebody? I get to go home with her baby, and what does she go home with? A big pile of grief.' We knew that it was everybody's choice, but we still felt a little bit responsible for causing this woman pain.

"Shauna walked out the door and went home. We took the baby. It's not like we took the baby and ran, but it almost felt like we did! We brought Thea home, set her down on the kitchen floor, looked at each other, and said, 'Okay. So now what?'

"We decided that we couldn't exactly return to sender, so we'd better figure this out! That first evening, we just sat and held Thea for a long time.

"The ten day waiting period wasn't that big a deal. There were no indications that Shauna would change her mind. We had taken the time to get to know her, and she, us.

"She phoned us on day seven. A good friend of ours had been in a serious car accident shortly before Thea was born. When Shauna phoned, one of her first questions was, 'How is your friend doing?' She didn't jump right in and say, 'How's my baby?', even though she had released him seven days before. That really impressed us.

"During that phone call, we asked her if she still felt she had made the right decision. She said, 'Yeah. Of course!' We knew right then that it wasn't iffy.

"She has affirmed her decision so many times. One day we were talking about what a happy little girl Thea is. She said, 'If I had kept her and if I had stayed with the birth father, she wouldn't be. The environment wouldn't have fostered that at all.'

And sometimes, if Thea is grumpy, Shauna will laugh and say, 'Ugh! I don't know how you do it. I'm glad it's you and not me!'

"I think she's thrilled to bits that she can come over. She consistently asks about our lives, and has worked to build a relationship with our family. We're not just people she uses to see the baby.

"It wasn't always easy, though. The first couple of times that Shauna came to visit, she stayed all day. We found that a little disconcerting. We knew that it wouldn't be healthy for her to keep coming over all day every week and after three months passed, we felt she needed to focus her life on something else. So we set times. We asked her what her day would look like and worked around that. These visits were a little less traumatic for her because she had somewhere to go afterwards instead of going home, pacing the floor, and falling apart. She had a focus and something to look forward to—like going to the gym—when she walked out the door.

"We've had a good relationship with Shauna's family from the beginning. We met her parents before Thea was born. We knew from what the adoption agency taught us that sometimes the parents of the birth mom will try to talk them out of the adoption. We thought that if we met them, and tried to build a relationship with them, they'd realize that we're normal and that we're not out to do their grandchild any damage.

"So we met Shauna's parents for dinner and asked them if they were interested in having ongoing contact. Apparently, before we arrived, they had told Shauna that they didn't want that. But when they met us, they changed their minds.

"We take Thea to Calgary once a year and Shauna's parents have driven up to Edmonton several times. They're very open and delighted that this has happened. They think it's wonderful for us, and for Shauna, and for Thea. We even had a big family bash in the backyard. Our parents and siblings came, and Shauna brought hers as well. It was quite a party!

"As for the marketing job the second time around—we didn't have to do it! Our second birth mother followed us into the community center where we volunteer and kind of cornered us and said, 'Have you guys considered adopting another child? I'm fifteen weeks pregnant and I'd like you to consider adopting my child.' It was bizarre!

"It was especially bizarre because as time went on, Victoria asked us nothing about ourselves. She thought we were wonderful and wasn't shy to say so, but she never knew anything about us!

"It became clear to us right from the beginning that she had an agenda. Part of Victoria's agenda was that we were going to adopt her, along with the baby. I don't think she had the first clue that there would be some limits on the relationship.

"It was hard letting her know what the boundaries were and that the relationship was about her daughter. And it took awhile for it to sink in to her that we weren't going to become her family. She saw the adoption as being all about her.

"Natalie was born sick and drug addicted, and spent two weeks in intensive care. When we brought her home, she went through drug withdrawal and had to be medicated for delirium tremens. She was a frail baby, so tiny and lethargic from the medication she was on that she almost didn't seem like a person. For a month, it was almost like she was just this tiny little object.

"The bonding process took longer than it did with our first baby. Natalie had some fierce competition! Our attention was being diverted by Thea, who was going through all her 'firsts' and was cute as a bug.

"She's part of us now, though, and we have no regrets.

"Dealing with Victoria has been difficult, though. She's so unstable. Her life has always been in chaos, and it always will be.

"We know that she'll disappoint Natalie many times. She'll say she's going to show up, and she won't. We won't whitewash it when it happens. But we'll need to let Natalie know that Victoria loves her, because we don't doubt that that's the truth. We'll say, 'Victoria has some problems and that she doesn't always function the way most people do, but she does love you.'

"We think that it's likely that she'll just disappear. That would be nice for us, in a sense, but that's not what's best for Nat. The hardest part would be working with Natalie's disappointment when she realizes that her birth mom never comes over and Thea's does all the time.

"We have to maintain a certain distance because we're the parents. We can't parent with the birth mothers peering over our shoulder. They have a certain amount of ownership of these children, understandably, but they have no control. That's tough for them, but the birth mother can't become your best friend. It just doesn't work.

"What we've come to realize is that these birth moms are very real people. They've had their struggles. They've got their dysfunctions just like we do. And they're afraid. The fact is, they have no legal control whatsoever. We could take both babies and move to Florida tomorrow and they have not one ounce of power over our decision. Once the court date has passed, it's over. We could do anything. It's nothing more than a gentleman's agreement!

"We hold all the cards. I think that's good, because it's not good for a child to be fought over back and forth. But I think that also gives us a lot of responsibility. We hold the cards, and we'd better be careful how we play them.

"We have to set our daughters up to succeed. We want them to feel accepted and welcomed from both sides, and to build successful relationships with their birth moms.

"I'll be candid. I think that couples need to be set up better to build relationships with the birth moms. The adoption agencies tend to emphasize their personal experience, saying that for the most part, these birth moms move on with their lives. They get married, the agency says, and you might see them three times the first year and after that, hardly at all. I don't believe that's true, and I don't believe that's what the birth moms want.

"I think that couples are set up for surprise, shock, and disillusionment. They're given the impression that they've got to tolerate the birth mom's presence for a couple of years, at which point she'll get married, move on, have her own family, and step out of the picture. The birth moms get pushed out of the picture, because the couples are threatened, to be quite frank. We've seen it over and over again.

"We met one gal who was saying that their birth mom had been by to visit about six times during the first year. She was just appalled. We said that ours came over every week, and then every two weeks, and now we're down to about once a month. She looked at us like we were from outer space! We thought, 'Lady. What are you thinking? You got the baby! You got the prize! Share it.'

"There needs to be good work done with adoptive couples to help them build lifelong relationships with their birth moms. The days of lying to your kids and saying, 'No, you're not adopted,' have long passed."

CHAPTER 16

Counseling Clients Who Place After Parenting

"We often talk about what it's going to be like to meet their brother one day."

—Sandra, birth mother, now age 38

One of a peer counselor's more unique opportunities is to work with a woman who has children, but for whom placing a subsequent child is the best option. Counselors often make the mistake of assuming that because a client is married or parenting, she would never seriously consider adoption. For some women, however, parenting yet another child is not a possibility. If the adoption option is not presented, a client may choose abortion instead, a decision that will adversely affect herself, her children and, of course, the unborn baby.

To a woman who is successfully rearing one or more children, the mere mention of the word 'adoption' may seem puzzling or insulting. A counselor should carefully explain that although the possibility of placing may seem outlandish to some, there are women who decide that parenting is not in the best interests of either themselves or their children. A harried single mother struggling to support a toddler may find the prospect of rearing another child daunting, especially since she already has so little time to herself. A married woman with older children may find an unplanned pregnancy equally disconcerting: even if she has the financial resources to raise the child, she may not feel physically or emotionally able to begin changing diapers and enduring temper tantrums all over again.

Women who choose to place after parenting, a peer counselor should emphasize, are typically good mothers. Many have risen to the challenge of parenting in less than ideal circumstances and have well-adjusted, healthy children as proof. Because of circumstances beyond their control, however, they have pursued the avenue of adoption. Unable to control their circumstances, they have taken control of the situation by making a life-affirming choice and sacrifice.

WHY WOMEN PLACE

Twenty-two-year-old Anjali came into the Center with an active three-year-old in tow. As the toddler proceeded to rid a shelf of its books, Anjali tearfully described her current predicament. A single mother, she had managed to procure a flexible job that allowed her to spend sufficient time with her son. When a promising new boyfriend entered her life, however, the stability she had worked so hard for began to unravel. Four months pregnant, Anjali knew that if she had to parent a second child, she would need an additional part-time job and a less cramped, more expensive, apartment. Her time and affection, Anjali realized, would be divided unequally between the two children, her eldest being short-changed as she struggled to meet the demands of an infant. She too would pay a price: her goal of taking evening classes at a local college would never materialize.

Anjali's fears were not unfounded. Studies have shown that single mothers who successfully parent their first child will have lower success rates with each subsequent child. For a single mother whose ability to parent will be compromised by an additional child, adoption can be an attractive option. In Anjali's case, her decision to place enabled her to pursue her diploma, while meeting her son's physical and emotional needs. Her daughter, in turn, was given a two-parent family that allowed her to remain in contact with her birth mother and half-brother.

Women who place after parenting are not always young or motivated to place due to financial constraints. For Abby, a 31-year-old mother of one, the decision was made to preserve her marriage. During a particularly rocky period, Abby and her husband went their separate ways. The couple decided to reconcile their differences six months later, but by then, Abby was already pregnant through a friend who had taken his role as her 'comforter' too far. The couple decided against parenting for fear that the child would not be fully accepted by Abby's husband. The baby, they realized, would serve as a constant reminder of the affair.

In the case of Lehana, the decision to place was made for her children's benefit. Having reared three children single-handedly for six years, the 41-year-old knew how thin she would be spread in caring for a fourth. Her greatest concern was the burden that a new infant would place on her 11-year-old daughter, for she recognized that she could not raise the baby without the young girl's assistance. Unwilling to deprive her daughter of her childhood, Lehana chose to place instead.

Leah, a 37-year-old mother of two, also placed for her children's sake. After going through a bitter divorce, Leah became involved with the friend of an acquaintance. The relationship was short-lived: her lover announced that he was married and wanted nothing more to do with Leah or the unborn child. Leah's ex-husband, in turn, used the romantic liaison as evidence that she was an unfit mother. Facing a long custody battle, as well as the stress of entering the workforce after thirteen years as a homemaker, Leah realized that she could not raise an infant by herself. Her decision to place was finalized when she recognized how emotionally insecure the divorce had made her two children. By placing her baby in a secure, stable home, Leah was able to direct her energy into the children who needed her more.

Women who place after parenting are intimately acquainted with the concept of sacrifice. Rather than choosing abortion or to bring a newborn into a less than ideal situation, these women face intense grief for the good of their marriages, their children, and themselves. Ironically, a client will often feel like a selfish failure if she benefits from her choice. In reality, placing a child for adoption was the greatest sacrifice she could have made for her child.

THE CHALLENGES OF PLACING AFTER PARENTING

Those who have never been educated about adoption are often resistant to the concept of openness. When faced with the convoluted scenario of a parent who is placing her children's sibling, many balk at the mere suggestion that an open relationship is possible. Even the birth mother may feel compelled to close the adoption, recognizing the additional complications brought on by her status as a parent.

Part of the reality of living in the 21st Century is that life is extremely complicated. A peer counselor should remind the client that the days of the cohesive, two-parent family have passed. Many children are now being raised by single parents or by couples who have combined their families into new units. Children may have an assortment of parents, being shuffled between households and living with full-siblings, half-siblings, step-siblings, or cousins. Part of effective parenting consists not so much of making life uncomplicated, but of helping children navigate through these complications. In a situation that is less than ideal, a good parent can help her children acquire valuable life skills.

In planning an open adoption, a client must first consider what will be most beneficial for her children. Today, the trend in North America is toward greater openness in adoption, and a woman who is seeking a closed adoption should carefully consider the long-term repercussions. When her children become adults, will they resent the fact that they had little or no contact with their adopted sibling? How will the children feel when they meet their sibling for the first time as adults? What are the benefits of maintaining ongoing contact, and do they outweigh the disadvantages?

Both the birth mother and the adoptive couple need to understand that the adoption plan should not be based on what will make the adults comfortable but on meeting the needs of the children involved. Many adopted children embrace their flesh-and-blood siblings without reservation. Whereas an adopted child may resent its birth mother for placing, it will not feel rejected by its siblings, knowing that they had no control over the situation. Should adults stand in the way of a friendship due to insecurity, both the adoptee and its siblings may be deprived of a fulfilling, lifelong connection.

Part of ensuring that this connection will be maintained is to anticipate and address sources of potential conflict between the birth mother and the adoptive couple. When a birth mother has never parented, the adoptive mother will enjoy an additional sense of security. If she is older and more mature than the birth mother, and has a stable marriage and a home, she may feel a sense of superiority, knowing that she has the tools required to be a more effective parent. A young birth mother may very well look up to her.

If a birth mother is also a parent, however, the dynamic will change considerably. There is the distinct possibility that the birth mother will be the same age or older than the adoptive parents. If the adoptive couple has not parented before, the birth mother may prove intimidating. She may inwardly resent the way in which the adoptive parents are rearing the child, and may be prone to offering unwanted advice. The type of animosity seen in the relationship between a mother-in-law and her daughter-in-law can easily surface. The adoptive mother will be more prone to question whether she is, in fact, a 'real' mother.

In order to prevent the formation of an adversarial relationship, a birth mother may deliberately choose to place with an older couple or a couple that is already parenting. She should strive to affirm the adoptive mother, praising the child and the way it is being parented. She should also avoid being possessive or motherly at all costs, knowing that her actions may sabotage the relationship.

The birth mother should be warned that her unique situation may conjure up emotions unfelt by other birth mothers. When she sees that the adoptive child and its siblings share similar personality traits, for example, she may question why she is parenting one, and not the other. She may feel guilty for favoring the company of the adopted child to the children she is parenting, or, conversely, for feeling closer to the children she has kept. A birth mother may also find herself pondering what the family dynamic would have been like had she decided against placing. These feelings, the client should be assured, are normal.

SHOULD PEER COUNSELORS SERVE AS CHILD PSYCHOLOGISTS?

One question that is commonly raised by peer counselors is whether they have a responsibility to deal with children directly. Should part of a Pregnancy Center's mandate be not only to support birth mothers, but their children as well?

The answer is a definitive 'no.' Counselors are neither equipped nor trained to work with children. To move beyond the role of a peer counselor is inappropriate, especially since a child's emotional well-being is at stake. If the situation requires outside help, clients should be put in contact with a qualified chartered psychologist or a certified social worker with experience in the area of adoption.

CHILDREN AND THE LOSS OF A SIBLING

Women often fear the repercussions of 'robbing' their children of a sibling. Can a young child, they ask, understand the complex circumstances surrounding the adoption? Will it believe that any child can be 'given away' at its mother's whim? Will the loss and consequent grief be emotionally harmful? Will a child forever resent its mother for separating it from flesh and blood? Can the separation of siblings ever be justified?

Many of these concerns are legitimate. If a child is old enough to observe that its mother is pregnant, it will naturally want to know why it cannot have a new brother or sister. The child may eagerly anticipate the arrival of its sibling, only to have its mother return home empty-handed and emotionally distraught. Even a child who is too young to understand the significance of its mother's swollen belly will be painfully aware that all is not well in its family. It may even believe itself to be the source of the tension that it cannot name.

Honesty is critical. A common tendency is to try to shield children, putting up a brave front to conceal grief. Some women believe that their children are unaware of the turmoil, when, in reality, the secrecy around the adoption is creating significant anxiety. Children are not fools: they will sense that something is wrong but will be too afraid to ask questions. In most cases, a secret will do more damage than the truth.

If a woman chooses to place, she should explain her decision long before the baby arrives. A child will suffer unnecessarily if it is allowed to anticipate the baby's birth, only to discover, during the last month of the pregnancy, that the infant will not be coming home. At the same time, the client should be committed to placing before she tells her children. As in any adoption scenario, no decision is final until the baby is born and the papers are signed. However, there is a period of indecision for most women. If, during this time of uncertainty, a client openly flip-flops between placing and parenting, her children may assume that she is double-minded and question the wisdom of her decision.

During the period of decision-making, clients should be warned that small children have disproportionately large ears. A mother, in other words, should avoid confiding in other adults when there is a risk of being overheard. She should also limit her confidants to a select group of trusted people. Adoption should be an approachable topic, but not one that is freely discussed at length within the hearing range of a child.

When the adoption decision is first introduced, clients should be prepared to answer difficult questions. When one woman told her three children about her adoption plan, the youngest begged her not to go through with her decision. "Don't give my brother away, Mommy," the four-year-old pleaded. "I don't want to be the baby anymore. I want someone else to be the baby." In response, the client affirmed that the decision would make everyone sad, but explained why it was the best for everybody—including the little girl.

A perceptive child may assume that since a baby can be 'given away,' it too might be placed for adoption. In order to prevent anxiety and insecurity, the client should address this issue directly, regardless of whether the child has expressed concern. A client might say, for example, "I'm placing this baby for adoption. Do you think I might place you one day?" Once the child responds, the mother can explain that from the moment she knew about this child, she made a 'forever' commitment to parent. Now, however, the family's circumstances have changed and life has become more complex. The new baby, the mother can explain, will be given a 'forever family' of its own, one that will love it very much. And even though it will live with its new family, its birth family will always love it too.

Children should be invited to voice their doubts, insecurities, and anger. The reality that every person in the family will experience these emotions should not be concealed. Birth mothers are often afraid to exhibit their grief, leaving children to assume that the unspoken sadness is their fault. If a client can allow herself to cry in front of her children, or to openly admit that she is having 'a sad day,' her children too will feel permission to grieve. Families can even weep together, sharing the pain of missing a baby.

Balance, of course, is crucial. A woman should not have a breakdown in front of her children or publicly sob on a daily basis, for her children will be unable to process pain of this intensity. Likewise, there is no need to have a family discussion after each counseling session a woman attends. If a birth mother avoids processing her own grief, however, she will convey the message that like its mother, the child has no right to grieve the loss of its sibling. An unhealthy pattern can be set up in front of inquisitive eyes: when grief comes, work harder and get on with one's life.

In addition to grieving the loss of a sibling, children must also overcome other obstacles. Since a woman who places after parenting may have become pregnant through an inappropriate or adulterous relationship, her children may be exposed to uncomfortable realities. For a child who has reached puberty, the mere thought that its mother is a sexual being is extremely disconcerting. Equally mortifying to the birth mother may be the prospect of having to explain an illicit affair and to face condemnation by her own child. In some instances, women opt for abortion rather than face the judgment of their adolescent children.

To complicate matters, children will inevitably be confronted by their friends and peers. Young children are prone to announcing, to one and all, that their mother is having a baby that will be given away once it is born. The origin of the baby—and why someone would rid herself of an infant after going to the effort of creating it—can become a popular topic among a class of first graders. Among older or savvier children, questions about the birth mother's motives and integrity make come in to play.

Once again, a client must be straightforward with her children. Before problems arise, she can approach a younger child's teachers at school and explain the situation and how it might impact the child's behavior over the next year. She can ask the child directly what its friends are saying about the situation. If the birth mother became pregnant through an affair, and negative criticisms or rumors are circulating, she should speak age appropriate truth into her child's life. She might say, for example, that she made a poor decision and cared for a man that would not make 'a good daddy.' Although she made a mistake, she can emphasize, the baby's life was never a mistake. The infant was made for a purpose, a purpose that it will discover in its adoptive family.

If a birth mother has children who are adolescents, honesty is imperative. Choosing a seemingly easy way out of the situation, such as procuring an abortion, may prove detrimental. A fourteen-year-old girl who discovers that her mother has had an affair and an abortion, for example, will have fewer reservations when it comes to her own sexual behavior. The message the birth mother is conveying is clear: when in trouble, take the easy way out and be sure to cover your tracks. In contrast, children will respect a parent who can admit that she made a mistake and will do what needs to be done to amend the situation. Although a birth mother may be judged to some extent, she will not lose the credibility she would have had her children stumbled upon a secret.

Some of the most destructive criticism may come from the children's own father. If the marriage has dissolved, or if the pregnancy was rooted in the woman's infidelity, her ex-husband may throw the adoption in her face. Revenge can be easily had if a man can pit the children against their mother by using the adoption as a source of ammunition.

If a man attempts to use the adoption as proof that the birth mother is a bad person, she should openly admit that she made a mistake and ask for the children's forgiveness. The client should then take the highroad, resisting the urge to return the criticism. The counselor can remind an indignant birth mother that her children's identities are inextricably linked to the identity of their parents; to denigrate the reputation of one parent is to attack the personhood of each of his children.

INCORPORATING SIBLINGS INTO AN OPEN ADOPTION

As the due date approaches, the client should carefully plan the hospital experience. She should consider which of her children should visit, measuring the pros and cons of each individual child based on its age, temperament, and interest. One child may long to meet its new sibling, while another might be too young, anxious, or unaware to benefit from the experience.

Since hospitals can be frightening places, mothers should prepare their children for what they will encounter. More importantly, a client should repeatedly emphasize that the baby will not be coming home. A child will often harbor the fantasy that the adoption plan will change once the baby is born and everyone sees how beautiful it is. Other children will realize, upon meeting their siblings for the first time, what they are about to lose. Mothers should anticipate an objection or a passionate outburst, and respond graciously. When the daughter of one client begged to mother the child herself, her mother graciously replied, "I think it's wonderful that you're so generous and loving to your sister, but this decision is best for everyone."

Women who are parents should strive to maintain some level of openness for the sake of their children. When an open adoption closes, the result is devastating to both the birth mother and the children involved. A woman should therefore avoid building the expectation in her children that they will visit their sibling every two weeks. Since some relationships will not last, the client should be prepared for the worst. If the relationship dissolves, she should reassure her children that although they will not see their sibling for a long time, they will undoubtedly connect with their brother or sister as adults. The majority of adult adoptees contact their siblings when they are older, and many forge lasting bonds.

In some scenarios, an adoptive relationship will create a different problem altogether. When a child visits its sibling, it may very well observe that the child who was 'given away' actually ended up in a preferable environment. In addition to losing a sibling, the older child may have had a chaotic life, being raised by a single mother, being forced to watch a marriage dissolve, or simply living in a low-income household in which every penny had to be accounted for. Its adopted sibling, in contrast, may have become the shining star in the lives of two amazing, loving, stable parents, living in a large house with every toy imaginable. To add to the older child's resentment, the adopted child will likely be blissfully unaware of the circumstances surrounding its birth or the intense pain caused by the adoption.

When the discrepancy is obvious, a child may bluntly state that it would like to be adopted as well. Resentment may last into adulthood: some siblings of adult adoptees have reported wishing that they had also been placed. Women must therefore be prepared to explain why a child cannot live with the adoptive couple. This issue can be extremely painful; counselors must weigh the maturity level of a client before bringing up the topic, as some women will be unable to interpret this concern as anything but a criticism.

If a client has serious concerns about her children's ability to cope with the issues surrounding adoption, she should be advised to seek family counseling. A peer counselor can help her to locate a psychologist who specializes in children or to find other resources available to women caught in difficult circumstances.

THE QUESTION OF HOME VISITS

A client with children may request to have a session in the context of her own home. In some cases, medical limitations may make a home visit the only option, and a counselor can go after receiving authorization from the director of her Center. However, in the majority of cases, home visits are counterproductive and should be discouraged. Because the children are in a familiar environment, they will likely cast off their best behavior and interrupt the session. Furthermore, when a birth mother and her counselor meet in a non-professional setting, the dynamic of the relationship can change. Rather than maintaining a counselor/client dichotomy, the tendency is to become pals, a dynamic that can easily limit the peer counselor's ability to lead and direct conversations that will facilitate the adoption process.

Pregnancy Centers should be prepared to accommodate women with children. One counselor found a creative way to hold a productive session despite the presence of two youthful guests. Her client, a single mom for whom child care was not a financial possibility, brought her two small children into the Center. Rather than feeling impatient or annoyed by the spirited toddlers, the counselor set up a video in the next room and asked another counselor to periodically check in on the children. She then reassured the client that it was more important that she follow through with her commitment to attend regular counseling sessions than it was to worry about the disruptions her children might cause.

HELPING CHILDREN GRIEVE

Children do not have the luxury of weekly counseling at a Pregnancy Center, nor can they turn to a peer for advice. A client may therefore find herself in a difficult position, serving as her children's primary counselor while concealing a good portion of her own grief. Unlike a birth mother who has no children, she must maintain her composure, running a family during times of great emotional and physical stress.

The following suggestions can be used by clients to help children understand and prepare for the loss of a sibling.

Enlist the help of another trusted adult

An intuitive child who senses how painful the adoption is for her mother will often avoid raising the subject for fear of hurting her mother even more. Another child may feel divided: although loyal to his mother, he may also experience significant anger, believing that she is needlessly burdening the family through her selfish decision. An unusually sensitive child, in turn, may cling to the fantasy that she can alter the situation by taking care of the infant herself or assuming the responsibility of making her mother happy again.

A favorite aunt, a close adult friend, or a playmate's mother can be a safe person in whom a child can confide. A client should be encouraged to ask a familiar, trusted friend to verbally reinforce her decision to place and to act as a sounding board for the children. The children's confidant may choose to attend a counseling session with the client in order to prepare for the difficult task at hand.

Prepare a family album for the adopted child

Children can be included in some of the most meaningful rituals in the adoption process—the creation of a 'Dear Baby' letter and the selection of a gift. Sifting through family pictures to create a photo album or searching for a treasure in a local toy store can be beneficial on several levels. First, young children will be able to connect the pregnancy with a real child. Their unborn sibling will become a person instead of a difficult concept. Second, the immense value of this unborn child will be affirmed. Children can see, first-hand, that rather than being shuffled off to a complete stranger, the baby is being lovingly placed, valued, and remembered. Third, the process of working together as a family will create a sense of cohesion. Joy—and grief—need not isolate the members of a family.

Gifts given to the placed child can have a symbolic significance, connecting it to its siblings. For example, both the baby and a sibling can receive matching teddy bears. If the older child has a favorite book, the birth mother can deliberately buy the adopted sibling an identical copy.

"Dear Baby" letters often prove especially meaningful. An older child can tell the baby all about himself in a letter, while a younger child can express herself by creating a special drawing for the baby. If a family decides to create a photo album or a scrapbook, each child can contribute, selecting a favorite photograph, decorating a page with pencil crayons or felts, or writing down a favorite memory.

Give each child a journal

One client who kept a journal realized that her children might also benefit from this mode of self-expression. Since her two sons and her daughter had observed her recording her thoughts, they were pleased when she gave them each a small journal. The woman's youngest son, who had not yet learned to write, was encouraged to draw what he felt. Whenever he observed his siblings journaling, he too would enthusiastically 'write' in his journal, though not all of his drawings were on topic. The client eventually observed that when her children processed their grief, her own grief process was validated.

Read age-appropriate books on adoption

One of the exciting fringe benefits of the open adoption movement is the proliferation of books geared to children around adoption. The majority of these books are aimed at helping adoptees understand their unique status and place in the family constellation. However, children whose siblings are to be placed will also benefit from these books. Their mother's explanations will be reinforced by the authority of the printed word.

A client can introduce a picture book by saying, "Maybe your baby sister's adoptive family will read her this book when she's your age," and then draw correlations between the protagonist's experience and the child's. An older child, in turn, can read novels or real life accounts in which adoptees share their experiences.

Create rituals to commemorate the adopted sibling

Children can be given the opportunity to participate in rituals that will help them revisit their grief. At Christmas, for example, a child can make a Christmas tree ornament for its adopted sibling or create a special card. The family may hang up a stocking decorated with the adopted child's name.

It is crucial, however, to respect each child's individual needs. No child should be forced to participate in a ritual. For some children, the grieving process may take two weeks, since that which is out of sight is also out of mind. If a child is forced to grieve as an adult would, it may develop an unhealthy fixation with its absent sibling. Birth mothers should be reminded that each child will grieve in its own way and according to its emotional capability. As a child goes through different developmental stages, so too will its interpretation of the adoption. A three-year-old will respond differently to the loss of its sibling by the time it reaches the age of six.

In order to give a child the opportunity to participate in rituals, while respecting its right to be inconsistent or disinterested, a birth mother can give the child a picture of itself with its sibling, or leave a photo album in an accessible place. The child can then feel a connection with its sibling whenever the need arises.

IN THEIR OWN WORDS

Sandra's Story

"I had been separated from my husband for six months when I fell into an unhealthy relationship. Three weeks later, on my thirtieth birthday, I found out I was pregnant.

"I was a single mom at home with three children under the age of ten. My ex was trying to convince me that I was mentally ill and couldn't parent the three children I had. I didn't know what I was going to do, or where I was going to turn.

"My very first reaction was to get an abortion, since it would have been so easy. That lasted a day. At that point, I went for professional counseling.

"At the beginning, the counseling was more about me than the pregnancy—getting me healthy, so that I could make healthy choices.

"As much as I wanted the baby, I didn't know if I could parent another child. I didn't know if I'd crack: I already had as much on my plate as I could handle.

"I was watching my children go back and forth between their dad's house and my house, and I could not see doing that to another child. The children had so much on their plates already, going through the divorce and dealing with the anger, the pain, the fighting, the conflict. Having a baby on top of all that would have been the straw that broke the camel's back.

"My counselor recommended that I go to the Pregnancy Care Centre. So I met with a peer counselor who educated me about the reality of adoption. At first I couldn't wrap my head around adoption. I believed, as I learned later, some of the myths, like 'How could I love a child, and yet give it away?'

"Some weeks I would go home completely intending to release this baby for adoption. Then I'd see my peer counselor again and go home thinking, 'I'm keeping this baby!'

"As the months went by, whenever I would lean towards wanting to keep the baby and parent, I had tension and turmoil inside. And then when I began to think about adoption, or read books and articles about it, I had peace. It was the weirdest thing: how could I have peace about this decision?

"I began to follow these feelings of peace and contentment, and to seriously consider releasing for adoption.

"I told my children fairly early on that I was considering adoption. It was really hard: I had to spend a lot of time reassuring them that they were born into a marriage with a mommy and a daddy who loved them very much, that they were planned and wanted. I didn't want them to think that I could give them away too.

"My situation was particularly difficult because my ex-husband was counteracting what I was saying. When the children went to his house for the weekend, they would come back Sunday night and tell me that he had said, 'How could she give up her baby?'

"My eight-year-old was particularly distraught when she came home. She said, 'That's my brother. How could you give my brother away?'

"I was really open and honest with her, explaining that there was only so much of Mommy to go around. I said that I didn't plan this pregnancy, that I had made some poor choices, and that now I needed to make the best choices I could. I said that as much as I loved this baby, I didn't have enough love and energy to be a good mom to him. I talked a lot about how there wasn't a father for this child. I stressed that this baby needed a mommy, a daddy, and a home that loved him, and then I talked about people that couldn't have babies.

"Jordan, my youngest, really didn't have much trouble with it.

"My oldest son, Joshua, was like, 'Please tell me we're not going to have this baby!' He remembered what it was like when we had Jordan—how exhausted I was and how much energy it took to have a baby around. He was dreading the thought that another baby would come in, and that it would be just the four of us taking care of him.

"I had to be careful to let him know that this was my decision. I didn't want Joshua to feel like he could be part of the reason why we didn't keep this baby.

"My daughter Madeleine was emotionally attached to the baby. I felt a lot of guilt that I had brought this onto her plate. I basically continued to reassure her that she was chosen, prepared for, planned for, and wanted.

"As for me, I kept myself at a distance from the situation. Being a mom, I felt like the three kids I had were my whole life and my whole world. I thought, 'If I allow myself to bond with this baby at all, I won't be able to follow through with the adoption.'

"I came up with an adoption plan. I wanted the parents to be financially stable, because if the finances were okay, that would be one huge thing out of the way in terms of their marriage and the amount of stress they had to deal with. I wanted them to have been married for a long time, and to have adopted a child already. I didn't want my son to be the only adopted child in the family, and I wanted to know that the couple's parenting skills were good.

"I read through a bunch of portfolios, and when I got to the family I ended up picking, I just had peace. So much of my world was guided by peace then. I was all over the place in terms of my mind and my emotions, and I was trying to become healthy and understand what's good in a family. The one thing that was constant was the peace—and the 'not peace.' I tended to move wherever I had peace, and I had complete peace about this couple.

"When Austin was born, I knew what a miracle he was and thought about how much he looked like his dad. I cried a lot, but part of me was detached. It was nothing like holding Madeleine, or Joshua, or Jordan. I honestly felt like he was somebody else's child.

"It was like I was so sure that I needed to place that I tempted myself in certain ways to see if I could keep him. I nursed him because I thought that maybe if I did that, I wouldn't be able to give him up—that that would be the attachment that wouldn't let me follow through with my decision.

"It wasn't. I still knew what I had to do.

"I didn't let the kids come to the hospital because they were very young and I thought it would be harder for them to let go of Austin if they did. I didn't want to bring them any more pain, and to be honest, I don't know if I could have handled seeing the kids with the baby.

"After the court date, the adoptive couple asked to see me and I took Joshua with me. He got to hold Austin, and when we went home, I cried.

"While I was still pregnant, I chose to have a semi-open adoption. Being a mom, and very set in my ways as a parent, I was afraid I'd want to tell them how to parent that baby. I also thought it would be so painful to see him.

"After having the baby, I just got through the first couple of years. But as I started learning more about open adoption, and as I became healthier, I realized that it would have been good to be part of my child's life—for me, and for him, and for the adoptive couple.

"I called the couple up and they let me meet Austin. He was three years old. That was really strange because he was so much like Madeleine—they were almost identical. It was so overwhelming because Madeleine was the one who seemed so attached to him throughout the whole pregnancy, and still, to this day, is the one to come and ask questions about her brother.

"I kept saying to the couple, over and over, 'He's just like Madeleine.' I'm sure that scared them because in the end, they decided not to open up the adoption.

"Still, I left with a sense of joy that he was healthy and had a lovely home and lots of love and support—everything that he needed. As much as I was hurt, and sad, and missing him, I just knew things were going to be okay.

"In terms of the children, it's been the hardest for Madeleine through the years. Whenever we get packages—letters, and photos, and artwork Austin has made—I show her. In the first years, Madeleine just cried and said, 'It's not fair! I wish you never gave him away!'

"I just had to allow her to have those feelings. We had a lot of conversations, and I let her cry and hugged her, and said that it's okay to feel this way, but I still believed it was the best decision. Austin was in a wonderful home.

"Sometimes after I've gone to birth mother's celebrations, I'll talk to Madeleine about the different moms that have come and shared stories of how their sons and daughters have grown up, and how they've gotten together. She's much better now.

"I don't regret choosing adoption. My children had more of me; they had me more as a whole person and a whole mommy. I believe I was able to give my children more love and more security than I would have with this baby.

"Austin has a very solid home and a whole family that hasn't suffered through a divorce. In that sense, he has so much more than my kids have.

"My children have learned a lot through this experience. They've learned that you should hold your head up high, and that you're worth something and valuable even when you do make mistakes.

"As for me, I was able to grow and rise above where I was when I got pregnant."

CHAPTER SEVENTEEN

Spiritual Care

"I want my daughter to know that she is the reason I'm here. For a long time I didn't feel like God was real. Now I know He is: I just have to look at her to see God in my life."

—Chantal, birth mother, age 30

At the heart of PCC ministry is a desire to reach people with the truth of the Gospel, recognizing that the most significant gift a client can leave with is a personal relationship with Jesus Christ. Opportunities are ample, for adoption counseling is, by nature, long-term and supportive. Because women are led through an initial point of crisis and a complex grief process to a state of resolution, both counselor and client enter deep emotional and spiritual terrain. The opportunity to present the Gospel arises from the relationship that develops during this vulnerable state and is directly proportionate to the level of care that a woman is given. A client will most vividly see Christ, in other words, in a counselor who is physically and emotionally present in the midst of her pain, showing consistency and integrity.

CARING FOR A CLIENT SPIRITUALLY

The essence of spiritual care is prayer. Before a client even steps in the door of the Center, a peer counselor can minister to her, praying that God will turn a pregnancy scare or an unplanned child into a significant spiritual experience. By bringing a client before God, a counselor will be reminded of the woman's value and of God's hand in a life that seems out of control. Prayer will also unite Pregnancy Center staff in a common purpose. For an anxious counselor dealing with a particularly difficult or emotionally draining client, prayer can be a powerful reminder that she is not isolated from her colleagues.

Prayer can even become a habit among the unchurched. One effective, non-invasive way of bringing the spiritual into conversation is to suggest that a client pray for her child on a daily basis. Even a birth mother with no religious background will find prayer a tangible way to care for her child. For most women, the miracle of creating a new life brings a new spiritual dimension into focus; a client will start to look beyond life's surface and past herself. As she beings to pray, she will also begin to question to whom she is praying. A counselor can find a spiritual point of reference—something as basic as a woman's belief in an afterlife—and open the door to further discussion.

If a birth mother is receptive, her counselor should emphasize that the life she has carried was never a mistake, in God's eyes, but a priceless human being entrusted to her. Although she may not be able to physically rear her child, she can become its spiritual parent. What child, after all, would not be deeply comforted to know that someone has been passionately praying for it every day of its life? The client, in turn, will begin to see that she is part of something remarkable, rather than the cause of something shameful.

Prayer can also give the birth mother a sense of hope. On occasion, a client will search endlessly through potential adoptive couples, rejecting them all in the belief that the 'perfect couple' exists. A birth mother of this sort can be encouraged to make the best choice possible, and then to trust God. By praying for her child and its parents, she can find comfort and a sense of control when she feels most powerless. Even if the adoption is closed at some point, she will still have a connection with her child that can never be severed.

A client who comes to faith after placing will find great consolation in the power of prayer. If she placed her child in a non-Christian home, she may experience considerable anxiety about whether the child will ever be exposed to the faith that has impacted her own life. Once again, the birth mother can become proactive, trusting that God will heed her prayers. A counselor can also point out, in this scenario, that there is no guarantee that a child placed in a religious home will become a genuine Christian. Likewise, when God has his heart set on a child, no upbringing, however godless, can keep the two apart.

A peer counselor need not always be the one to initiate a spiritual discussion. Often the adoption process itself will bring women to a point of spiritual awakening. For some women, the entrustment ceremony proves a significant marker. With formality and ceremony come memories of other spiritual events, including weddings or funerals that clients have attended in the past. Women with some religious background often desire to have a priest or pastor officiate the ceremony, thus reopening a door that may have been closed for years.

Birth Mothers' Support Groups can also mark the beginning of a spiritual experience. Group facilitators may choose resources and materials that reflect a Christian philosophy, but should be careful to edit them in a way that will prevent clients from feeling preached at or alienated. Indeed, it is the clients within the group that are often the most eager and effective evangelists. Birth mothers rarely have an agenda when sharing their stories; they will relate, without pretension, the impact that the adoption process has had on their spiritual journey. Other women are unlikely to feel threatened by a peer who expresses a belief that God's hand has been evident at certain points in the adoption process. Adoption is, after all, a spiritual process that taps into needs that these women may only be beginning to sense.

Although group leaders should not shy away from discussing spiritual issues, they should always allow clients to ask the questions. Because birth mothers are particularly vulnerable, a respectful counselor will consciously avoid pushing them in a spiritual direction. The Holy Spirit will have far more impact than any manipulative or heavy-handed tactic, however well-intentioned.

The Postmodern Client

Today's client can often seem enigmatic, for her values and world view may differ radically from the views held by her more senior counselor. There is, in fact, a tremendous gap between the philosophies of baby boomers—post-war babies who made their debut between 1946 and 1964—and the children of Generation X who were born after 1964.

Generation X ers and 'Millennials'—those who came of age at the turn of the century—tend to see the world through a postmodern lens. Whereas baby boomers relied on reason in the search for truth ("I think, therefore I am"), Generation X ers dismiss the notion of one coherent truth and pursue their individual paths with the dictum, "I feel, therefore I am." While boomers subscribed to a secular humanist philosophy, believing that the world was getting better and that problems could be solved through social engineering, Generation X ers believe that the solutions imposed by their parents' generation only created larger problems.

Known also as members of the 'latchkey' or 'lonely' generation, Generation X ers have had to contend with issues of abandonment caused by absent parents. Naturally cynical, they generally view their parents' materialism and workaholic drive with disdain. To them, relationships and community hold paramount value.

Although many have never set foot in a church, members of Generation X are extremely receptive to spiritual ideas. However, the 'four spiritual laws' that convicted past generations will only offend this generation. The imposition of any spiritual 'law' is repugnant to those whose highest value is 'tolerance' and the belief that each individual has the right to pursue his own form of truth. Furthermore, members of Generation X resent being 'told' anything; real communication takes place through dialogue, and only after a relationship has been established. An invitation to describe their spiritual journeys can open doors that authoritative preaching has slammed shut.

In the postmodern world, the process of conversion is a lengthy one. Whereas the majority of baby boomers have had some exposure to Christian teachings, Generation X ers are, as a whole, biblically illiterate. They may be vaguely familiar with Christ's death and resurrection, but wholly ignorant of its significance. Therefore, in order to grasp the concept of salvation, X ers must first be taught the fundamentals of the Gospel. These basic truths must then be repeated: a decision will typically be reached only after the Gospel has been presented, in its entirety, fourteen times (compared to seven times for baby boomers). Finally, the new Christian should be given time to contend with biblical teachings, one truth at a time. Despite the authenticity of an X er's commitment, she will inevitably have difficulty accepting the concept of absolute biblical truth because of her notion that everything is subjective. Revelation will inevitably be an ongoing experience.

10 Tips for Reaching Generation X

1. Avoid using 'Christianese,' or religious jargon. Words such as 'justification' and 'sanctification' will mean nothing to a non-believer, let alone fifty percent of Christians!

2. Witnessing should not be a scheduled event, and conversion will seldom follow a timetable. While one woman may be immediately receptive to the Gospel in its entirety, another may remain closed for months, or even years. Share only when the timing is prompted by the Holy Spirit.

3. Prayer and preparation are critical. Before a counseling session begins, pray that God will help you to be the person that this particular client needs. Some women may require a compassionate listener; others may respond to a more confrontational style of counseling.

4. Avoid the temptation to share a gospel of 'tolerance.' Although members of Generation X will be drawn to God's unconditional love, they must also be introduced to his holiness. X ers may balk at the idea of a God who holds them accountable for their actions. However, your objective is to share the truth, not to make clients feel good.

5. Throw out the formulas. Generation X ers will not respond to a processed religious package, but can be reached through dialogue. Ask questions and allow the client to discover the answers herself.

6. Be transparent. Remember that you do not have all of the answers, nor are you immune to grief or anger. Clients will respect a counselor that is human and vulnerable.

7. Commitment is essential. Always follow through with your word.

8. If a client makes a decision for Christ, recognize that her journey is only beginning. She will need to be taught the fundamentals of the faith, encouraged to join a church, and nurtured into a mature believer who will, in turn, reach others.

9. Do not despair if a new 'Christian' mixes Buddhism, New Age philosophy, and a smattering of Wicca into her faith. The tendency to blend the best of each faith is common. Trust that the Holy Spirit will cull out that which is untrue.

10. Always remember that no woman will walk through your door by accident: clients are there by divine appointment. The most outrageous, hopeless, or vulgar woman may also prove to be the most spiritually receptive.

From the Postmodern, to the Pew

One peer counselor, a member of Generation X, came to know Christ as a pregnant teenager. Craving contact with God, "Semira" frequently joined her friends at a nearby restaurant to explore the unknown through animated conversation and spiritual speculation. Fuelled by drug highs, the group of teenagers explored the ideas presented in such works as James Redfield's popular spiritual manual, *The Celestine Prophecy.*

Semira's introduction to the faith came from an unlikely source. Her best friend had a brother who, after being arrested and charged for stealing a car, was required to perform community service. His encounter with the law led him to a local church where he was asked to do yard work and other basic maintenance. Enamored with neither lawn nor garden, he chose instead to sit upon the church steps, strumming his guitar. The youth pastor found him and said that if he wrote a song about Jesus, he could consider his community service with the church complete. The teenager quickly became excited about the church, and in his enthusiasm, invited both his sister and Semira.

When recounting her experience, Semira cannot name a specific date in which she became a Christian. A typical Generation X er, what she does know is that her gradual coming to Christ occurred because a youth pastor had established a relationship, genuinely caring for and counseling the small group of teens. Semira was deeply moved when this very pastor, after committing a serious sin, returned to the church, made a sincere confession, and was received with grace.

Having experienced an unplanned pregnancy and the trials of early parenthood, Semira longed to help other women in crisis. When she came to the Pregnancy Care Center, eager to volunteer, she considered herself a Christian, but did not yet understand some of the fundamentals of her faith. Only after reading some of the material the Center offered and consulting the Bible did she realize that she could no longer hold a pro-choice stance. And, true to her generation, it took Semira over a year to recognize the contradiction of professing Christianity while living with her boyfriend. Discipled by mature Christians, Semira continued to grow and to re-examine her beliefs. Today, few would question the authenticity of her faith.

EVANGELISM

For some peer counselors, the word 'evangelism' evokes distasteful images. It is often viewed as a mandatory part of being a Christian, an activity fraught with the danger of missing a critical opportunity or fumbling foolishly through the 'four spiritual laws' with an equally uncomfortable client. While a peer counselor will probably be required to venture out of her comfort zone, or to expend extra time and emotional energy in a client in crisis, evangelism need not be a traumatic experience.

Genuinely caring for a client, for example, can speak volumes. If a birth mother who is accustomed to being used and taken advantage of suddenly receives support at no cost, she will begin to take notice. Her curiosity will be further aroused when she discovers that the Center is a non-profit agency run largely by volunteers and donors. Unnerved by the unconditional love she has received, she may very well ask her peer counselor to explain why people would donate time and energy for no obvious reward. A counselor can then begin to share her faith.

Birth mothers long to be respected and will thrive in an environment in which they are affirmed. Many have to contend with disrespect on a daily basis, and despite the wisdom of their decision to place, view themselves as shameful and incapable of parenting. A peer counselor has the opportunity to put a completely different spin on the subject. When a client makes a reasoned or unselfish decision, she should be praised. If she decides to place, her strength of character can be affirmed. Even if she falters, making a poor life choice, she can be reminded of past successes and of her unchanging worth. Counselors should offer specific, concrete, genuine feedback.

Clients can also be encouraged to consider the progress they are making. Rather than seeing past failures as a record of her inadequacy, a client can begin to view significant events as signposts in her spiritual journey. A birth mother who once lived only to drink and socialize can, in retrospect, see her crisis pregnancy as a turning point. Not only did she find support at the Center, but she chose to give life and to ensure, though adoption, that the life given would be a fulfilling one. However difficult the journey, the birth mother has moved from living a life devoid of meaning to one forever changed by the creation of a new human being.

When opportunity arises, a counselor can not only share Christ's love through her compassion for a client but present the Gospel. The method of doing so will reflect individual styles. Whereas one counselor may take an intellectual approach, presenting truth in a logical, reasoned manner, another may choose to share her personal testimony, approaching the Gospel from a more emotional angle. While one counselor may be confrontational, sharing Christ in a bold manner, her colleague may prefer a less direct approach, inviting a client to attend church or a concert. Some counselors may feel comfortable with several evangelistic styles, matching their approach with the individual client's needs.

Although becoming a Christian can radically alter a woman's life, counselors should be careful to avoid presenting Christ as an alternative to grieving. Christian or not, women will inevitably experience tremendous pain as they go through the adoption process. A client who insists that she has given her burden over to God and packages her emotions into neat spiritual compartments is only deceiving herself. One counselor encountered a client who over-spiritualized everything to the point of dominating her birth mother's group with religious rhetoric. Rather than expressing anger or anguish over the child she had recently placed, the birth mother stated that she was doing well, through the grace of God. The counselor recognized signs that all was not well, including the fact that the client had not informed her family about the adoption. When gently pressed, the client fell apart, revealing her fragility and despondency.

Perhaps one of the most painful aspects of counseling is watching a client fluctuate between a spiritual awakening and obvious self-destruction. A client may choose to be abstinent, for example, and then suddenly return requesting yet another pregnancy test. Others may become involved with more serious perils. One counselor was heartbroken to learn that a client, who was close to making a commitment to Christ and piecing together the fragments of her life, chose to get inebriated during a brief relapse and was brutally raped. After months of counseling, the client appeared to be in a worse predicament than when she had first entered the Center.

However distressing, trauma is sometimes the very thing that will compel a woman to seek change. After placing her son with a Christian couple, one woman faithfully attended a birth mother's group and gave a convincing account of how well she was processing her grief. Before long, however, she disappeared, evading her peer counselor's calls and snubbing other birth mothers. Several of her concerned friends reported seeing her at parties and at bars, and eventually word spread that she was pregnant. A year later, she showed up at her birth mother's group with a four-month-old baby. She admitted that she had been previously in denial and was now prepared to deal with her grief. Her second pregnancy, she explained, had been a turning point in her life.

A client who engages in old habits while espousing new ideas is never a lost cause. One counselor was exasperated when an 18-year-old client frequented bars with her friends throughout her pregnancy, unwinding in a familiar atmosphere despite her new convictions. One day, when she was seven months pregnant, she entered an old haunt, and suddenly recognized it for what it was. "I wanted to stand up on the table and say, 'Look, this is where this gets you!'" she recounted to her counselor. From that point on, she began attending church in search of more fulfilling friendships. She eventually came to faith.

Nevertheless, the stakes are high when dealing in a ministry of this nature. If clients do not begin to resolve some of their spiritual issues throughout the adoption process, the chance that they will become pregnant again is high. A client who has placed without grieving will likely choose abortion the second time around, thinking it a less painful alternative. If spiritually nurtured, however, women may avoid compounding their grief with more poor decisions. And, even if they experience failure, they will be able to return to the Center, recognizing that the love shown there is unconditional.

IN THEIR OWN WORDS

Darla's Story

"I was raised in a Christian family, and my mom always taught me to pray. When I got pregnant at twenty-four, I went back to that.

"I had gone far away. With the relationship I was in, I was the farthest from God that I'd ever been. And my boyfriend didn't want anything to do with me or the baby.

"I went to God because the other option was suicide . . . or abortion. I went back to God, and He turned a bad thing into a really good thing. He brought John and Mary my way.

"I grew closer to Him through the situation. Even though it might sound cliché, I prayed my way through it. It was God's strength that pulled me through because on my own, I couldn't have done it."

Kendra's Story

"My journey began long before I was pregnant. I knew, growing up, that there was a God, but I didn't know anything about Him. My parents didn't go to church or talk about God, so I really knew nothing. I knew that there were a lot of religions out there, but I didn't understand what made them different, or why people believed what they believed.

"I started dating a fellow who was a Sunni Muslim. I was really interested in his religion, and was going through the process of looking into what it took to convert. And that's when I found out that I was pregnant.

"The moment I knew I was pregnant I had this overwhelming feeling that this was a gift from God. Not any God—my God. I somehow knew that I was never to be alone again.

"Throughout my pregnancy, I came to the Center for counseling. My counselor always prayed with me before I left, which was awesome. After I placed Jeremy for adoption, she prayed with me to receive the Lord. My counselor said, later, that it was the worst prayer and lead-up that she had ever done with anyone. She said it wasn't her; it was definitely a God thing. I agree that it didn't matter what she said. It wasn't about her.

"Looking back, I see that I needed Jeremy to show me the path I needed to take in life. He was—and still is—a gift from God."

Erin's Story

"I was in a self-destructive phase after I placed my daughter for adoption. Because I was so lonely and desperate for attention, I got involved with all sorts of guys looking for 'love.' But I only ended up feeling worse, especially about myself. I got severely depressed and even considered suicide at one point, but the thought of my daughter growing up to find out what I had done kept me from doing anything. I was hospitalized twice for depression and for post traumatic stress disorder after sleeping at a friend's house and being sexually assaulted by her older brother.

"When things became unbearable, I went to check in at the hospital because I was feeling suicidal once again. After I cried for hours and they still would not admit me, I became completely calm. All I could think about was how this was my last resort and since they too had shut me out, there was only one way out. I was so calm because I already knew in my head that I had a full prescription of anti-depressants and sleeping pills sitting on my nightstand at home. I planned to take those, along with some aspirin and alcohol, and fall asleep forever. I felt so low that even the thought of my daughter didn't budge my decision.

"My PCC counselor met me at the hospital. Since we had a close relationship, she immediately knew why I had become calm. I remember her begging the hospital, with tears in her own eyes, to keep me, even for just one night. They ended up keeping me in emergency overnight and then started me on an out-patient counseling program. My counselor really did save my life.

"Through all the bad things that had occurred in my life, there was one woman who never lost faith in me and prayed for me, and who helped me on my path to knowing God. That was my PCC counselor. She never forced religion or God on me. I simply felt cared about and was made aware that I was being prayed for."

CHAPTER EIGHTEEN

In Their Own Words

"It's not about me, and it's not about the adoptive parents. It's about the child."

—Nicki, birth mother, age 17

As preparations were made to write this book, we recognized that some of the individuals who work with birth mothers or adoptive couples may be troubled by our positive attitudes towards open adoption. Indeed, many today still believe that open adoption is not only confusing for children, but a risky and complicated venture that leads to grief more often than not.

We openly recognize that in some cases, open adoption does not work. We recognize the pain that a birth mother, an adoptive couple, and a child will face when an adoption plan or an adoptive relationship falls apart. Even when some measure of success is achieved, we are aware that the process is far from flawless.

However, we have seen—far more frequently—open adoptions that have been successful over the long term. We have seen birth mothers caught in difficult circumstances make decisions that have changed them in profound ways, emotionally and spiritually. In many cases, these adoptions would not have taken place without some degree of openness and choice; many women would not even consider entrusting a child to a nameless, faceless couple.

We have also seen adoptive parents and children who have weathered the storms of open adoption, and who are now advocates for more openness. In their experience, children long to know about their birth parents. As the most important member of the adoption constellation in the minds of both sets of parents, the child is given a sense of its heritage in an open adoption, and the reassurance that it was loved, not 'given away.'

We believe that those who are working in the adoption field must be willing to embrace all of the options surrounding adoption, and to help clients find the most suitable alternative. In order to be effective, counselors must deal with their own biases and reservations in order to counsel clients in a way that is not fear-based. An individual who values life must be prepared to travel through uncharted waters, entering a journey without a map and with few clear markers. The alternative—leaving women uninformed about the wide range of alternatives available—may prove detrimental to both mother and child.

For those of us who facilitate peer counseling in the adoption field comes the realization that we stand on the sidelines coaching, encouraging, and cheering. The people with the most valid comments on the process are those who are the most intimately affected by adoption: birth mothers, birth fathers, adoptive parents, and adoptees. The following words are their own:

WHY DID YOU CHOOSE TO PLACE?

"I wanted my child to eat, and I couldn't afford to feed myself. I wanted my child to have a two-parent family. I wanted everything wonderful for my child—nothing negative. Adoption wasn't the first thing I thought of, but it was the best thing."

—*Jacqueline, birth mother, age 23*

"My father was not part of my life emotionally, even though he was in my life physically. I needed a father, and I felt I needed to give this child a father."

—*Amber, birth mother, age 20*

DID YOU EVER FEEL THAT YOUR DECISION TO PLACE WAS SELFISH?

"At first I really felt like I needed to do what was best for this baby. But when I talked with my counselor, it came out that I needed to do what was best for me: whatever was best for me was the best thing for the baby. At first I felt really guilty—what a selfish decision since I got myself into this situation! As it turns out, the best thing for me was the best thing for my daughter, by far."

—*Emily, birth mother, age 25*

"I remember thinking at first that I was so selfish for not parenting this child. But I still wanted my son in a two-parent family like I'd grown up in. Even now, I look at my situation (I'm a single mother), and I know that the reason I didn't place my second child was because I couldn't handle it—I couldn't go through that again. *That* was the selfish decision."

—*Nicki, birth mother, age 17*

DID YOU EVER CHANGE YOUR MIND DURING THE PROCESS?

"It never even crossed my mind. I'm really solid with my decisions, and very black and white. Twenty days after I found out I was pregnant, I was pretty sure I wasn't going to parent."

—*Emily, birth mother, age 25*

"I was young. My mind was set. I never changed my mind."

—*Aurora, birth mother, age 16*

"Of course I had thoughts, but I never really changed my mind. I sometimes thought, 'What would it be like to raise a child with no income or education?' But in the end, I thought, 'What would it be like for the baby?'"

—*Rosanne, birth mother, age 25*

HOW DO YOU FEEL ABOUT ADOPTION COUNSELING?

"My counselor dropped me. After I had the baby, she said she'd call and she didn't. I may have pushed her a little bit, but I really wish she'd pushed me back. I really wish she'd hounded me—anything to get me to come in and talk."

—Jacqueline, birth mother, age 23

"It was important to know that I had someone on my side who would walk through the steps with me. I had so many questions, from how I would find a couple to how I would get over placing my son."

—Kendra, birth mother, age 23

"I think I would have been completely lost without counseling. I never would have understood adoption and how healthy and positive it can be for everyone involved."

—Sandra, birth mother, now age 38

"I never received adoption counseling: a social worker facilitated the adoption. Today I see these girls who placed in open adoptions who get the help they need and go through the grief cycle. I see these birth mothers, and they're such amazing women. They're young: they're the same age as I was when I placed in a closed adoption. But in a couple of years some of them move on with their own lives, marry, and have kids. I know that they'll still have to deal with things, but in two, three, four, five years these women come out so much farther ahead. How long did it take me? Eighteen years."

—Michelle, birth mother, now age 45

WHERE WOULD YOU BE IF YOU HAD NOT PLACED?

"I'd be very bitter. I had had an abortion before I became pregnant with Elizabeth. It got so bad that I wouldn't even touch my boyfriend. I felt, 'Why would you want to be near me? I killed your first child.' That's where I was.

"We didn't do anything—hug, hold hands, anything!—for six months. Then I felt sorry for him. I was on the pill, but after only one time, I got pregnant again. Talk about being a poster child for 'it only takes once!'

"I wouldn't be here if it hadn't been for Elizabeth. I wouldn't have been able to get counseling."

—Jacqueline, birth mother, age 23

WHY ARE PEOPLE AFRAID OF OPENNESS IN ADOPTION?

"Open adoption denies couples of their dream of being married and having their own children. They adopt, but they still hang on to that dream. If another person is introduced into the equation, they can't pretend that it's their birth child anymore."

—Mary, adoptive mother

"When an adoptive couple is first handed that baby, the emotions are overwhelming. You become parents at that second—as surely as anyone who pushes a baby out. To then let into your consciousness the fact that this is not fully your baby in every way is extremely challenging."

—Linda, adoptive mother

WHAT IS YOUR GREATEST FEAR ABOUT ADOPTION?

"My biggest fear, if I'm really honest, is that the emotional bond between my child and her birth mother will take over some day. Will I lose the bond I have with my child?

"We're trying to safeguard against that by building in more openness than we ever imagined. Then the birth mother becomes a regular part of life instead of a fantasy."

—*Linda, adoptive mom*

"My fear is that our second daughter's birth mom will disappear. The whole rejection thing might happen. How do you tell your child that you gave her mom the opportunity and she didn't come around?"

—*Mary, adoptive mom*

"What if I can't have another child? What if I gave away my only one? It's my biggest fear around adoption. It might even be my biggest fear ever.

—*Jacqueline, birth mother, age 23*

"I sometimes fear that there will be a death—that my daughter or the adoptive couple will die."

—*Amber, birth mother, age 20*

"I'm afraid that the adoptive mom will back off even more. And maybe she'll tell my daughter things that aren't untrue but that would suggest I'm not fit to be a parent. How will I be portrayed? What will my daughter think of me?"

—*Emily, birth mother, age 25*

"My biggest fear is the fact that everything is based completely on trust. Once they have the baby, they also have the right to tell me stay out of their lives."

—*Erin, birth mother, age 17*

"For every fear that I have, the adoptive couple tends to have an opposite and related fear. My biggest fear was that they would turn their backs on me and never let me see my child again. Their fear was that I would ask for him back.

—*Kendra, birth mother, age 23*

WHAT DO YOU MOST DISLIKE ABOUT ADOPTION?

"I hate the misunderstandings and misconceptions people have about adoption."

—*Julie, birth mother, age 21*

"I hate always having to be the bigger person. I feel that in the relationship I have with the adoptive parents, I'm giving and giving and giving and giving—and only receiving a little bit.

"On the whole, I know I made the best decision and I don't have regrets at all. I just hate having to say to people, 'Oh, it's terrific! Oh, it's great!', because there are days when it's not terrific and it's not great."

—*Emily, birth mother, age 25*

"I hate birth fathers who don't take responsibility. We have to face the public with our bellies sticking out, and the birth fathers don't have to tell anyone. They don't have to be there. They don't have to do anything. They can just walk away."

—Kendra, birth mother, age 23

"I'm ashamed that my family views the adoption as such a negative. I don't view it as something negative at all. Two absolutely wonderful people have a beautiful daughter, and a little girl has a beautiful family."

—Michael, birth father, age 17

WHAT WOULD YOU LIKE TO SAY TO ADOPTIVE PARENTS?

"Most of the women who place are young and they are all very fragile emotionally. These women have given you a piece of themselves, so please make it easier on them. If you promise them visits, follow through. If you say you'll send photos and letters, then please do. You have no idea of how important these things are to a woman's grief and recovery process."

—Erin, birth mother, age 17

"Don't take your birth mom for granted."

—Julie, birth mother, age 21

"Don't put too much energy into raising your child like she's 'adopted.' It's done, it's happened, so just raise her like a normal kid. That's what my parents did: there's never an emphasis whatsoever on me being adopted. Kids are kids—let them be kids."

—Ana, adoptee from a closed adoption, 17

"I think it must be very hard to be an open adoptive parent, and I don't think I could open my home to a child and their whole birth family. I need to commend those who do; I think they're amazing. I'm so glad that God has put people with immense courage on earth."

—Emily, birth mother, age 25

WHAT WOULD YOU LIKE TO SAY TO BIRTH MOTHERS?

"Keep it as open as possible. I remember people saying that to me over and over and over and over again. I was like, 'No! I want it closed.' But keep it as open as possible; keep the lines of communication open. Whatever it is—whether you think it's stupid or not—talk about it."

—Nicki, birth mother, age 17

"What's easier at the time is not always better. I have all the respect in the world for the courage of birth mothers. At the time you chose to give up your child for adoption, you could have made an easier decision—not a better one."

—Jacob, adoptive father

"I would definitely like to thank my birth mom, because I've got a really good life. I couldn't see myself living any other way right now."

—Ana, adoptee from a closed adoption, 17

WHAT HAVE YOU LEARNED ABOUT LOVE?

"I found that I have a lot of love to give, but that maybe I haven't given enough love to people in my family or my friends. I'd really like to give more. Since having a child, I've found it easier to give love."

—*Emily, birth mother, age 25*

"Love is something that sometimes gets lost. What you thought was a relationship, what you thought had the groundwork and all the qualities of a friendship, may suddenly die."

—*Michelle, birth mother, now age 45*

"Love cannot just be there: you have to work at it, whether it's with the adoptive couple, your son or daughter, or your parents. You always have to work at relationships. The unconditional love is there, but it's also how far you take it."

—*Kendra, birth mother, age 23*

HOW HAS ADOPTION CHANGED YOUR LIFE?

"Before I got pregnant, I thought my life was about who I was dating. My identity wasn't in myself; it was in that other person. I've since realized that I'm my own individual person.

"I also realized, with Jeremy, that money wasn't everything. The stuff that I thought was important before I got pregnant wasn't important. Family is important. Relationships and communication are important."

—*Kendra, birth mother, age 23*

"I was completely dead-set against having children. My motto was that children are great, as long as you can give them back at the end of the day. Now all I want to do is be a mom."

—*Jacqueline, birth mother, age 23*

"I realize now that I have to sacrifice for my children, whether it's Ben or Meghan. Doing what I don't want to do is sometimes best for them."

—*Nicki, birth mother, age 17*

"I think that any experience that large forces you to grow up. You're dealing with subject matter that you can't handle if you're still thinking like a child. You can't be selfish, you can't be spontaneous: you have to sit down and think about what impact your decision will have over the next twenty, thirty years. You have to make a grown-up decision and you have to deal with a lot of 'grown-ups' in the process: the adoption agency, the adoptive-parents-to-be, the medical professionals—everyone. Everyone involved is considerably older than a seventeen-year-old, and they won't come down to your level. You have to come up to theirs."

—*Michael, birth father, age 17*

"I don't know if it's just growing up and getting older, or whether it's the open adoption, but I think part of this whole process is this idea that life does not always turn out the way you always dreamed it would. You have a vision for the way things should be that goes back to when you were five years old. Life does not turn out that way. And yet, somehow, I firmly believe that it's through those situations that God takes the stuff that we think is just the worst—our broken dreams—and turns it into something better than we could have ever dreamed of. That's been part of the process for me."

—*Jacob, adoptive father*

WHAT IS YOUR BIGGEST DREAM FOR THE FUTURE?

"My dream for my adopted daughter is that one day, she'll help me advocate for open adoption."

—*Linda, adoptive mother*

"I want a relationship with my son like the one I had with my youth group leaders. They were some of my best friends, but they were not my parents. A youth group leader can hang out with kids, do stupid things, and just be friends."

—*Nicki, birth mother, age 17*

"My dream is to go for coffee with my daughter some day."

—*Jacqueline, birth mother, age 23*

WHAT BRINGS YOU THE MOST SADNESS?

"For me, the sadness is in knowing that the adoptive parents will know my daughter so much better than I will. They're going to know her inside and out."

—*Chantal, birth mother, age 30*

"It's difficult when your mothering instincts kick in and you just want a baby to hold."

—*Julie, birth mother, age 21*

"I may have forever lost my chance to parent."

—*Emily, birth mother, age 25*

WHEN DO YOU FEEL THE GREATEST JOY?

"When my son calls me 'Julie-mom' and kisses me."

—*Julie, birth mother, age 21*

I have infinite joy when I make eye contact with my daughter, no matter when, or where, or in what context. I remember looking into her eyes the day she was born: she didn't even know what she was looking at, but I'd never, ever felt joy like that. When I look at her now, I know she knows who she's looking at."

—*Emily, birth mother, age 25*

APPENDIX

Chapter Two: "Options in Adoption"

ADOPTION LAWS

The following guide will assist Centers in researching the adoption laws of their specific jurisdictions. A Center director should be able to address all of the following issues with current, legally accurate information based on the respective state or provincial laws:

Child Welfare laws

Research the individual state or provincial laws, typically found under the Child Welfare or Child Endangerment Act.

Adoption avenues

Contact Child Welfare, the Children's Aid Society, or Social Services—depending on what exists in the jurisdiction—to access information on how adoption is handled in a particular province or state. In most jurisdictions, there are several avenues through which to pursue an adoption. There are exceptions, however, including Quebec, Canada, where adoption is facilitated solely through Social Services.

Government adoption

Examine the rules governing adoptions facilitated by Social Services. What degree of openness will the government allow? Are there policies that will restrict contact between the birth mother and child?

Agency adoption

Research the status of private adoption agencies. What fees does the agency charge? Are adoptive couples required to pay all service charges? What kind of counseling or provisions is available for both the adoptive family and the birth mother? Is there a state or provincial licensing requirement? If so, the Pregnancy Center's executive director and board must decide whether the Center will refer clients to non-licensed agencies in that jurisdiction.

Private adoption

Obtain the rules governing private or third party adoption. The executive director should carefully examine the advantages and disadvantages of this option. Is there the potential, for example, that money will be made through the exchange of a child? What fees are involved? When will the home study be conducted? In some jurisdictions, a lawyer-facilitated adoption may not involve a home study until the adoption order goes to court. In such cases, the child may be a year old before this happens.

The adoption process

Collect information about the specifics of the adoption process. When is the client required to sign the 'consent to release' forms? What kind of paperwork must she complete? What paperwork and information about the adoptive couple will she receive? Will she be required to make a court appearance at any time during the adoption? How long is the period between the signing of the papers and the placement of the child in the adoptive couple's home, and the granting of the final adoption order?

Other technical details may apply. Depending upon state or provincial legislation, the baby may be required to spend time in a foster home before the adoption is finalized. In some cases, babies may only be placed from outside of the hospital. When examining the latter possibility, the executive director must differentiate between state and provincial laws, and hospital policy.

Financial compensation

In some jurisdictions, the birth mother may openly receive payment to compensate for her inability to work during the latter stages of her pregnancy. In other jurisdictions, the adoptive couple or agency may not be permitted to cover any of the woman's expenses, as payment can be considered the 'purchase' of the baby. When dealing with this issue, Pregnancy Centers should explore whether the exchange of money for expenses must go through the adoption agency or a lawyer.

Reversing the adoption decision

Prepare for the eventuality that some clients will change their minds about placing. Is there a waiting period in which the client can change her decision without repercussion? What actions must she take if she decides to parent a child that has already been placed? What penalties will be held against her? Will the penalties differ based on when she changes her mind?

The rights of the putative father

Find out what laws exist concerning the putative father's rights. Will the client be required to notify the birth father about her decision to place? Is his signature required? How will the marital status of the client impact the adoption plan? What are the birth father's legal rights if a woman chooses not to name the father on the infant's birth certificate?

In some cases, a woman may actually leave her state or province in order to evade the putative father's rights. The client should be informed of residency requirements—the length of time she must live in the new region before placement is legal. In some cases, the child must have been conceived in the province in which it is placed; in others, only the place of birth is relevant.

Clients will need to be advised of the legal problems that may arise should they flee the birth father. Under what circumstances can the putative father's right to notification be waived? Can these rights be waived in the case of rape and if so, is the woman required to report the sexual assault to police? If a restraining order is in place due to the birth father's violence, is the client required to go to court before placing?

Aboriginal groups

Determine whether the laws concerning aboriginal groups differ from laws governing other people groups.

Adoption contracts

As open adoption becomes more common, the practice of creating an adoption contract or agreement concerning the level of openness is also gaining in popularity. Centers should explore whether these contracts have any legal impact in the adoption process in their specific jurisdictions. Will the courts grant visitation for non-custodial parents?

Chapter 7: "'Dear Baby' Letters and Gifts"

"Dear Baby" Letter Format

The following guidelines can be used to write a 'Dear Baby' letter. Letters may vary: some women may choose to write a portion of the letter while in hospital, or after the baby is born. Others might wish to write a series of letters.

Dear Baby,

The salutation should be as personalized as possible. If the client is aware of the baby's sex, or has named it before birth, she should use the most intimate address possible.

I am writing this letter because...

The birth mother should explain why she is writing the letter, whether it be to reassure the child of her love, to explain her decision to place, or to affirm the parents she has lovingly chosen.

Here are some of the reasons I decided to place...

This part of the letter should describe some of the birth mother's reasons for placing. She should explain who she is and what stage she is at in life. She should also gently describe her relationship with the birth father, being careful not to make disparaging or inappropriate comments.

I chose your adoptive parents because...

The birth mother can emphasize how carefully her decision was made, affirming the value of the adoptive couple.

These are my hopes, prayers, and dreams for you...

The birth mother should envision the future, describing the person she hopes her child will become.

This is what you mean to me now...

In the conclusion, the birth mother should express how meaningful this child has been to her. She can describe what it felt like to carry the baby in her womb and refer to intimate moments they have shared.

The birth mother should also indicate what she hopes will happen in the future. For example, a woman placing her child in an open adoption might write, 'I hope that we can develop a special friendship throughout the years.' A woman placing her child in a closed adoption might state, 'I anxiously await the day when you will contact me. I can't wait to see the person you have become.' Should the birth mother intend to remain anonymous, she should provide an explanation as to why, perhaps acknowledging that life and circumstances sometimes set people on different paths. Nevertheless, the fact that the child will always remain in her heart should be emphasized.

Love,
Your birth mother

Sample 'Dear Baby' Letter

Dear Kaitlyn,

I hope and pray that you will never wonder why you are where you are. All I can tell you is that you are where God wants you to be—the place you are supposed to be. "For I know the plans I have for you," declares the Lord. "Plans to prosper you and not to harm you, plans to give you a hope and a future." (Jeremiah 29:11)

Finding out that I was pregnant with you was frightening, but at the same time I was completely thrilled! I love every second that I know you are inside me and growing, and becoming who you are meant to be. You are the reason for me. You are the reason I know, with all my heart, soul, and mind, that God is merciful and loving. God turned this situation into something beautiful and divine.

You were made out of love. I loved Joe when we made you, and I still love him as a precious friend. However, the love we shared was not one that was meant to be romantic and shared for life, but to create a new member for another family—for your mom, your dad, and your big brother.

Not many people get to choose their parents, but I was able to choose yours. They are loving, strong, happy, and together. I have no doubt that they deserve you. Most importantly, you deserve them!

There is no way that I will be able to give you all that I had when I was growing up and I couldn't live with myself if I denied you the things I had. I had a mom and a dad who were there for me all the time. I know that your parents will do that for you too. They will love you extra because they have patiently waited for God to bring you into their family and make it complete. I am carrying you so that you can be with them: I am having you for your mom and dad. They are who you were made to be with.

Making this choice for you is what I am most proud of in my life. I am giving you a better life without any thought about how hard it will be for me to let you go. To keep you with me would be selfish. I love you with the most pure and peaceful love that I have ever known and that is why I made this choice.

I remember the first time I heard your heartbeat. I remember the first time I felt you move inside me. I remember the first time I saw you on the ultrasound. Every night we listen to music together and I read you the book, *Just the Way You Are*. You remind me that you are with me by getting the hiccups every day! I pray that after you are born, we will continue to bond and love. I have hopes for our relationship and I know that with the Lord's hand, we will have something extraordinary.

I promise that I will never let a day go by in which I don't think of you, pray for you, love you and miss you. Always know that we are under the same sky—God's sky—and that you are the most precious gift in my heart! Always and forever!

Your birth mother,

Chantal

Sample 'Dear Baby' Letter

Dear Jeremy,

I love you so very much and this is why I write this letter to you today. I have had to make the hardest decision of my life and I want you to know why. As you know, I decided I couldn't raise you myself and placed you with your Mom and Dad. I did this because you are a very special person and I had to do what I thought was best for you.

I am a full-time student who lives at home with my parents, and I also work part time at a bookstore. I have several years to go before I can finish my education and settle down. I want you to know that you were conceived out of love, but because of many complicated reasons, your birth father and I are no longer together.

Since the moment I found out I was pregnant, I have thought of you and what would be best for you. I have many hopes and dreams for both of us. Because of my dreams for you, I have placed you with your loving family because they are the parents I could only dream of being! I want you to have the best opportunities life could offer. At this time in my life, the only thing I could offer is love. I could have thought of myself and dropped out of school to raise you, but I think we would have been hard struck for money and I wouldn't be able to give you everything I wanted to.

From the moment I found out about you, I felt you were a little boy. The ultrasound confirmed my feelings. I can't explain why, but I was so happy to be having a boy.

I believe you were meant to be born and that you were meant to make a difference in this world. Even with you still inside, you have made a difference. I feel you kicking me and I wonder if you are going to be a soccer player, or a football player—or even a hockey player in the NHL. I wonder if you are going to be a doctor, a lawyer, or a pilot. I have dreams of you getting a good education and going to college or university. I have hopes that you will do your best in life and will always know I love you.

It has been almost two weeks since you were born. The night you were born was a very wonderful night. There were many people at the hospital waiting for your arrival, including your mom and dad, my parents and brother, and my best friend Gabrielle, who flew in from Toronto just for you. Your birth father was at the hospital too.

What a difference you have made in so many people's lives! You are a very beautiful baby and I love you even more. I have been over twice to visit with you and your parents since you were born. Seeing you for the first time with them was very hard for me, but also very reassuring. It helped me to see that I was making the right decision. I see in their faces how much they love you and how much they can offer you. We have decided to make this an open adoption so we can keep in contact. I can see you whenever I want to.

Jeremy, I want you to know that I am very proud of you and happy that I have made the right decisions for us both. I will always love you!

Your birth mother,

Kendra

Chapter 9: "The Entrustment Ceremony"

SAMPLE CEREMONY INVITATION

"Children are a gift from God; they are His reward."
Psalm 127:3

ROBERT WARREN
COLEMAN-LIETZ

Born
November 9, 2002 at 3:13 a.m.
Weight: 7 lb 4 oz
Length: 21 inches

To
Karen Coleman (birth mother) and Mark Lietz (birth father)

Lovingly Surrendered To
Ernest and Alice Blumhardt

[opposing page]

ENTRUSTMENT SERVICE
First Baptist Church

Reverend Brent Matthews officiating
Karen and Mark, trusting God,
lovingly pass their son, **Robert Warren**
into the care of **Alice and Ernest**

"Blessed are you who hunger now, for you will be satisfied.
Blessed are you who weep now, for you will laugh."
Luke 6:21

SAMPLE ORDER OF SERVICE

Entrustment Service

For

LISA JANETTE

April 7, 2003

Welcome ....Diane Campbell, officiator
Poetry Reading .... Gloria Phelps, birth grandmother
Reflections and Statement............................... Lisa Whitney, birth mother
Response .... Barbara and Jim Fisher, adoptive parents
Pledge and Vows
Guest Affirmations
Entrustment of Lisa Janette

Sample Birth Mother's Address

Dear Kelly and Dean,

I chose you to parent Elliott Adam because of your faith in Christ, and because I love this child more than words can express.

I believe that you have the ability to provide Elliott with a loving, two-parent family, and I am excited that you will have the opportunity to experience the joy and excitement of being parents for the first time. You have shown yourselves to be down-to-earth, warm people who are ready to welcome a child into your home, making him a priority and sacrificing whatever is necessary in order to love and protect him.

There are many things that I wish that I could do for this beautiful boy:

> I wish that I could be the one to see his first smile and to figure out what makes him laugh.

> I wish I could be there to protect him from hurt and harm, holding him in my arms when he discovers that life is hard.

> I wish I could be the one to tell him every day that he is loved.

> I wish I could be the one to discover all the reasons that he is the most special child in the world.

As I place this baby into your care, I am trusting that you will do all of the things that I will not be able to. I trust that God will give you the strength, patience, and courage to be good parents.

I thank you for being willing to enter into an open adoption: it means so much to me to know that I will be able to see this child again and to watch you grow as parents and as a family. I commit to praying for each of you every day.

I know that tremendous grief lies ahead of me, but I believe that this child will also be a source of great joy in the years to come. My grief will be worth seeing Elliott grow up in a loving, secure home.

Dean and Kelly, I will now place this child in your arms.

Sample Covenant

An Adoption Covenant

IT is no accident that God has brought us together, for together we can accomplish what we could not do apart. Together, we give this child the great necessities of life: the roots of security and the wings of opportunity. We all have hope in our hearts. We collectively offer a blend of security and nurture. It was love for children that put us on converging paths. Now it is our love for this unique child which unites us for the shared journey ahead.

WE stand committed to our ideals. We believe that children have an innate dignity. We are convinced that children should never be viewed as possessions to be hoarded, but rather are best understood as gifts from God to be selflessly loved. We believe that children need security and stability, and we recognize that they depend on the adults in their lives for these comforts. We believe that relationships thrive in an atmosphere of honesty and mutual respect. We recognize that if any one of us is diminished, we all are.

THEREFORE, we pledge to:

1. Place the child's interests above our own.
2. Be honest in all of our interactions.
3. Take the time to consider situations from the perspective of others.
4. Protect and honor the reputation of others in this relationship.
5. Consult each other before introducing new people to the arrangement.
6. Stay flexible and open to new possibilities.
7. Convey newly discovered medical information.
8. Be direct in the expression of feelings.
9. Consider mediation in the event of major misunderstanding or disagreement.
10. Consider sharing our experience for the benefit of others.

WE make this pledge as an expression of love, integrity, and goodwill. We ask God's blessing on our covenant.

Signed this date: _____ By: _____

Birth mother

_____

Birth father

_____

Adoptive mother

Witness

_____

Adoptive father

Sample Prayer Of Blessing

Father,

I thank you for the love and courage it took for Heidi to give the gift of life and a loving family to little Daniella. I ask you to give Heidi strength in her time of grief, and joy in her future. Let her always remember that the sacrifice she is making today is an unselfish expression of love. Give her peace with her decision.

Thank-you for those who are here today to love and support Heidi. I pray that you will give them the strength and wisdom to comfort and encourage Heidi in the days ahead.

I thank you, Father, for Caroline and Darren, and for your hand in preparing them to start a family in this special way. Give them the wisdom, insight, and courage to raise Daniella in the way that is best for her. Bless them as they become parents.

Father, I thank you for the gift of Daniella, a beautiful and deeply loved baby girl. Let her know that she is loved by many. Let her always seek your guidance in her life. May she become all that you have intended her to be.

We pray these things in the name of He who understands both our pain and joy.
Amen

Sample Address Made By A Peer Counselor

(For a Christian birth mother)

Welcome. I feel privileged to share this most personal moment in your lives, Janelle, Cory, and Nathan.

We want to welcome each of you who are with us today to witness the entrustment of Alexandra Natalie. You are important people in the lives of Janelle, Cory, and Nathan, and in the new life of this beautiful baby girl.

For most of you, this is the first time you have attended an entrustment ceremony. Entrustment services serve as a formal celebration of the placement of a child into an adoptive family, and because love is being expressed in its highest form, there will be both joy and pain. This service will bear witness to the love and sacrifice of a birth mother, and the love and joy of an adoptive couple. This service will allow us to publicly support and affirm them, and to ask God's blessing on each of the parties involved.

Ephesians 1:5 says that "in love, God adopted us through Jesus Christ." We know that God understands all of the emotions in the entrustment ceremony this afternoon. He knows the joy of adopting a child into His family. He also knows the love and sacrifice involved in releasing a child. God loved us so much, you see, that He wanted us to belong to His family. This love came at a cost: God had to release His son Jesus Christ, allowing him to come from heaven to earth and die for us.

God could only do this because of His tremendous love for us. For this reason, He understands the sacrifice you are making, Janelle, by releasing Alexandra into the care of Cory and Nathan.

He also understands the longing and joy of Cory and Nathan, and what it is like for them to adopt Alexandra into their family and to love her as their own daughter.

God is here at this entrustment service, understanding the joy of Cory and Nathan, and the unselfish love and sacrifice of Janelle. Little Alexandra does not understand what has happened, yet, but one day she will know that she is indeed twice blessed. She has the love of Janelle, who was willing to release her daughter into the love and care of a family. Alexandra also has the love and acceptance of Cory and Nathan as they welcome her into their lives and family.

Alexandra is truly blessed, for she is twice loved.

Chapter 13: "Dealing with the Birth Father"

Abuse can take many forms, being directed in physical, sexual, environmental, or psychological ways:

Physical:

> hitting, slapping, punching, kicking, or pushing
> choking
> using a weapon, or threatening to use one
> arm twisting, hair pulling, or forcing someone up against a wall
> restraining someone, or locking them in a room

Sexual (with a spouse or partner):

> forcing someone to have intercourse
> forcing someone to engage in unwanted sexual behavior
> adultery or the use of pornography
> using sex to manipulate
> 'hounding' for sex
> being rough
> refusing to have any sexual or intimate contact whatsoever

(with a child)

A child should never be inappropriately subjected or exposed to sexual contact, activity, or behavior, including:

> fondling or intercourse
> exposure to an adult's genital area
> exposure to pornography or sexual fantasies
> exposure to inappropriate sexual conversation or joking
> being exposed for sexual stimulation or amusement
> prostitution

Environmental:

> harming pets
> damaging or throwing out a partner's clothing or possessions
> breaking things
> locking a partner in or out of the house
> completely cutting off a partner's access to the phone
> preventing a partner's access to friends or family
> abusing those close to the victim

Emotional/Verbal/Psychological:

> publicly humiliating or denigrating a partner
> insults, name calling, laughing in one's face
> threatening to harm oneself
> failing to come home
> yelling, intimidation, threats of violence
> inappropriate expression of jealousy
> real or suggested involvement with another man or woman

Chapter 14: "Birth Mothers' Support Groups"

Sample Formats For Birth Mothers' Support Groups

Seasonal

Valentine's Day

Theme: Relationships and Love

Snack: Valentine cake decorated with the name of each baby, red fruit punch, candy hearts with messages

Welcome and Introduction: Please tell us about your funniest or worst date—the date that still makes you flinch.

Teaching and Sharing Time: [Divide into three groups. In ten minutes, each group should create a definition of 'love.']

> How would you define love?
> What is society's definition of love?

Read the definition of love from I Corinthians 13:4-8a. Please describe someone in your life who:

> Is always patient with you.
> Is glad when good things happen to you.
> Brags about you—not himself.
> Does not insist on having her own way.
> Did not hold a grudge.
> Became angry when someone else was wronged.
> Celebrated when good triumphed.
> Never gave up on you.
> Never lost faith in you.
> Always hoped for the best for you.
> Stuck with you through both the good and bad times.
> Will love you forever.

You have described the kind of love each of you are capable of giving. You demonstrated this love when you placed the welfare of the child that you carried in your body, gave birth to, and loved deeply, above your own needs. This love is also the love you deserve to receive. Do not settle for a cheap substitute.

Seasonal

Christmas

Theme: The reality of Christmas

Snack: Gingerbread women (and gingerbread men, depending on how hostile the group is towards birth fathers)

Welcome and Introduction: Please describe your first memory of Christmas. What was your worst Christmas memory?

Teaching and Sharing Time: Some of you are facing your first Christmas after baby. We all have images of what the holiday should entail: a family celebration, ornaments and lights, gifts crammed under a tree, laughter, warmth, and an abundance of food. However, this conception of Christmas—played up by the media—is a myth. For many people, Christmas is a lonely or stressful time. We are often disappointed because our expectations and hopes cannot live up to reality.

> If you have survived at least one post-baby Christmas, please share the story of that Christmas. What was meaningful, and what was most difficult? What do you wish you had done differently?

> For those of you who are facing your first Christmas since giving birth, please share some of your thoughts and fears about the holiday. How do you plan to cope?

The first Christmas, we should recall, was certainly difficult for the original players in the story:

Mary was probably only fifteen, unmarried, and pregnant. In her culture, death was the penalty for illegitimacy. We can safely assume that she was shamed by her family and friends. Joseph, her fiancé, knew that the child was not his, but he married Mary to protect her. Mary and Joseph knew that the child she was carrying was special. Do you suppose that anyone else did?

The young couple would have been considered the working poor in those days. To register to pay taxes, the couple had to travel a long way to a small town. Transportation would have been primitive by today's standards: Mary probably rode on a donkey. She would have missed her family. There was no midwife, no hospital, no epidural, no birth coach—not even a second rate motel with a bed. She may have given birth in a cattle yard, a barn, or in a dark and dirty cave. With only an inexperienced husband to help, this young teenager gave birth to her first child, a son.

This is what Christmas celebrates, yet somehow, we have forgotten the history of the holiday. Those who are poor, afraid, grieving, and lonely do not have a place in our modern version of the story. Perhaps by recalling the Christmas story, we can put the season in perspective.

What are some of the ways we can survive the most difficult times of the holiday? [i.e. live through each day as it comes, take the time to grieve in privacy, begin a new Christmas tradition, such as buying an ornament for each year of your child's life, etc.]

Topical

Theme: Anger

Snack: Devil's food cake, hot tamales

Welcome and Introduction: What single event made you the most angry during your pregnancy or adoption? How did you respond?

Teaching and Sharing Time: Anger can be an explosive response to the belief that our significance is being questioned or denied. Consider the following:

> On a scale of one to ten (ten being the angriest), where are you now in terms of your anger? Remember, anger is a normal, healthy part of the grieving process.

> With whom are you angry? (i.e. your social worker, the adoptive mother, the birth father, your parents, your friends, etc.)

> How do you express your anger? (i.e. sarcasm, physical violence, silence, etc.)

The only long-term solution to anger is to deal with its root cause. When you are angry, analyze the situation. If you are reacting to something that seems insignificant, you may need to delve deeper to uncover what is really bothering you.

When dealing with anger, vengeance will only bring temporary relief. Planning a constructive confrontation is a far more productive method of dealing with the issue. Try using the 'sandwich' approach when talking to someone who has wronged you:

> The bread: Start by saying something positive (i.e. apologize for your part in the dispute).

> The meat: State the negative (i.e. 'This is what is upsetting me...').

> The bread: End with another positive message (i.e. 'I really care about you and I hope that we can work through this.').

This approach is much easier to swallow than a meaty chunk of criticism!

Conclusion: What are some other positive ways to deal with anger? (i.e. exercise, writing a letter that will never be sent, venting to a person that you trust, etc.)

Topical

Theme: Dealing with guilt imposed by others

Snack: Chocolate chip cookies

Welcome and Introduction: Can you think of someone in your life who refuses to see you as an adult? How does he or she go about making you feel like a child?

Teaching and Sharing Time:

The decision to place is usually made after extensive pondering, prayer, and pain. The process becomes no less complicated when friends or family question your ability to make a decision that is in the best interest of both you and your baby. Guilt is often a powerful tactic that people use (whether consciously or unconsciously) to voice their disapproval.

How many of you heard the following remarks during your decision-making process? What message was really being conveyed?

'Your baby needs to have two parents.' (You would be selfish to parent.)

'How could you give away your own child?' (You must not have a heart!)

'I could never do that!' (I would love my baby too much to give it away.)

or, if you considered changing your mind about the placement:

'Imagine what the adoptive couple must be going through!' (The birth mother's pain, in other words, is of a lesser significance.)

When you make a choice, you will always wonder what might have been had you selected another path. Each choice has its own peaks and pitfalls—no path is free of problems or without its rewards. Choose your path and do not apologize: what is, is. Make the best choice possible, and then use it to learn and grow.

SAMPLE RESPONSE Journal ENTRIES

"Cheryl," September 10 entry
Session topic: Anger

> I'm glad I finally came to Group! It was nice hearing from other birth moms, but it didn't help in a way because I still don't know what to do. Parent or adopt??? Will I ever know what to do?

Facilitator Response

We were glad to see you tonight, and we hope to see you again! It's okay to flip-flop in your decision-making: you're making a major life-changing choice, one that will impact both you and your baby. It's certainly not easy, and it's good that you're not taking your decision lightly.

"Carly," October 12
Session topic: How family members deal with adoption

> Today was my first time. I don't really have anything to write. Hopefully next time!

Facilitator Response

The first time is always the hardest! We hope you'll hang in there—you're a welcome addition to the group.

"Jessica," November 15 entry
Session topic: Relationships and Dating

> Tonight was challenging! I still don't believe I will EVER meet that special someone (no matter what you guys say!), but it's nice to hear that some of the group feels the same way. Most of us have been burned. At least we have each other to complain to!

> Oh well . . . no matter how bad the man situation is, at least I'm not dating Bryan anymore. I'd sooner be celibate forever than do that again! —Jess

> P.S. My sister read somewhere that this whole dating/marriage thing is like being a little kid waiting for their birthday: "You know it'll come sometime, but the rest is a surprise!"

Facilitator Response

Jessica, your responses are always amusing: I look forward to reading them. Thank-you for your honesty in group today!

"Kira," January 7 entry
Session topic: Baby's first birthday

> Good session—emotional! The 'big day' isn't for a couple months, but it's good to start getting ready. Thanks for the encouragement!

Facilitator Response

Kira, you have come a long way this past year. I'm sure you'll get through the 'big day' too!

"Mei-Ling," March 15 entry
Session topic: Adoptive mothers

I really loved Group tonight! It's so amazing talking to people who have been through the same thing, and who genuinely support and care for each other. Thank you so much for your help and encouragement!

Tonight reaffirmed some things I've been thinking about lately—it's almost like God knew what I needed to hear. Like I said earlier, I still have some major anger to deal with, but I feel a lot better now about the issues I've been having with "Carrie" [the adoptive mother]. I'm meeting with her in two weeks, so wish me luck!

Facilitator Response

I'll be thinking about you and praying for you. I'm impressed by the way you've handled the issues so far, and I'm confident you'll continue to deal with them with integrity.

"Brianna," April 17 entry
Session topic: Guilt

It's almost like tonight's session was all about me! Kristin will be exactly fourteen months in a week, and I'm so glad I placed her—her family is wonderful! But I still struggle a lot. I always wonder what it will be like when I have kids of my own. Will Kristin hate me for keeping them and not her? I also think maybe I could have done more to make the relationship I had with her dad work out. If we had stayed together, we probably could have parented. We're both old enough!

The worst thing is when I go out with my friends and actually start having a good time. I feel awful! How could I go out and have fun when I couldn't even take care of my own baby? I know I did the right thing, but I can't stop feeling this way.

Facilitator Response

Thank-you so much for your honesty, Brianna. It helps to talk through these feelings. When you're feeling guilt, you might want to think about why you made the decision to place, why you chose a wonderful family for Kristin. Then concentrate on making good choices for the future, since you can't change the past.

About the Author

Carmen Wittmeier obtained her Master of Arts in English at the University of Alberta and has worked as a writer, editor, researcher, and reporter. She currently teaches English literature at Langara College in Vancouver, British Columbia.

ISBN 141206788-X